THE RULING ELDER
The Warrant, Nature, and Duties of the Office in the Presbyterian Church

by
Samuel Miller, D.D.
Professor of Ecclesiastical History and Church Government
in the Theological Seminary at Princeton

www.solafidepublishers.com

The Ruling Elder: The Warrant, Nature, and Duties
of the Office in the Presbyterian Church
by Samuel Miller

Originally Published in 1835
by Joseph Whetham
Philadelphia

Reprint Edition © 2015
Sola Fide Publishers
Post Office Box 2027
Toccoa, Georgia 30577
www.solafidepublishers.com

Cover and Interior Design by
Magnolia Graphic Design
www.magnoliagraphicdesign.com

ISBN-13: 978-0692590881
ISBN-10: 0692590889

FOREWORD

To the Ministers and Elders of the Presbyterian Church in the United States.

Reverend and Respected Brethren,
The substance of the following Essay was delivered from the pulpit, in the form of a sermon, more than twenty years ago, and subsequently published. In consequence of repeated solicitation from some individuals of your number, I have thought proper to alter its form, to enlarge its limits, and to adapt it, according to my best judgment, to more general utility. It has long appeared to me that a more ample discussion of this subject than I have hitherto seen, is really needed. And if the present volume should be considered as, in any tolerable degree, answering the desired purpose, I shall feel myself richly rewarded for the labour which has attended its preparation.

Such as it is, my venerated friends, I inscribe it, most respectfully, to you. My first prayer in regard to it is, that it may be the means of doing some good: my next, that it may be received by those whom I have so much reason to respect and love, as a well intended effort to benefit the Church of God.

I am aware that some of my brethren do not concur with me in maintaining the Divine authority of the office of the Ruling Elder; and, probably, in several other opinions respecting this office advanced in the following pages. In reference to these points, I can only say, that, as the original publication, of which this is an enlargement, was made without the remotest thought of controversy, and even without adverting, in my own mind, to the fact, that I differed materially from any of my brethren; so nothing is more foreign from my wishes, in the republication, than to assail the opinions or feelings of any brother. I have carefully re-examined the whole subject. And, although, in doing this, I have been led to modify some of my former opinions in relation to a few minor points. Yet in reference to the Divine warrant and the great importance of the office for which I plead, my convictions have become stronger than ever. The following sheets exhibit those views, and that testimony in support of them, which at present, satisfy my own mind, and which I feel confident may be firmly sustained. How far, however, the considerations which have satisfied me may impress more impartial judges, I cannot venture to foretell. All that I dare to ask in their behalf is, that they may be seriously and candidly weighed.

But there is one point in regard to which I anticipate no diversity of opinion. If the statement given in the following Essay, concerning the duties incumbent on Ruling Elders, be correct, it is certain that very inadequate views of those duties have been too often taken, both by those who conferred, and those who sustained the office; and that there is a manifest and loud call for an attempt to raise the standard of public sentiment in reference to the whole subject. That we make so little of this office, compared with what we might do, and ought to do, does really appear to me one of the deepest deficiencies of our beloved Church. That a reform in this respect is desirable, is to express but half the truth. It is necessary; it is vital. It has pleased the sovereign Disposer to cast our lot in a period of mighty plans, and of high moral effort, for the benefit of the world. In the subject of this volume, I am inclined to think, is wrapped up one of those means which are destined, under His blessing, to be richly productive of moral energy in the enterprises of Christian benevolence, which appear to be every day gathering strength. When the rulers of the Church shall, in the genuine spirit of the humble, faithful, and laborious Paul, "magnify their office;" when they shall be found cordially and diligently co-operating with those who "labour in the word and doctrine," in inspecting, counselling, and watching over the "flocks" respectively committed to their "oversight in the Lord;" and when they shall be suitably honoured and employed, in their various appropriate functions, both by pastors and people; this change will, I believe, be, at once, one of the surest precursors, and one of the most efficient means, of the introduction of brighter days in the Church of God.

So far as we can anticipate events, this important change must begin with the teachers and rulers of the Church themselves. On every one of you, therefore, if my estimate of the subject be correct, devolves a high and most interesting responsibility. That you may have grace given you to acquit yourselves of this responsibility, in a manner acceptable to our common Master, and conducive to the signal advancement of His kingdom; and that future generations, both in the Church and out of it, may have reason to "rise up and call you blessed," is the fervent prayer of,

Reverend and Respected Brethren,
Your friend and fellow-servant
in the house of God,
SAMUEL MILLER.

Princeton,
April 20, 1831.

CONTENTS

CHAPTER ONE

Introductory remarks – Nature of the Church – Visible and Invisible Church – Unity of the Church – A form of government for the Church appointed by Christ – Nature and limits of ecclesiastical power – Summary of the doctrine of Presbyterians on this subject – The proper classes of officers in a Church completely organized – Positions intended to be established, as affording a warrant for the office of Ruling Elders – pages 11-24.

CHAPTER TWO

Testimony from the order of the Old Testament Church – Import of the term Elder – Specimen of the representations given of this class of officers – Elders of the Synagogue – Authorities in reference to the government of the Synagogue – The titles, duties, number, mode of sitting, &c., of the Elders of the Synagogue – Quotations from distinguished writers on this subject – Burnet – Goodwin – Lightfoot – Stillingfleet – Grotius – Spencer – Clark – Neander – pages 25-39.

CHAPTER THREE

Evidence from the New Testament Scriptures – Model of the Synagogue transferred to the Church – Specimen of the passages which speak of the New Testament Elders – Particular texts which establish the existence of this class of Elders in the Primitive Church – Objections to our construction of these passages – Answered – pages 41-59.

CHAPTER FOUR

Testimony of the Christian Fathers – Clemens Romanus – Ignatius – Polycarp – Cyprian – Origen – Gesta Purgationis, &c., Optatus – Ambrose – Augustine – Apostolical Constitutions – Isidore – Gregory – Facts incidentally stated by the Fathers concerning Ssme of the Elders – Syrian Christians – pages 61-86.

CHAPTER FIVE

Testimony of the witnesses for the truth in the Dark Ages – Waldenses – Albigenses – Bohemian Churches – Calvin derived this feature in his ecclesiastical system from the Bohemian Brethren – pages 87-97.

CHAPTER SIX

Testimony of the Reformers – Zuingle – Œcolampadius – Bucer – Peter Martyr – John A. Lasco – Calvin – Whitgift – Dean Nowell – Ursinus – Confession of Saxony – Szegeden – Magdeburgh Centuriators – Junius – Zanchius – Parus – Piscator – Cartwright – Greenham – Estius – Whitaker – Ruling Elders generally established in the Reformed Churches – pages 99-118.

CHAPTER SEVEN

Testimony of eminent Divines since the Reformation – Owen – Baxter – English Puritans – of New England – Goodwin – Hooker – Cotton – Davenport – Thorndike – Cotton Mather – Edwards – Kromayer – Baldwin – Suicer – Whitby – Watts – Doddridge – Neander – Dwight – pages 119-139.

CHAPTER EIGHT

Ruling Elders necessary in the Church – The importance of discipline to the purity of the Church – Discipline cannot be maintained without this class of officers, or persons of equivalent powers – The pastor alone cannot maintain it – The whole body of the Church cannot conduct it in a wise and happy manner – Prelatists and independents both obliged to provide substitutes for them – This provision, however, inadequate – pages 141-156.

CHAPTER NINE

Nature of the Ruling Elder's office – Analogy between their office and that of secular rulers – Their duties as members of the Church Session – Their more private and Constant Duties as "Overseers" of the Church – Their Duties as members of higher judicatories – Question discussed whether they ought to be called Lay-Elders – Duties of the Church members to their Elders – Elders ought to have a particular seat assigned them – pages 157-175.

CHAPTER TEN

Distinction between the office of Ruling Elder and Deacon – The persons whose appointment to take care of the poor is recorded in the sixth chapter of the Acts of the Apostles, were the first Deacons – The question discussed, whether they were Deacons at all – Whether the first Deacons were preachers and baptizers? – Deacons were never ecclesiastical rulers – The office of Deacon dropped by many Presbyterian Churches – The offices of Ruling Elder and Deacon united in the same men, in Scotland and the United States – This not desirable – Reasons for this opinion – pages 177-198.

CHAPTER ELEVEN

The qualifications proper for the office of Ruling Elder – It is not necessary that they be aged persons – It is of the utmost importance that they have unfeigned and approved piety – That they possess good sense, and sound judgment – That they be orthodox, and well informed in Gospel truth – That they have eminent prudence – That they be of good report among them who are without – That they be men of public spirit – That they be men of ardent zeal, and importunate prayer – pages 199-211.

CHAPTER TWELVE

Of the election of Ruling Elders – Who are proper Electors – Ought they to be elected for life, or only for a limited time? – Of the number of Elders proper for each Church – Of those who may be considered as eligible to this office – Whether a man may be a Ruling Elder in more than one Church at the same time – pages 213-224.

CHAPTER THIRTEEN

Of the ordination of Ruling Elders – Ordination a necessary designation to office – Proofs from Scripture – The laying on of hands – Not always connected with the special gifts of the Spirit – This ceremony ought to be employed in the ordination of Ruling Elders – Probable reason of its falling into disuse – Authorities in favour of its restoration – Who ought to lay on hands in the ordination of Elders – Advantages of imposing hands in ordaining this class of officers – Should Elders lay on hands in the ordination of Ministers – pages 225-244

CHAPTER FOURTEEN

On the resignation of Ruling Elders – Their removal from one Church to another – The method of conducting discipline against them – pages 245-250.

CHAPTER FIFTEEN

The advantages of conducting discipline upon the Presbyterian plan – It is founded on the principle of representation – It presents one of the best barriers against clerical ambition and encroachments – Furnishes one of the best securities for preserving the rights of the people – Furnishes to Ministers efficient counsel and support – Favourable to despatch and energy – Accomplishes that which cannot be attained in any other way – Favourable to union and co-operation in enterprises of Christian benevolence. – pages 251-267.

CHAPTER ONE

Introductory

Our once crucified, but now exalted Redeemer, has erected in this world a kingdom which is His Church. This Church is either visible or invisible.

By the invisible Church we mean, the whole body of sincere believers, of every age and nation, "that have been, are, or shall be gathered into one, under Christ, the glorious Head thereof." Part of these are already made perfect in heaven. Another portion are at present scattered over the earth in different denominations of professing Christians, though not certainly distinguishable from others by the human eye. And the remainder are in future to be gathered in by the grace of God; when the whole number of the "redeemed from among men," will be united in one holy assembly, which is the "spouse," the "body of Christ, the fulness of Him that filleth all in all."

By the visible Church is meant the body of those who profess the true religion, together with their children. It is that body which is called out of the world, and united under the authority of Christ, the Head, for the purpose of maintaining Gospel truth and order, and promoting the knowledge, purity, comfort, and edification of all the members. When we use the term *Church*, as expressive of a visible, professing body, we either mean the whole visible Church of God throughout the world, or a particular congregation of professing Christians, who have agreed to unite together for the purpose of mutual instruction, inspection, and edification.[1]

The word *Church* is also employed in Scripture to designate a Church Judicatory; that is, the Church assembled and acting by her representatives, the Elders, chosen to inspect, and bear rule over the whole body. This, it is believed, will be evident to those who impartially consult Matthew xviii. 15-18; and compare the language of the original here with that of the original, and the Greek translation of the Seventy, of Deuteronomy xxxi. 28-30.

The visible Church is a spiritual body. That is, it is not secular or worldly, either in its nature or objects. The kingdom of Christ "is not of this world." Its Head, laws, ordinances, discipline, penalties, and end, are all spiritual. There can be no departure from this principle; in other words, there can be no connexion between the Church and the State; no enforcement of ecclesiastical laws by the power of the secular arm, or by "carnal weapons," without departing from "the simplicity that is in Christ," and invading both the purity and safety of His sacred body.

This great visible Church is one, in all ages, and throughout the world. From its first formation in the family of Adam, through all the changes of the Patriarchal, Mosaic, and Christian dispensations, it has been one and the same; having the same di-

---

1. It has been asserted by some, that the term *Church* not only means, strictly, a religious assembly, a body of professing people; but that it cannot be applied, with propriety, to any thing else; and that it is altogether improper to apply it, as is often done, to the building in which the assembly is wont to convene for worship. This is, undoubtedly, a groundless scruple. Under the Old Testament economy, it is plain that the word *Synagogue* was indiscriminately applied both to the public assembly and to the edifice in which they worshipped. Besides the word *church* is evidently derived from the Greek words, κυριου οικος, "the house of the Lord;" and therefore, may be considered as pointing quite as distinctly to the edifice as to the worshippers. Nay it is highly probable that the word in its original use had a primary reference to the house rather than to the assembly. And even if it were not so, still the understanding and use of the word in this double sense, if once agreed upon, cannot be considered as liable, so far as is perceived, to any particular objection or abuse.

vine Head, the same ground of hope, the same essential characters, and the same great design. Diversity of denomination does not destroy this unity. All who profess the true religion, together with their offspring, however divided by place, by names, or by forms, are to be considered as equally belonging to that great family denominated the Church. The Presbyterian, the Episcopalian, the Methodist, the Baptist, and the Independent, who hold the fundamentals of our holy religion, in whatever part of the globe they may reside, are all equally members of the same visible community; and, if they be sincere, will all finally be made partakers of its eternal blessings. They cannot, indeed, all worship together in the same solemn assembly, even if they were disposed to do so; and the sin and folly of men have separated into different bodies those who ought to "walk together." Still the visible Church is one. All who "hold the Head," of course, belong to the body of Christ. "We, being many," says the inspired Apostle, "are one body in Christ, and every one members one of another." Those who are united by a sound profession to the same almighty Head; who embrace the same "precious faith;" who are sanctified by the same Spirit; who eat the same spiritual meat; who drink the same spiritual drink; who repose and rejoice in the same promises; and who are travelling to the same eternal rest, are surely one body; in a sense more richly significant than can be ascribed to millions who sustain a mere nominal unity.

This unity is very distinctly recognized, and very happily expressed, by Cyprian, a distinguished Christian Father of the third century. "The Church," says he, "is one, which, by its fruitful increase, is enlarged into a multitude. As the rays of the sun, though many, are yet one luminary; as the branches of a tree, though numerous, are all established on one firmly rooted trunk; and as many streams springing from the same fountain, though apparently dispersed abroad by their overflowing abundance, yet have their unity preserved by one common origin; so the Church, though it extends its rays throughout the world, is one Light. Though every where diffused, its unity is not broken. By the abundance of its increase, it extends its branches through the whole earth. It spreads far and wide its flowing streams; yet it has one Head; one Fountain; one Parent; and is enriched and enlarged by the issues of its own fruitfulness."[2]

It is ever also to be borne in mind that the Church is not a mere voluntary association, with which men are at liberty to connect themselves or not, as they please. For, although the service which God requires of us is throughout a voluntary one: although no one can properly come into the Church but as a matter of voluntary choice: although the idea of either secular or ecclesiastical compulsion is, here, at once unreasonable and contrary to Scripture: yet as the Church is Christ's institution, and not men's; and as the same divine authority which requires us to repent of sin, and believe in Christ, also requires us to "confess Him before men," and to join ourselves to His professing people; it is evident that no one is at liberty, in the sight of God, to neglect uniting himself with the Church. Man cannot, and ought not, to compel him; but if he refuse to fulfil this duty, when it is in his power, he rejects the authority of God. He, of course, refuses at his peril.

Of this body, Christ alone, as before intimated, is the Head. He only has a right to give laws to His Church, or to institute rites and ordinances for her observance. His will is the supreme guide of His professing people; His word their code of laws; and His glory their ultimate end. The authority of Church officers is not original, but subordinate and delegated: that is, as they are His servants, and act under His commission, and in His name, they have power only to declare what the Scriptures reveal as His will, and to pronounce sentence accordingly. If they attempt to establish any other terms of communion than those which His word warrants; or to undertake to exercise authority in a manner which He has not authorized, they incur guilt, and have no right to exact obedience.

In this sacred community, government is absolutely necessary. Even in the perfectly holy and harmonious society of heaven, there is government; that is, there is law and authority,

---

2. *De Unitate Ecclesiæ*. Sect. iv.

under which the whole celestial family is united in perfect love, and unmingled enjoyment. Much more important and indispensable is government among fallen depraved men, among whom "it is impossible but that offences will come," and to whom the discipline of scriptural and pure ecclesiastical rule, is one of the most precious means of grace. To think of maintaining any society, ecclesiastical or civil, without government, in this depraved world, would be to contradict every principle of reason and experience, as well as of Scripture and to think of supporting government without officers, to whom its functions may be intrusted, would be to embrace the absurd hope of obtaining an end without the requisite means.

The question, Whether any particular form of Church government is so laid down in Scripture, as that the claim of divine right may be advanced on its behalf, and that, of consequence, the Church is bound in all ages, to adopt and act upon it; – will not now be formally discussed. It has been made the subject of too much extended and ardent controversy, to be brought within the compass of a few sentences, or even a few pages. It may not be improper, however, briefly to say, that it would, indeed, have been singular, if a community, called out of the world, and organized under the peculiar authority of the all-wise Redeemer, had been left entirely without any direction as to its government: – That the Scriptures, undoubtedly, exhibit to us a form of ecclesiastical organization and rule, which was, in fact, instituted by the Apostles, under the direction of infinite Wisdom that this form was evidently taken, with very little alteration, from the preceding economy, thus giving additional presumption in its favour: – that we find the same plan closely copied by the churches for a considerable time after the apostolic age: – that it continued to be in substance the chosen and universal form of government in the Church, until corruption, both in doctrine and practice, had, through the ambition and degeneracy of ecclesiastics, gained a melancholy prevalence: – and, that the same form was also substantially maintained by the most faithful witnesses for the truth, during the dark ages – until the great body of the Reformers took it from their hands, and established it in their respective ecclesiastical connexions.

These premises would appear abundantly to warrant the conclusion, that the form of government which answers this description, is the wisest and best; that it is adapted to all ages and states of society; and that it is agreeable to the will of Christ that it be universally received in His Church. All this the writer of the following Essay fully believes may be established in favour of Presbyterianism. There seems no reason, however, to believe, with some zealous votaries of the hierarchy, that any particular form of government is in so rigorous a sense of divine right, as to be essential to the existence of the Church; so that where this form is wanting, there can be no Church. To adopt this opinion, is to take a very narrow and unscriptural view of the covenant of grace. After yielding to the visible Church and its ordinances all the importance which the word of God warrants, still it cannot be doubted, that on the one hand, men in regular external membership with the purest Church on earth, may be hypocrites, and perish; and on the other, that all who cordially repent of sin, and receive the Saviour in spirit and in truth, will assuredly obtain eternal life, although they never enjoyed the privilege of a connexion with any portion of the visible Church on earth. The tenor of the Gospel covenant is – "He that believeth on the Son of God hath eternal life, and shall not come into condemnation, but is passed from death unto life; but he that believeth not the Son, shall not see life, but the wrath of God abideth on him."

Still it is plain, from the word of God, as well as from uniform experience, that the government of the Church is a matter of great importance; that the form as well as the administration of that government is more vitally connected with the peace, purity, and edification of the Church, than many Christians appear to believe; and, of consequence, that it is no small part of fidelity to our Master in heaven, to "hold fast" the form of ecclesiastical order, as well as the "form of sound words" which He has delivered to the saints.

The existence of ecclesiastical rulers, presupposes the existence and exercise of ecclesiastical power. A few remarks on the nature, source, and limits of this power may not be irrelevant as a part of this preliminary discussion.

When we speak of ecclesiastical power, then, we speak of that which, much as it is misunderstood, and deplorably as it has been perverted and abused, is plainly warranted, both by reason and Scripture. In fact, it is a prerogative which common sense assigns and secures to all organized society, from a family to a nation. The doctrine attempted to be maintained by the celebrated Erastus, in his work, *De Excommunicutione,* viz*:* that the exercise of all Church power, however modified, is to be rejected, as forming an *imperium in imperio,* is one of the most weak and untenable of all positions. The same argument would preclude all authority or government subordinate to that of the State, whether domestic, academical, or financial. The truth is, there not only may be, but there actually are thousands of *imperia in imperio,* in every civil community in the world; and all this without the least danger or inconvenience, as long as the smaller or subordinate governments maintain their proper place, and do not claim, or attempt to exercise, powers which come in collision with those of the State.

Now the power exercised by the Church is of this character. Christ is the Sovereign. His kingdom is spiritual. It interferes not with civil government. It may exist and flourish under any form of political administration; and always fares best when entirely left to itself, without the interference of the civil magistrate. Accordingly, it is notorious, that the power of which we speak was exercised by the Church in the days of the Apostles, and during the first three centuries of the Christian era, not only without any aid from the secular arm, but while all the civil governments of the world were firmly leagued against her, and following her with the bitterest persecution. But the moment the Church became allied with the State, that moment the influence of each on the other became manifestly mischievous. The State enriched, pampered and corrupted the Church; and the Church, in her turn, gradually extended her power over the State, until she claimed, and in some instances gained, a haughty supremacy over all rulers and governments. This is an ecclesiastical power which the Bible no where recognizes or allows. It is the essence of spiritual usurpation; and can never have a place but where the essential character of the religion of Jesus Christ is misapprehended or forgotten. This abominable tyranny, so long and so wickedly maintained in the name of the meek and lowly Saviour, who, instead of countenancing, always condemned it; – has prejudiced the minds of many against ecclesiastical power in any form. On account of this prejudice it is judged proper to state, with some degree of distinctness, what we mean when we speak of the Church of Christ as being invested with power for the benefit of her members, and for the glory of her almighty Head.

It is evident that even if the Church were a mere voluntary association, which neither possessed nor claimed any divine warrant, it would have the same powers which are universally conceded to all other voluntary associations; that is, the power of forming its own rules, of judging of the qualifications of its own members, and of admitting or excluding, as the essential principles and interests of the body might require; and all this as long as neither the rules themselves, nor the execution of them, infringed the laws of the State, or violated any public or private rights. When a literary, philosophical, or agricultural society claims and exercises powers of this kind, all reflecting people consider it as both reasonable and safe; and would no more think of denying the right to do so, than they would think of denying that the father of a family had a right to govern his own household, as long as he neither transgressed any law of the State, nor invaded the peace of his neighbours.

But the Christian Church is by no means to be considered as a mere voluntary association. It is a body called out of the world, created by divine institution, and created, as its members believe, for the express purpose of bearing testimony for Christ, in the midst of a revolted and rebellious world, and maintaining in their purity the truth and ordinances which He has appointed. The members of this body, therefore, by the act of uniting themselves with it, profess to believe certain doctrines, to be under obligation to perform certain duties, and to be bound to possess a certain character. Of course, the very purpose for which, and the very terms on which the Master has formed this body, and bound its members together, necessarily imply, not only the right, but the duty, of refusing to admit those who are manifestly hostile to the essential principles of its institution, and of casting out those who, after their admission, as manifestly depart from those principles. To suppose less than this, would be to suppose that a God of infinite wisdom has withheld from a body, formed for a certain purpose, that which is absolutely necessary for its defence against intrusion, insult, and perversion; in other words, for its own preservation.

Hence the Apostle Paul, after the New Testament Church was erected, speaks (1 Cor. xii. 28) of "governments," as well as "teachers" being set in it by the authority of God. He expressly claims, (2 Cor. x. 8) an "authority" which God had given to His servants as rulers in the Church, "for edification, and not for destruction." And he exemplifies this authority by representing it as properly exercised in casting out of the Church, any one who was immoral or profane (1 Cor. v). Hence the officers of the Church are spoken of as "guides" ($\eta\gamma o\upsilon\mu\varepsilon\nu o\iota$), "overseers," or "bishops" ($\varepsilon\pi\iota\sigma\kappa o\pi o\iota$) and "rulers" ($\pi\rho o\varepsilon\sigma\tau\omega\tau\varepsilon\varsigma$) – and it is declared to be their duty, not only to instruct, warn, and entreat; but also to "rebuke," or authoritatively to admonish and censure. They were commanded by the authority of the Head of the Church (1 Cor. v.; Tit. iii. 10) to "reject," to "put away from them," after using proper admonition, those who were grossly heretical or immoral. In short, in that period of gospel simplicity, and purity, the Church claimed no authority over any but her own members; and even over them, no other authority than that which related to their character, duties, and interests as members, and was deemed essential to her own well-being.

And as this power of the Church is not self-created or self-assumed, but derived from her gracious and almighty Head; and as it is, and can, of right, only be, exercised over her own members; so it is merely spiritual in its nature; in other words, it claims no right whatever to inflict temporal pains or penalties. It cannot touch the persons or property of those to whom it is directed. It addresses itself only to their judgments and consciences. It includes only a right to instruct, warn, rebuke, censure, and cast out, that is, to exclude from the privileges of the body. This last step is the utmost length to which it can go. When the Church has excluded from her pale those toward whom this power is directed – in other words, when she has declared them out of her communion or fellowship – she has done every thing to which her power extends. All beyond this is usurpation and oppression. The great end of Church Government is not to employ physical force; but moral weapons only. It can never invade the right of private judgment. It can never exert its power over any but those who voluntarily submit to it. And it prescribes no sanctions but those which have for their object the moral benefit of the body itself, and also of the individuals to whom they are awarded. The Gospel knows nothing of delivering men over to the secular arm, to be punished for offences against the Church. The Church might, therefore, exert her whole power, in its plenary extent, though all the governments of the world were arrayed against her in the bitterest hostility, as they have once been and as they may again be found.

And, as all the power of the Church is derived, not from the civil government, but from Christ, the almighty King of Zion; and as it is purely spiritual in its nature and sanctions; so the power of Church officers is merely ministerial. They are strictly servants, who are to be governed, in all things, by the pleasure of their Employer. They have only authority to announce what the Master has said, and to decide agreeably to that will which He has made known in His word. Like ambassadors at a foreign court, they cannot go one jot or tittle beyond their instructions. Of course, they have no right to set up a law of their own. The Bible is the great statute-book of the body of which we speak; the only infallible rule of faith and practice. And nothing can be rightfully inculcated on the members of the Church as truth, or demanded of them as duty, but that which is found in that great charter of the privileges as well as the obligations of Christians.

To complete the view of that ecclesiastical power which we consider as implied in Church government, it is only necessary to add that it is given solely for the benefit of the Church, and not for the aggrandizement of Church officers. Tyrants in civil government have taught, and acted upon the principle, that the great end of all political establishments is the exaltation of a few at the expense of the many. And it is deeply to be deplored that the same principle has been too often apparently adopted by bodies calling themselves Churches of Christ. Nothing can be more opposite than this, to the spirit and law of the Redeemer. The "authority" which the Apostle claims as existing, and to be exercised in the Church, he represents as given "for edification, and not for destruction" (2 Cor. x. 8); – not for the purpose of creating and pampering classes of "privileged orders," to "lord it over God's heritage;" not to build up a system of polity, which may minister to the pride or the cupidity of an ambitious priesthood; not to form a body, under the title of clergy, with separate interests from the laity of the Church. All this is as wicked as it is unreasonable. No office, no power is appointed by Jesus Christ in His Church, but that which is necessary to the instruction, the purity, and the happiness of the whole body. All legitimate government here, as well as elsewhere, is to be considered as a means, not an end; and as no further resting on divine authority, than we can say in support of all its claims and acts, "thus saith the Lord;" than it is adapted to build up the great family of those who profess the true religion, in knowledge, peace, and holiness unto salvation.

The summary of the doctrine of Presbyterians, then, concerning ecclesiastical power, may be considered as comprehended in the following propositions:

1. That the Lord Jesus Christ is the only King and Head of the Church, the Fountain of all power; and that no man or set of men, have any right to consider themselves as holding the place of His vicar, or representative.

2. That the Bible contains the code of laws which Christ has enacted, and given for the government of His Church; and that it is the only infallible rule of faith and practice.

3. That His kingdom is not of this world; and of course, that the Church can take no cognizance of any other concerns than those which relate to the spiritual interests of men.

4. That the power of Church officers is not original, or

inherent, but altogether derived and ministerial. They have no other authority than, as His servants, and in His name, to proclaim the truth which He has declared, and to urge to the performance of those duties which He has commanded.

5. That nothing can be lawfully required of any one as a member of the Church, excepting what is expressly taught in Scripture; or, by good and necessary consequence to be inferred from what is expressly taught there.

6. That the Church being instituted by Christ for the chief purpose of maintaining in their purity the doctrines and ordinances of Christ, is authorized and bound by Him to refuse to admit to her fellowship those who are known to be hostile to this purpose, and to exclude such as are found to offend against this purpose after admission.

7. That the discipline and penalties of the Church are wholly of a moral kind, consisting of admonition, entreaty, warning, suspension, and excommunication; and that exclusion from the fellowship of the body is the highest penalty that can be inflicted on any delinquent.

8. That the apostolic Church, though under the bitterest persecution, was instructed by the inspired Apostles, to exercise the power mentioned, and did actually exercise the same; and is to be considered as therein exemplifying and teaching the principles which ought to regulate the Church in all ages.

9. That the Church can exercise no authority over any others than her own members.

10. That none can be compelled to be members, or to submit to her authority any longer than they choose to do so.

11. That the authority of the Church cannot be lawfully exercised for any other purpose than to promote the purity, order, and edification of the whole body; and that of course, any exercise of Church power which has for its object the aggrandizement of ecclesiastics, at the expense of the body of the Church, is an unscriptural abuse. And,

12. Finally; that all civil establishments of religion, in any form, or under any denomination, are wrong; contrary to the spirit of Christianity; injurious to the best interests of the Church;

and really more to be deprecated by the enlightened friends of piety, than the most sanguinary persecution that can be inflicted by the arm of power.

In every Church completely organized, that is, furnished with all the officers which Christ has instituted, and which are necessary for carrying into full effect the laws of His kingdom, there ought to be three classes of officers, viz: at least one Teaching Elder, Bishop, or Pastor; a bench of Ruling Elders, and Deacons. The first to "minister in the word and doctrine," and to dispense the sacraments; the second to assist in the inspection and government of the Church; and the third to "serve tables;" that is, to take care of the Church's funds destined for the support of the poor, and sometimes to manage whatever relates to the temporal support of the Gospel and its ministers.

The following Essay will be devoted to the consideration of the second class of these officers, namely, Ruling Elders; and the points which it is proposed more particularly to discuss, are the following: the Church's warrant for this class of officers; the nature, design, and duties of the office itself; the qualifications proper for those who bear it; the distinction between this office, and that of deacons; by whom Ruling Elders ought to be elected; in what manner they should be ordained; the principles which ought to regulate their withdrawing or being deposed from office, removing from one Church to another, &c.; and, finally, the advantages attending this form of government in the Church.

The question, whether the Church has any warrant for this class of officers, will have different degrees of importance attached to it by different persons. Those who believe that no form of Church government whatever can justly claim to be, in any sense, of divine right, will, of course, consider this inquiry as of small moment. If the Church be at perfect liberty, at all times, to adopt what form of government she pleases, and to modify, or entirely to change the same at pleasure; then no other warrant than her own convenience or will, ought to be required. But if the writer of the following pages be correct in believing, that there is a form of government for the family of God laid down in Scripture, to which it is the duty of the Church, in all ages, to conform; then the inquiry which it is the purpose of several of the succeeding chapters to pursue, is plainly important, and demands our serious attention.

It is believed, then, that the following positions, in reference to the office now under consideration, may be firmly maintained, viz: that under the Old Testament economy in general, and especially in the Synagogue service, Elders were invariably appointed to exercise authority and bear rule in ecclesiastical society; that similar Elders, after the model of the Synagogue, were appointed in the primitive Church, under the direction of inspired Apostles; that we find in the writings of some of the early Fathers, evident traces of the same office as existing in their times; that the Waldenses, and other pious witnesses for the truth, during the dark ages, retained this class of officers in the Church, as a divine institution; That the Reformers, with very few exceptions, when they separated from the corruptions of Popery, restored this office to the Church; that a number of distinguished divines and Churches, not otherwise Presbyterian, who have flourished since the Reformation, have remarkably concurred in declaring for the same office; and, finally, that Ruling Elders, or officers of a similar kind, are indispensably necessary in every well ordered congregation. Each of these topics of argument is entitled to separate consideration.

CHAPTER TWO

Testimony From the Order of the Old Testament Church

It is impossible fully to understand either the spirit, the facts, or the nomenclature of the New Testament, without going back to the Old. The Christian religion is founded upon that of the Jews; or rather is the completion of it. The latter was the infancy and adolescence of that body of which the former is the manhood. And it is remarkable, that no class of theologians more strenuously contend for the connexion between the Jewish and Christian economies, and the impracticability of taking intelligent views of the one, without some previous knowledge of the other, than most of those who deny the apostolic origin of the class of officers now under consideration. With all such persons, then, we join issue. And, as a very large part of the titles and functions of ecclesiastical officers were, evidently, transmitted from the ceremonial to the spiritual economy, it is indispensably necessary, in order fully to understand their character, to go back to their source.

The term *Elder*, corresponding with זקן in Hebrew, and πρεσβυτερος in Greek, literally signifies an aged person. Among the Jews, and the eastern nations generally, persons advanced in life were commonly selected to fill stations of dignity and authority, because they were supposed to possess most wisdom, gravity, prudence, and experience. From this circumstance, the term *Elder*, became, in process of time, and by a natural association of ideas, an established title of office.[1]

Accordingly, the Jews gave this title to most of their officers, civil as well as ecclesiastical, long before Synagogues were established. From the time of Moses, they had Elders over the nation, as well as over every city, and smaller community. These are repeatedly represented as inspectors, and rulers of the people; as "officers set over them;" and, indeed, throughout their history, there is every reason to believe that the body of the people never, themselves, exercised governmental acts; but chose their Elders, to whom all the details of judicial and executive authority, under their divine Legislator and Sovereign, were constantly committed.

The following specimen of the representation given on this subject in various parts of the Old Testament will suffice, at once, to illustrate and establish what is here advanced. Even while the children of Israel were in Egypt, they seem to have had Elders, in the official sense of the word; for Jehovah, in sending Moses to deliver them, said, "Go, and gather the Elders of Israel together, and say unto them, the Lord hath visited you, and hath seen what is done to you in Egypt;" Exodus iii. 16. In the wilderness, the Elders of Israel are spoken of as called together by Moses, appealed to by Moses, and officially acting under that divinely commissioned leader, on occasions almost innumerable. These Elders appear to have been of different grades, and endowed, of course, with different powers; Exod. xvii. 5; xviii. 12; xxiv. 1, 9; Numbers xi. 16; Deut. xxv. 7-9; xxix. 10; xxxi. 9, 28. From these and other passages, it would seem, they had seventy

---

1. It has been often remarked, that the ancient official use of this word, as implying wisdom and experience, is still preserved in many modern languages, in which *Seigneur*, *Signor*, *Senator*, and other similar words, are used to express both dignity and authority. It is evident that all these words, and some others which might be mentioned, are derivatives from the Latin word *Senior*. It is no less plain, that the title of the magistrates of cities and boroughs, who are called *Alderman* or *Eldermen*, is from the same origin with our modern term *Elder*. Many of the titles of respect, both in the Eastern and Western world, were it proper to take time for the purpose, might be traced beyond all doubt to a similar source.

Elders over the nation; and besides these, Elders over thousands, over hundreds, over fifties, and over tens, who were all charged with inspection and rule in their respective spheres. Again, we find inspectors and rulers of the people, under the name of Elders, existing, and on all public occasions, acting in their official character, in the time of Joshua; during the period of the Judges; under the Kings, especially during the most favoured and happy season of their kingly dominion; probably during the captivity in Babylon; and, beyond all doubt, as soon as they returned from captivity, and became settled in their own land; until the Synagogue system was regularly established as the stated means of popular instruction and worship.

When the Synagogue service was instituted, is a question which has been so much controverted, and is of so much real uncertainty that the discussion of it will not be attempted in this place, especially as it is a question of no sort of importance in the inquiry now before us. All that it is necessary for us to assume, is that it existed, at the time of our Lord's advent, and for a considerable time before; and that the Jews had been long accustomed to its order and worship; which no one, it is presumed, will think of questioning. Now, whatever might have been its origin, nothing can be more certain, than that, from the earliest notices we have of the institution, and through its whole history, its leading officers consisted of a bench of Elders, who were appointed to bear rule in the congregation; who formed a kind of Consistory, or ecclesiastical judicatory, – to receive applicants for admission into the Church; to watch over the people, as well in reference to their morals, as their obedience to ceremonial and ecclesiastical order; to administer discipline when necessary; and, in short, as the representatives of the Church or congregation, to act in their name and behalf; to "bind" and "loose;" and to see that every thing was "done decently and in order."

It is not forgotten that a few eminent writers, following the celebrated German errorist, Erastus, have contended that there was no ecclesiastical government among the Jews distinct from the civil; and that, of course, there were no rulers of the Synagogue, separate from the civil judges. Those who wish to see this error satisfactorily refuted, and the existence of a distinct ecclesiastical government among that people clearly established, may consult what has been written on the subject, by the learned Gillespie,[2] by professor Rutherford,[3] by Bishop Stillingfleet,[4] and others; from whose writings they will be convinced, beyond all reasonable doubt, that the civil and ecclesiastical judicatories were really distinct; that the persons composing each, as well as their respective spheres of judgment were peculiar; and that the latter existed long after the civil sovereignty of the Jewish people was taken away.

There has been, indeed, much diversity of opinion among learned men, concerning a variety of questions which arise in reference to these Elders of the Synagogue; as, for example, whether there was a difference of rank among them; whether some were teachers as well as rulers, and others rulers only; whether there was any diversity in their ordination, &c., &c. But while eminent writers on Jewish antiquities have differed, and continue to differ, in relation to these points, they are all perfectly agreed in one point – namely, that in every Synagogue there was a bench of Elders, consisting of at least three persons, who were charged with the whole inspection, government, and discipline of the Synagogue; who, as a court or bench of rulers, received, judged, censured, excluded, and, in a word, performed every judicial act, necessary to the regularity and welfare of the congregation. In this general fact, Vitringa, Selden, Voetius, Marck, Grotius, Lightfoot, Blondel, Salmasius, and, indeed, so far as I can now recollect, all the writers on this subject, who deserve to be represented as high authorities, substantially agree. And in sup-port of this fact, they quote Philo, Josephus, Maimonides, Benjamin of Tudela, and the great mass of other Jewish witnesses, who are considered as holding the first rank among Rabbinical authorities. Indeed, they speak of the fact as too unquestionable to demand any formal array of testimony for

---

2. *Aaron's Rod, &c.* Lond. 4to. 1646.

3. *Divine Right of Church Government, &c.* Lond 4to. 1646.

4. *Irenicum.* Part 2. Chapter 6.

its confirmation.[5]

Accordingly, we find various passages in the New Testament history, which refer to these Ruling Elders, as belonging to the old economy, then drawing to a close, and which admit, it would appear, of no other interpretation than that which supposes their existence. The following specimen will suffice; Mark v. 22. "And, behold, there cometh one of the rulers of the Synagogue, Jairus by name; and when he saw him he fell at his feet;" Acts xiii. 15. "And after the reading of the law and the prophets, the rulers of the Synagogue sent unto them, saying, Ye men and brethren, if ye have any word of exhortation for the people, say on." On this latter passage, Dr. Gill, an eminent master of oriental, and especially of rabbinical learning, in his Commentary, writes thus: "The rulers of the Synagogue sent unto them: that is, those who were the principal men in the Synagogue; the Ruler of it, together with the Elders; for there was but one Ruler in a Synagogue, though there were more Elders; and so the Syriac version here renders it, the Elders of the Synagogue." By this language, as I understand the Doctor, he does not mean to intimate that the other Elders of whom he here speaks, did not bear rule in the Synagogue; but that there was only one, who, by way of eminence, was called, "the Ruler of the Synagogue;" that is, who presided at their meetings for official business. It is plain, however, that, even in this assertion, he is in some degree in error; for more than once we find a plurality of persons in single Synagogues spoken of as "Rulers."

The learned Vitringa, who, undoubtedly, is entitled to a very high place in the list of authorities on this subject, is of the opinion, that all who occupied a place with the bench of Elders in the Synagogue, were of one and the same rank or order; that they all received one and the same ordination; and were, of

---

5. When the unanimous agreement of these learned writers is asserted, it is not meant to be alleged that they all entertain the same views of the Elders of the *Synagogue,* as to all particulars; but simply that they all unite in maintaining that there was, in every Synagogue, such a bench of Elders, who conducted its discipline, and managed its affairs.

course, equally authorized to preach, when duty or inclination called them to this part of the public service, as well as to rule. And in this opinion he is joined by some others, whose judgment is worthy of the highest respect. But, at the same time, this eminent man freely grants, that a majority of the Elders of the Synagogue were not, in fact, ordinarily employed in teaching or preaching; that this part of the public service was principally under the direction of the chief ruler, or head of each Synagogue, who attended to it himself, or called on one of the other Elders, or even any other learned Doctor who might be present, and who was deemed capable of addressing the people in an instructive and acceptable manner: and that the chief business of the mass of the Elders was *to rule*.[6] The correctness of this opinion has been questioned. A number of other writers, quite his equals, both in talents and learning, and especially quite as conversant with Jewish authorities, have maintained that a majority of the Elders in the Synagogue were neither chosen nor set apart to the function of teaching, but to that of ruling only. But, in the want of absolute certainty which exists on this subject, and for the sake of argument, I am willing to acquiesce in Vitringa's opinion. Suppose it to have been as he alleges: – this is quite sufficient for our purpose. If it be conceded, that there was, in every Synagogue, a bench of Elders, who, as a judicial body, were entrusted with the whole government and discipline of the congregation: – that a majority of these Elders seldom or never preached, but were, in fact (whatever right they might have had) chiefly occupied as ecclesiastical rulers; and that all ecclesiastical matters, instead of being discussed and decided by the congregation at large, were constantly committed to the judicial deliberation and decision of this Eldership; if these things be granted – and they are granted, in substance, by every writer with whom I am acquainted, entitled to be referred to as an authority; – it is all that can be considered as material to the purpose of our argument. This will appear more fully in the sequel.

    These officers of the Synagogue were called by different

---

6. *De Synagoga Vetere*. Lib. iii. Par. i. Cap. 7.

names, as we learn from the New Testament, and from the most respectable Jewish authorities. The most common and familiar name, perhaps, was that of Elders, as before stated at large. They were also called rulers of the Synagogue; a title of frequent occurrence in the New Testament, as applied to the whole bench of the Elders in question; but which would seem, from some passages, to have been, at least, sometimes applied, by way of eminence, to the principal ruler in each Synagogue, which principal ruler appears, however, to have been of the same general rank, or order, with the rest, and to have had no other precedence than that which consisted in presiding and taking the lead in the public service. These officers were further called Heads of the Synagogue, Overseers, or Bishops, Presidents, Orderers, or Regulators of the affairs of the Synagogue, Guides, &c. &c. These titles are given at length by Vitringa,[7] Selden,[8] and others, with the original vouchers and exemplifications of each; showing that they all imply bearing rule, as well as the enjoyment of pre-eminence and dignity.

And as these Elders were distinguished from the common members of the Synagogue by appropriate titles, indicating official honour and power; so they had also distinct and honourable seats assigned them, when the congregation over which they ruled was convened. The place of sitting usually appropriated to them was a semi-circular bench, in the middle of which the chief ruler was placed, and his colleagues on each side of him, with their faces toward the assembly, and in a certain position with respect to the Ark, the principal door, and the cardinal points of the compass. This statement is confirmed by the learned Thorndike, a distinguished Episcopal divine of the 17th century. In speaking of the Consistory, or bench of Elders, in the Synagogue, and describing their manner of sitting in public worship, he makes the following statement, in the form of a quotation from Maimonides, and confirms it abundantly from other sources:

"How sit the people in the Synagogue? The Elders sit with

---

7. *De Synagoga Vetere*, Lib. iii. Par. i. Cap. 1, 2, 3.

8. De Synedriis – passim.

their faces towards the people, and their backs towards the Recall (the place where they have the copy of the law;) and all the people sit rank before rank, the face of every rank towards the back of the rank before it; so the faces of all the people are towards the Sanctuary, and towards the Elders, and towards the Ark; and when the Minister of the Synagogue standeth up to prayer, he standeth on the ground before the Ark, with his face toward the sanctuary, as the rest of the people."[9]

The number of the Elders in each Synagogue was not governed by any absolute rule. In large cities, according to certain Jewish authorities quoted by Vitringa, the number was frequently very large. But even in the smallest Synagogues, we are assured, as mentioned in a former page, that there were never less than three, that the judicatory might never be equally divided.

Such were the arrangements for maintaining purity and order in the Synagogues, or parish churches of the old economy, anterior to the advent of the Messiah. It would seem to be impossible for any one to contemplate this statement, so amply supported by all sound authority, without recognising a striking likeness to the arrangements afterwards adopted in the New Testament Church. That this likeness is real, and has been maintained by some of the ablest writers on the subject, the following short extracts will sufficiently establish.

The first quotation shall be taken from Bishop Burnet. "Among the Jews," says he, "he who was the chief of the Synagogue was called *Chazan Hakeneseth,* that is, the Bishop of the Congregation, and *Sheliach Tsibbor,* the angel of the Church. And the Christian Church being modelled as near the form of the Synagogue as could be, as they retained many of the rites, so the form of their government was continued, and the names remained the same." And again: "In the Synagogues there was, first, one that was called the Bishop of the Congregation. Next the three Orderers, and Judges of every thing about the Synagogue, who were called *Tsekenirn,* and by the Greeks, πρεσβυτεροι or γεροντες. These ordered and determined every

---

9. *Discourse of the Service of God in Religious Assemblies.* Chap. 3. p. 56.

thing that concerned the Synagogue, or the persons in it. Next to them, were the three *Parnassin,* or Deacons, whose charge was to gather the collections of the rich, and to distribute them to the poor. The term *Elder*, was generally given to all their Judges: but chiefly to those of the great Sanhedrim. So we have it in Matt. xvi. 21, Mark viii. 3, xiv. 43, and xv. 1, and Acts xxiii. 14." "A great deal might be said to prove that the Apostles, in their first constitutions, took things as they had been modelled to their hand in the Synagogue. And this they did, both because it was not their design to innovate, except where the nature of the Gospel dispensation obliged them to do it; as also, because, they took all means possible to gain the Jews, who we find were zealous adherers to the traditions of their fathers, and not easily weaned from those precepts of Moses, which by Christ's death were evacuated. And if the Apostles went so great a length in complying with them in great matters, as circumcision and other legal observances (which appears from the Acts and Epistles), we have good grounds to suppose that they would have yielded to them in what was more innocent and less important. Besides, there appears, both in our Lord Himself, and in His Apostles, a great inclination to symbolize with them as far as was possible. Now the nature of the Christian worship shows evidently, that it came in the room of the Synagogue, which was moral, and not of the temple worship, which was typical and ceremonial. Likewise this parity of customs betwixt the Jews and Christians, was such that it made them taken by the Romans, and other more overly observers, for one sect of religion. And, finally, any that will impartially read the New Testament, will find that when the forms of government or worship are treated of, it is not done with such architectonal exactness, as was necessary, if a new thing had been instituted, which we find practised by Moses. But the Apostles rather speak as those who give rules for the ordering and directing of what was already in being. From all which it seems well grounded and rational to assume, that the first constitution of the Christian Churches was taken from the model of the Synagogue, in which these Elders were separated, for the discharge of their employments, by an imposition of hands, as all Jewish writers do clearly witness."[10]

The second testimony shall be that of Dr. Thomas Godwin, an English divine of great erudition, especially in oriental learning. In his well-known work, entitled *Moses and Aaron*, we find the following passage: "There were in Israel distinct Courts, consisting of distinct persons; the one principally for Church business; the other for affairs in the commonwealth; the one an ecclesiastical Consistory; the other a civil Judicatory. The secular Consistory was named a Sanhedrin, or Council; the spiritual, a Synagogue. The office of the ecclesiastical court was to put a difference between things holy and unholy, and to determine appeals in controversies of difficulty. It was a representative Church. Hence is that, *Dic Ecclesæ*. Matt. xviii. 16."[11]

The next quotation shall be taken from Dr. Lightfoot, another Episcopal divine, still more distinguished for his oriental and rabbinical learning. "The Apostle," says he "calleth the minister *Episcopus* (or Bishop), from the common and known title of the *Chazan* or Overseer in the Synagogue." And again: "Besides these, there was the public minister of the Synagogue, who prayed publicly, and took care about reading the law, and sometimes preached, if there were not some other to discharge this office. This person was called, שליח ציבור, the angel of the Church, and חזן הכנסת the *Chazan,* or Bishop of the congregation. The Aruch gives the reason of the name. The *Chazan*, says he, is שליח ציבר, the angel of the Church (or the public minister), and the *Targum* renders the word ראה by the word חזה, one that oversees. For it is incumbent on him to oversee how the reader reads, and whom he may call out to read in the law. The public Minister of the Synagogue himself read not the law publicly; but every Sabbath he called out seven of the Synagogue (on other days fewer), whom he judged fit to read. He stood by him that read, with great care, observing that he read nothing either falsely or improperly, and called him back, and corrected him, if he had

---

10. *Observations on the First and Second Canons, &c.* pp. 82, 83, 84, 85. Glasgow, 12mo. 1673.

11. *Moses and Aaron*, book 5, chapter i.

failed in any thing. And hence he was called *Chazan,* that is, Ἐπίσκοπος, Bishop, or Overseer. Certainly the signification of the words Bishop and Angel of the Church, had been determined with less noise, if recourse had been had to the proper fountains, and men had not vainly disputed about the signification of words taken I know not whence. The service and worship of the temple being abolished, as being ceremonial, God transplanted the worship and public adoration of God used in the Synagogues, which was moral, into the Christian Church; viz: the public ministry, public prayers, reading God's word, and preaching, &c. Hence the names of the ministers of the Gospel were the very same, the Angel of the Church, and the Bishop, which belonged to the Ministers in the Synagogues. "There was in every Synagogue, a bench of three. This bench consisted of three Elders, rightly and by imposition of hands preferred to the Eldership." "There were also three Deacons, or *Almoners,* on which was the care of the poor."[12]

In another place, the same learned orientalist says, describing the worship in the Jewish Synagogue: "In the body of the Church the congregation met, and prayed and heard the law, and the manner of their sitting was this: The Elders sat near the Chancel, with their faces down the Church: and the people sat one form behind another, with their faces up the Church, toward the Chancel and the Elders. Of these Elders there were some that had rule and office in the Synagogue, and some that had not. And this distinction the Apostle seemeth to allude unto, in that much disputed text, 1 Tim. v. 18. The Elders that rule well, &c., where 'the Elders that ruled well' are set not only in opposition to those that ruled ill, but to those that ruled not at all. We may see, then, whence these titles and epithets in the New Testament are taken, namely, from the common platform and constitution of the Synagogues, where *Angelus Ecciesiæ,* and *Episcopus* were terms of so ordinary use and knowledge. And we may observe from whence the Apostle taketh his expressions, when he speaketh of some Elders ruling, and labouring in word and doctrine, and some

---

12. Lightfoot's *Works*, Vol. i. p. 308. Vol. ii. pp. 133.

not; namely, from the same platform and constitution of the Synagogue, where 'the Ruler of the Synagogue' was more singularly for ruling the affairs of the Synagogue, and 'the minister of the Congregation,' labouring in the word, and reading the law, and in doctrine about the preaching of it. Both these together are sometimes called jointly, 'the Rulers of the Synagogue;' Acts xiii. 15; Mark v. 22; being both Elders that ruled; but the title is more singularly given to the first of them."[13]

Again, he says: "In all the Jews' Synagogues there were *Parnasin,* Deacons, or such as had care of the poor, whose work it was to gather alms for them from the congregation, and to distribute it to them. That needful office is here (Acts vi) translated into the Christian Church."[14]

The fourth quotation shall be taken from Dr. (afterwards Bishop) Stillingfleet, who, in his *Irenicum*, maintains a similar position with confidence and zeal; the following is a specimen of his language: "That which we lay, then, as a foundation, whereby to clear what apostolical practice was, is that the Apostles, in forming Churches, did observe the customs of the Jewish Synagogue."[15] And in support of this position, particularly in reference to the Eldership of the Synagogue, he quotes a large number of the most distinguished writers, both Jewish and Christian. It is due to candour, indeed, to state, that Stillingfleet does not admit that any of the Elders, either of the Synagogue, or of the primitive Church, were lay-elders, but thinks they were all invested with some kind of clerical character. This, however, as before remarked, does not at all affect the value of his testimony to the general fact, that, in every Synagogue there was a Consistory, or Judicatory, of Elders, and that the same class of officers was adopted, both name and thing, in the apostolic Church, which he unequivocally asserts and proves.

In the same general doctrine, Grotius and Salmasius of

---

13. Lightfoot's *Works,* Vol. i. pp. 611, 612.

14. *Ibid,* i. 279.

15. *Irenicum*. Part 2. Chapter 6.

Holland, decisively concur. By Grotius, the following strong and unqualified language is used: "The whole polity, or order (regimen) of the Churches of Christ, was conformed to the model of the Jewish Synagogue." And again, speaking of ordination by the imposition of hands, he says: "This method was observed in setting apart the Rulers and Elders of the Synagogue: and thence the custom passed into the Christian Church."[16] Salmasius also, and other writers, of equally profound learning, might be quoted as unequivocally deciding, that the Synagogue had a bench of Ruling Elders, and that a similar bench, after that model, was constituted in the Christian Church. Especially, he contends that the Elders of the Church were, beyond all doubt, taken from the Eldership in the Synagogue.[17]

The learned Spencer, a divine of the Church of England, in the seventeenth century, teaches the same general doctrine, when he says: "The Apostles, also, that this reformation (the change from the Old to the New Testament dispensation) might proceed gently, and without noise, received into the Christian Church many of those institutions which had been long in use among the Jews. Among the number of these may be reckoned, the imposition of hands; bishops, elders, and deacons; excommunication, ordination, and other things familiar to learned men."[18]

Dr. Adam Clarke, whose eminent learning no competent judge will question, also bears testimony that in every Jewish Synagogue, at the time of the coming of Christ, and before, there was an ecclesiastical judicatory, or little Court, whose duty it was to conduct the spiritual government of each congregation. Among several places in which he makes this statement, the following is decisive: – In his Commentary on James ii. 2, he says: "In ancient times petty courts of judicature were held in the Synagogues, as Vitringa has sufficiently proved, De Vet. Syn. I. 3.; and it is probable that the case here adduced was one of a judicial kind; where of the two parties, one was rich, and the other

---

16. Grotii, *Annotationes in Act. Apost.* vi. xi.
17. *De Primatu Papæ.* cap. i.
18. *De Legibus Hebræoram*, Lib. iii. Dissert. 1. Cap. 2. Sect. 4.

kind; where of the two parties, one was rich, and the other poor; and the master or ruler of the Synagogue, or he who presided in this court, paid particular deference to the rich man, and neglected the poor person; though as plaintiff and defendant, they were equal in the eye of justice."

I shall cite on this subject only one more authority; that of the celebrated Augustus Neander, Professor in the University of Berlin, and generally considered as perhaps more profoundly skilled in Christian antiquities, than any other man now living. He is, moreover, a minister of the Lutheran Church, and, of course, has no sectarian spirit to gratify in vindicating Presbyterianism. And, what is not unworthy of notice, being himself of Jewish extraction, he has enjoyed the highest advantages for exploring the peculiar polity of that people. After showing at some length, that the government of the primitive Church was not monarchical or prelatical, but dictated throughout by a spirit of mutual love, counsel, and prayer, he goes on to express himself thus: "We may suppose that where any thing could be found in the way of Church forms, which was consistent with this spirit, it would be willingly appropriated by the Christian community. Now there happened to be in the Jewish Synagogue, a system of government of this nature; not monarchical, but rather aristocratical (or a government of the most venerable and excellent.) A council of Elders, וּקְנֵים, πρεσβυτεροι, conducted all the affairs of that body. it seemed most natural that Christianity, developing itself from the Jewish religion, should take this form of government. This form must also have appeared natural and appropriate to the Roman citizens, since their nation had, from the earliest times, been, to some extent, under the control of a Senate, composed of Senators, or Elders. When the Church was placed under a council of Elders, they did not always happen to be the oldest in reference to years; but the term expressive of age here, was, as in the Latin *Senatus*, and in the Greek γερουσια, expressive of worth or merit. Besides the common name of these overseers of the Church, to wit, πρεσβυτεροι, there were many other names given, according to the peculiar situation occupied by the individual, or rather his peculiar field of labour; as ποιμενες, shepherds; *ηγουμενοι,* leaders; *προεστωτες των αδελφων,* rulers of the brethren; and *επισκοποι,* overseers."[19]

Now, if, in the ancient Jewish Synagogue, the government of the congregation was not vested either in the people at large, or in any single individual, but in a bench of Elders; if this is acknowledged on all hands, as one of the clearest and most indubitable facts in Jewish antiquity; – and if, in the judgment of the most learned and pious divines that ever lived, both episcopal and non-episcopal, the New Testament Church was formed after the model of the Jewish Synagogue, and not after the pattern of the Temple service; – we may, of course, expect to find some evidence of this in the history of the apostolic Churches. How far this expectation is realized, will be seen in the next chapter.

---

19. Kirchengeschichte, Vol. i. pp. 283, 285.

CHAPTER THREE

Evidence in Favour of the Office From the New Testament Scriptures

In this chapter it is proposed to show, that the office in question is mentioned in the New Testament as existing in the apostolic Church; that it was adopted from the Synagogue; and that it occupied, in substance, the same place in the days of the Apostles, that it now occupies in our truly primitive and scriptural Church.

The first assertion is, that this class of officers was adopted in the Church of Christ, under its New Testament form, after the model of the Synagogue. Some have said, indeed, that the Apostles adopted the model of the temple, and not of the Synagogue service, in the organization of the Church. But the slightest impartial attention to facts will be sufficient, it is believed, to disprove this assertion. If we compare the titles, the powers, the duties, and the ordination of the officers of the Christian Church, as well as the nature and order of its public service, as established by the Apostles, with the Temple and the Synagogue systems respectively, we shall find the organization and service of the Church to resemble the Temple in scarcely any thing; while they resemble the Synagogue in almost every thing. There were Bishops, Elders, and Deacons, in the Synagogue; but no officers bearing these titles, or performing similar functions in the Temple. There was ordination by the imposition of hands in the Synagogue; but no such ordination in the Temple. There were reading the Scriptures, expounding them, and public prayers, every Sabbath day in the Synagogue; while the body of the people went up to the Temple only three times a year, and even then to attend on a very different service. In the Synagogue, there was a system established, which included a weekly provision, not only for the instruction and devotions of the people, but also for the maintenance of discipline, and the care of the poor; while scarcely any thing of this kind was to be found in the Temple. Now, in all these respects, and in many more which might be mentioned, the Christian Church followed the Synagogue model, and departed from that of the Temple. Could we trace a resemblance only in one or a few points, it might be considered as accidental; but the resemblance is so close, so striking, and extends to so many particulars, as to arrest the attention of the most careless inquirer. It was, indeed, notoriously, so great in the early ages, that the heathen frequently suspected Christian Churches of being Jewish Synagogues in disguise, and stigmatized them as such accordingly.

And when it is considered that all the first converts to Christianity were Jews; that they had been accustomed to the offices and service of the Synagogue during their whole lives: that they came into the Church with all the feelings and habits connected with their old institutions strongly prevalent; and that the organization and service of the Synagogue were of a moral nature, in all their leading characters, proper to be adopted under any dispensation; while the typical and ceremonial service of the Temple was then done away; – when these things are considered, will it not appear perfectly natural that the Apostles, themselves native Jews, should be disposed to make as little change in converting Synagogues into Christian Churches, as was consistent with the spirituality of the new dispensation? That the Synagogue model, therefore, should be adopted, would seem beforehand to be the most probable of all events. Nor is this a new or sectarian notion. Whoever looks into the writings of some of the early Fathers; of the Reformers; and of a large portion of the most learned men who have adorned the Church of Christ, subsequently to the Reformation, will find a very remarkable concurrence of opinion that such was the model really adopted in the organization of the apostolic Church. Most of the distinguished writers whose names are mentioned in the preceding chapter, are, as we have seen, unanimous and zealous in maintaining this position.

Accordingly, as soon as we begin to read of the Apostles organizing Churches on the New Testament plan, we find them instituting officers of precisely the same nature, and bestowing on them, for the most part, the very same titles to which they had been accustomed in the ordinary sabbatical service under the preceding economy. We find Bishops, Elders, and Deacons, every where appointed. We find a plurality of Elders ordained in every Church. And we find the Elders represented as "overseers," or inspectors of the Church; as "rulers" in the house of God; and the members of the Church exhorted to "obey them," and "submit" to them, as to persons charged with their spiritual interests, and entitled to their affectionate and dutiful reverence.

The following passages may be considered as a specimen of the New Testament representations on this subject. "And when they had ordained them Elders in every Church, and had prayed with fasting, they commended them to the Lord, on whom they believed;" Acts xiv. 23. "And when they were come to Jerusalem, they were received of the Church, and of the Apostles and Elders. And the Apostles and Elders came together to consider of this matter;" Acts xv. 4, 6. "And from Miletus, he (Paul) sent to Ephesus, and called the Elders of the Church; and when they were come unto him, he said unto them, Take heed unto yourselves, and to all the flock, over which the Holy Ghost hath made you overseers;" Acts xx. 20, 28. "Is any sick among you? Let him call for the Elders of the Church; and let them pray over him," &c.; James v. 14. "The Elders which are among you I exhort, who am also an Elder, and a witness of the sufferings of Christ and also a partaker of the glory that shall be revealed. Feed the flock of God that is among you, taking the oversight thereof, not by constraint, but willingly; not for filthy lucre, but of a ready mind; neither as being Lords over God's heritage, but being ensamples to the flock;" 1 Peter v. 1, 2, 3. "For this cause left I thee in Crete, that thou shouldest set in order the things that are wanting, and ordain Elders in every city, as I had appointed thee;" Titus i. 5. "Obey them that have the rule over you, and submit yourselves, for they watch for your souls as they that must give account;" Heb. xiii. 17. "And we beseech you, brethren, to know them which labour among you, and are over you in the Lord, and admonish you, and to esteem them very highly in love for their work's sake;" 1 Thess. v. 12, 13. "Let the Elders that rule well be accounted worthy of double honour, especially they who labour in the word and doctrine;" 1 Tim. v. 17. To whatever Church our attention is directed, in the inspired history, we find in it a plurality of Elders; we find the mass of the Church members spoken of as under their authority; and while the people are exhorted to submit to their rule, with all readiness and affection; these rulers are commanded, in the name of Christ, to exercise the power vested in them by the great Head of the Church, with firmness, and fidelity, and yet with disinterestedness and moderation, so as to promote most effectually the purity and order of the flock.

The circumstance of our finding it so uniformly stated that there was a plurality of Elders ordained in every Church, is certainly worthy of particular attention here. If there had been a plurality of these officers appointed only in some of the more populous cities, where there were probably several worshipping assemblies; where the congregations may be supposed to have been unusually large; and where it was important, of course, to have more than a single preacher; then we might consider this fact as very well reconcilable with the doctrine of those who assert, that all the Elders in the apostolic Church were official teachers. But as both the direction and the practice were to ordain Elders – that is, more than one, at least, in every Church, small as well as great – there is, evidently, very strong presumption that it was intended to conform to the Synagogue model; and if so, that the whole of the number so ordained could not be necessary for the purpose of public instruction; but that some were rulers, who, as in the Synagogue, formed a kind of congregational Presbytery, or consistory, for the government of the Church. The idea that it was considered as necessary, at such a time, that every

Church should have two, three, or four Pastors or Ministers, in the modern popular sense of those terms, is manifestly altogether inadmissible. But if a majority of these Elders, whatever their ordination or authority might be, were in fact employed, not in teaching, but in ruling, all difficulty vanishes at once.

Accordingly, the learned Vitringa, before mentioned, whose authority is much relied upon to disprove the existence of the office of Ruling Elder in the primitive Church, explicitly acknowledges, not only that there was then a plurality of Elders in every Church; but that, as in the Synagogue, the greater part of these were, in fact, employed in ruling only; and that although all of them were set apart to their office in the same manner, and were, ecclesiastically, of the same rank, yet a majority of them, from want of suitable qualifications, were not fitted to the public preachers, and seldom or never attempted this part of the service.[1]

But there are distinct passages of Scripture, which have been deemed, by some of the most impartial and competent interpreters, very plainly to point out the class of Elders now under consideration. In Romans xii. 6, 7, 8, the Apostle exhorts as follows: "Having then gifts, differing according to the grace given to us; whether prophecy, let us prophesy according to the proportion of faith; or ministry, let us wait on our ministering; or he that teacheth on teaching; or he that exhorteth on exhortation; he that giveth, let him do it with simplicity; he that ruleth, with diligence; he that showeth mercy, with cheerfulness." With this passage may be connected another, of similar character, and to be interpreted on the same principles. In 1 Cor. xii. 28, we are told: "God hath set some in the Church, first Apostles, secondarily Prophets, thirdly Teachers, after that miracles, then gifts of healing, helps, governments, diversities of tongues." In both these passages there is a reference to the different offices and gifts bestowed on the Church by her divine King and Head; in both of them there is a plain designation of an office for ruling or government, distinct from that of teaching; and in both, also, this

---

1. Vitringa, *De Synagoga Vetere*. Lib. ii. Cap. ii.

office evidently has a place assigned to it below that of Pastors and Teachers. Now, this office, by whatever name it may be called, or whatever doubts may be started as to some minor questions respecting its powers and investiture, is substantially the same with that which Presbyterians distinguish by the title of Ruling Elder.

Some, indeed, have said that the Apostle in 1 Cor. xii. 28 is not speaking of distinct offices, but of different duties, devolving on the Church as a body. But no one, it is believed, who impartially considers the whole passage, can adopt this opinion. In the whole of the context, from the 12th verse, the Apostle is speaking of the Church of God under the emblem of a body, and affirms that, in this body, there is a variety of members adapted to the comfort and convenience of the whole body. For the body, says he, is not one member, but many. "If the foot shall say, Because I am not the hand, I am not of the body, is it, therefore, not of the body? And if the ear shall say, Because I am not the eye, I am not of the body, is it, therefore, not of the body? If the whole body were an eye, where were the hearing? If the whole were hearing, where were the smelling? But now hath God set the members every one of them in the body as it hath pleased him. And if they were all one member, where were the body?" plainly implying that in every ecclesiastical, as well as in every natural body, there are different functions and offices; that all cannot be teachers; that all cannot be governors, or governments; but that to each and every functionary is assigned his proper work and duty.

Nor is this interpretation of the Apostle confined to Presbyterians. Peter Martyr, the learned Italian reformer, interprets the passage before us just as we have done. In his Commentary on 1 Cor. xii. 28, he speaks thus: "Governments. Those who are honoured with this function, are such as were fitted for the work of government, and who know how to conduct every thing relating to discipline righteously and prudently. For the Church of Christ had its government. And because a single pastor was not able to accomplish every thing himself, there were joined with him, in the ancient Church, certain Elders, chosen from among the people, well-informed, and skilled in spiritual things, who formed a kind of parochial Senate. These, with the pastor, deliberated on every matter relating to the care and edification of the Church. Which thing Ambrose makes mention of in writing on the Epistle to Timothy. Among these Elders the Pastor took the lead, not as a tyrant, but rather as a Consul presiding in a council of Senators." Many Episcopalians and others find in the passage the same sense. The Rev. Herbert Thorndike, before quoted, a learned divine of the Church of England, who lived in the reign of Charles I., speaks thus of the passage last cited. "There is no reason to doubt, that the men whom the Apostle, 1 Cor. xii. *28,* and Eph. iv. 11, called Doctors, or Teachers, are those of the Presbyters, who had the abilities of preaching and teaching the people at their assemblies; that those of the Presbyters who preached not, are called here by the Apostle, governments; and the Deacons, $αντιληψεις$, that is, helps, or assistants to the Government of Presbyters; so that it is not to be translated helps in governments, but helps, governments, &c. There were two parts of the Presbyter's office, viz: teaching and governing, the one whereof some attained not, even in the Apostle's times."[2]

But there is a still more pointed reference to this class of Elders in I Tim. v. 17. "Let the Elders that rule well be counted worthy of double honour, especially they who labour in the word and doctrine." It would seem that every person of plain common sense, who had never heard of any diversity of opinion on the subject, would, without hesitation, conclude, on reading this passage, that, at the period in which it was written, there were two kinds of Elders: one whose duty it was to labour in the word and doctrine, and another who did not thus labour, but only ruled in the Church. The Apostle declares that Elders who rule well are worthy of double honour, but especially those who labour in the word and doctrine. Now, if we suppose that there was only one class of Elders then in the Church, and that they were all teachers, or labourers in the word and doctrine, we make the inspired

---

2. *Discourse of Religious Assemblies.* Chap. iv. p. 117.

Apostle speak in a manner utterly unworthy of his high character. There was, therefore, a class of Elders in the apostolic Church who did not, in fact, or, at any rate, ordinarily, preach, or administer sacraments, but assisted in government; in other words, Ruling Elders.

For this construction of the passage, Dr. Whitaker, a zealous and learned Episcopal divine, and Regius Professor of Divinity in the University of Cambridge, of whom Bishop Hall remarks, that "no man ever saw him without reverence, or heard him without wonder," very warmly contends, "By these words, the Apostle evidently distinguishes between the Bishops and the Inspectors of the Church. If all who rule well be worthy of double honour, especially they who labour in the word and doctrine, it is plain that there were some who did not so labour; for if all had been of this description, the meaning would have been absurd; but the word "especially" points out a difference. If I should say that all who study well at the University are worthy of double honour, especially they who labour in the study of theology, I must either mean, that all do not apply themselves to the study of theology, or I should speak nonsense. Wherefore I confess that to be the most genuine sense by which Pastors and Teachers are distinguished from those who only governed; Romans xii. 8. Of this class of Elders Ambrose speaks in his commentary on 1 Tim. v. 1."[3]

The learned and venerable Dr. Owen gives his opinion of the import of this passage in still more pointed language. "This is a text," says he, "of incontrolable evidence, if it had any thing to conflict withal but prejudice and interest. A rational man, who is unprejudiced, who never heard of the controversy about Ruling Elders, can hardly avoid an apprehension that there are two sorts of Elders, some who labour in the word and doctrine, and some who do not so do. The truth is, it was interest and prejudice which first caused some learned men to strain their wits to find out evasions from the evidence of this testimony. Being found out, some others, of meaner abilities, have been entangled, by

---

3. Prælectiones, as quoted in Calderwood's *Altare Damascenum*, p. 681.

them. There are Elders, then, in the Church. There are, or ought to be so in every Church. With these Elders the whole rule of the Church is intrusted. All these, and only they, do rule in it."[4]

Equally to our purpose is the judgment of that acute and learned Episcopal divine, Dr. Whitby, in his Commentary on this passage: "The Elders of the Jews," says he, "were of two sorts; 1st, such as governed in the Synagogue, and 2dly, such as ministered in reading and expounding their scriptures and traditions, and from them, pronouncing what did bind or loose, or what was forbidden, and what was lawful to be done. For when, partly by their captivity, and partly through increase of traffic, they were dispersed in considerable bodies through divers regions of the world, it was necessary that they should have governors or magistrates to keep them in their duty, and judge of criminal causes; and also Rabbins, to teach them the law, and the tradition of their fathers. The first were ordained *ad judicandum, sed non ad docendum de licitis et vetitis,* i.e., to judge and govern, but not to teach. The second, *ad docendum, sed non ad judicandum,* i.e., to teach, but not to judge or govern." "And these the Apostle here declares to be the most honourable, and worthy of the chiefest reward. Accordingly, the Apostle, reckoning up the officers God had appointed in the Church, places teachers before governments;" Cor. xii. 28.

I am aware that a number of glosses have been adopted to set aside the testimony of this cogent text in favour of Ruling Elders. To enumerate and show the invalidity of them all, would be inconsistent with the limits to which this manual is restricted. But a few of the most plausible and popular may be deemed worthy of notice.

Some, for example, have said, that, by the Elders that rule well in this passage, civil magistrates are intended; while, by those who labour in the word and doctrine, ministers of the Gospel are pointed out. But it will occur to every reflecting reader that, at the time when the passage of Scripture under consideration was addressed to Timothy, and for several centuries after-

---

4. *True Nature of a Gospel Church*. Chapter vii. pp. 41, 142, 143.

wards, there were no Christian Magistrates in the Church; and to suppose that the Church is exhorted to choose heathen judges or magistrates, to compose differences, and maintain order among the followers of Christ, is in the highest degree improbable, not to say altogether absurd.

Others have alleged, that by the Elders that rule well are meant Deacons. It is enough to reply to this suggestion, that it has never been shown, or can be shown, that Deacons are any where in the New Testament distinguished by the title of Elders; and, further, that the function of ruling is no where represented as belonging to their office. They were appointed διακονειν τραπεζαις, "to serve tables;" Acts vi. 2, 3; – but not to act as rulers in the house of God. Of this, however, more in a subsequent chapter.

A third class of objectors contend, that the word μαλιστα, which our translators have rendered *especially,* ought to be translated *much;* that it is not to be considered as distinguishing one class of Elders from another, but as marking intensity of degree; in other words, that it is meant to be exegetical of those who rule well, viz: those who labour much, or with peculiar diligence, in the word and doctrine. On this plan, the verse in question would read thus: Let the Elders who rule well, that is who labour much in the word and doctrine, be accounted worthy of double honour. If this were adopted as the meaning of the passage, it would go to show that it is for preaching alone, and not for ruling well, that Elders are entitled to honour. But is it rational or consistent with other parts of Scripture, to suppose that no honour is due to the latter? It has also been contended, by excellent Greek critics, that the structure of the sentence will not naturally bear this interpretation. It is not said, δι μαλιστα κοπιωντες, as would have been the proper order of the words if such had been the meaning intended to be conveyed; but μαλιστα οι κοπιωντες: – not those who labour with especial diligence and exertion; but especially those who labour, &c. But the most decisive consideration is, that not a single case can be found in the New Testament in which the word has the signification here attributed to it. It is so generally used to distinguish one class of objects from another, that we may safely venture to say, it cannot possibly have a different meaning in the passage before us. A few decisive examples will be sufficient. In the same chapter, from which the passage under consideration is taken, (1 Tim. v. 8,) it is said: "If any man provide not for his own, and especially (μαλιστα) for those of his own house, he hath denied the faith," &c. Again; Gal. iv. 10: "Let us do good unto all men, but especially (μαλιστα) unto them who are of the household of faith." Again; Philip. iv. 22: "All the saints salute you, chiefly (μαλιστα) they of Cæsar's household." Thus, also, 2 Tim. iv. 13: "When thou comest, bring with thee the books, but especially (μαλιστα) the parchments." Further; 1 Tim. iv. 10: "Who is the Saviour of all men, especially (μαλιστα) of those who believe." Again; Titus i. 10: For there are many unruly and vain talkers, especially (μαλιστα) they of the circumcision." Now, in all these cases, there are two classes of objects intended to be distinguished from each other. Some of the saints were of Cæsar's household, and others were not. Good was to be done to all men; but all were not believers. There were many vain and unruly talkers alluded to, but they were not all of the circumcision: and so of the rest.

A fourth class of objectors to our construction of this passage, are certain prelatists who allege, that by the Elders that rule well, the Apostle intends to designate superannuated Bishops, who though too old to labour in the word and doctrine, were still able to assist in ruling. To this it is sufficient to reply, that, whether we understand the "honour" (τιμης) to which the Apostle refers, as intended to designate pecuniary support, or rank and dignity, it would seem contrary to every principle, both of reason and Scripture, that younger and more vigorous labourers in the word and doctrine, should have a portion of this honour awarded to them, superior to that which is yielded to those who have become worn out in the same kind of service. These aged, venerable, and exhausted dignitaries, according to this construction, are to be, indeed, much honoured, but less than their junior brethren, whose strength for labour still continues.

A further objection made to our construction of this passage is, that when the Apostle speaks of double honour (διπλης τιμης) as due to those who rule well, he refers, not to respect and regard, but to temporal support.[5] Now, say this class of objectors, as Presbyterians never give salaries to their Ruling Elders, they cannot be the kind of officers contemplated by the sacred writers in this place. But is it certain that by the original term here translated "honour," salary, or maintenance, is really intended? Why not assign to the word τιμη its more common signification, viz.: honour, high respect, reverence? It is common to say, that the illustration contained in the 18th verse, "Thou shalt not muzzle the ox that treadeth out the corn; and the labourer is worthy of his reward," seem to fix the meaning to temporal support. But those illustrations only carry with them the general idea of reward; and surely a reward may be of the moral as well as of the pecuniary kind. But supposing the inspired Apostle really to mean double, that is liberal maintenance, still this interpretation does not at all militate against our doctrine. It might have been very proper, in the days of Paul, to give all the Elders a decent temporal support, as a reward for their services. But if any Elders chose to decline receiving a regular stipend, as Paul himself seems to have done, he surely did not, by this disinterestedness, forfeit his office. It may be that Ruling Elders ought now to receive a compensation for their services, especially when they devote to the Church a large part of their time and talents. But if any are willing to render their services gratuitously, whether they be ruling or preaching Elders, every one sees that this cannot destroy, or even impair their official standing.

---

5. It is worthy of notice that Calvin, in his Commentary on this place, gives the following view of the Apostle's meaning when he speaks of "double honour." "When Chrysostom interprets the phrase *double honour*, as importing support and reverence, I do not impugn his opinion. Let those adopt it who think proper. But to me it appears more probable that a comparison is here intended between widows and elders. Paul had just before commanded to have widows in honour. But Elders are still more worthy of honour than they. Wherefore to these double honour is to be given." This interpretation is natural, and consistent. "Honour widows, says the Apostle, that are widows indeed;" but "let the Elders that rule well be counted worthy of double honour, especially those that labour in the word and doctrine." The same word is used to express honour, in both cases.

Accordingly, it will be seen in the sequel, that there is a concurrence of sentiment, in favour of our construction of this celebrated passage in Timothy, among the most distinguished divines of all denominations, Protestant and Catholic, Lutheran and Reformed, truly remarkable, and affording a very strong presumptive argument in favour of its correctness.

There is another class of passages, already quoted in a former part of this chapter, which is entitled to more formal consideration. I mean such as that found in 1 Thess. v. 12, 13. "And we beseech you, brethren, to know them which labour among you, and are over you in the Lord, and admonish you; and to esteem them very highly in love for their work's sake." Such also as that found in Heb. xiii. 17. "Obey them that have the rule over you, and submit yourselves; for they watch for your souls, as they that must give account," &c. Here the inspired writer is evidently speaking of particular Churches. He represents them as each having a body of Rulers "set over them in the Lord," who "watch over them," and whom they are bound to "obey." In short, we find a set of officers spoken of, who are not merely to instruct, and exhort, but to exercise official authority in the Church. Now this representation can be made to agree with no other form of government than that of the Presbyterian Church. Not with Prelacy; for that presents no ruler in any single Church but the Rector only. It knows nothing of a Parochial Council, or Senate, who conduct discipline, and perform all the duties of spiritual rule. Not with Independency; for according to the essential principles of that system, the body of the communicants are all equally rulers, and even the Pastor is only the chairman, or president, not properly the Ruler of the Church. But with the Presbyterian form of Church government, in which every congregation is furnished with a bench of spiritual Rulers, whom the people are bound to reverence and obey, it agrees perfectly.

There is only one passage more which will be adduced in support of the class of Elders before us. This is found in Matt. xviii. 15-17. Here it is believed that the 17th verse, which enjoins: "Tell it to the Church," has evidently a reference to the plan of discipline known to have been pursued in the Jewish Synagogue and that the meaning is, "Tell it to that Consistory or Judicatory, which is the Church acting by its representatives." It is true, indeed, that some Independents, of more zeal than caution, have confidently quoted this passage as making decisively in favour of their scheme of popular government. But when carefully examined, it will be found not only by no means to answer their purpose; but rather to support the Presbyterian cause. We must always interpret language agreeably to the well known understanding and habit of the time and the country in which it is delivered. Now, it is perfectly certain that the phrase: "Tell it to the Church," was constantly in use among the Jews to express the carrying a complaint to the Eldership or representatives of the Church. And it is quite as certain, that actual cases occur in the Old Testament in which the term *Church* (εκκλησια) is applied to the body of Elders. See as an example of this, Deuteronomy xxxi. 28, 30, comparing our translation with that of the Seventy, as alluded to in a preceding chapter. We can scarcely avoid the conclusion, then, that our blessed Lord meant to teach His disciples, that, as it had been in the Jewish Synagogue, so it would be in the Christian Church, that the sacred community should be governed by a bench of Rulers regularly chosen and set apart for this purpose.

In support or this construction of the passage before us, we have the concurring judgment of a large majority of Protestant divines, of all denominations. We have not only the opinion of Calvin, Beza, Paræus, and a great number of distinguished writers on the continent of Europe; but also of Lightfoot, Goodwin, and many others, both ministers of the Church of England, and the Independents of that country. It is worthy of remark, too, that Chrysostom, known to be an eminently learned and accomplished Father, of the fourth century, evidently understands this passage in the Gospel according to Matthew, as substantially agreeing with the views of Presbyterians; or, at any rate, as totally rejecting the Independent doctrine. Zanchius (in *Quart. Præcept.*) and Junius (*Controv.* iii. Lib. ii. Cap. vi.) quote him as asserting in his Commentary on this place, that by the Church to which the offence was to be told, we are to understand the *προεδροι και προεστωτες* of the Church.

It may not be improper, before taking leave of the Scriptural testimony in favour of Ruling Elders, to take some notice of an objection which has been advanced with much confidence, but which manifestly, when examined, will be found destitute of the smallest force. It has been said that great reliance is placed on the word *προεστωτες*, found in 1 Timothy v. 17, as expressive of the ruling character of the office under consideration; whereas, say these objectors, this very word, as is universally known and acknowledged, is applied by several of the early Fathers to Teaching Elders, to those who evidently bore the office of Pastors of Churches, and who were, of course, not mere rulers, but also "labourers in the word and doctrine." If, therefore, this title be applied to those who were confessedly teachers, what evidence have we that it is intended, in any case, to designate a different class? This objection is founded on a total misrepresentation of the argument which it is supposed to refute. The advocates of the office of Ruling Elder do not contend or believe that the function of ruling is confined to this class of officers. On the contrary, they suppose and teach that one class of Elders both rule and teach, while the other class rule only. Both, according to the doctrine of the Presbyterian Church, are *προεστωτες*; but one only "labours in the word and doctrine." When, therefore, cases are found in the early records of the Church in which the presiding Elder, or Pastor, is styled *προεστως,* the fact is in perfect harmony with the usual argument from I Tim. v. 17; the import of which we maintain to be this: Let all the Elders that rule well, be counted worthy of double honour, especially those of their number who, besides ruling, besides acting as *προεστες*, in common with the others, also labour in the word and doctrine.

It has also been contended that the whole doctrine of the Ruling, as distinct from the Teaching Elder, tends to weaken, if not wholly to destroy, the Presbyterian argument in favour of parity in the Gospel ministry, drawn from the fact, that both Scripture and early Christian antiquity represent Bishop and Presbyter as convertible titles for the same office. Presbyterians maintain, and I have no doubt, with perfect truth, that, in the language of the New Testament, a Bishop means the Pastor, or overseer of a single Church or parish; that Bishop and Presbyter are not titles which imply different grades of office; but that a Presbyter or Elder who has a pastoral charge, who is the overseer of a flock, is a Scriptural Bishop, and holds the highest office that Christ has instituted in his Church. Now, it has been alleged by the opponents of Ruling Elders, that to represent the Scriptures as holding forth two classes of Elders, one class as both teaching and ruling, and the other as ruling only, and consequently, the latter as holding a station not exactly identical with the former, amounts to a virtual surrender of the argument derived from the identity of Bishop and Presbyter.

This objection, however, is totally groundless. If we suppose *Elder*, as used in Scripture, to be a generic term, comprehending all who bore rule in the Church; and if we consider the term *Bishop*, as also a generic term, including all who sustained the relation of official inspectors or overseers of a flock, then it is plain that all Bishops were scriptural Elders; and that all Elders, whether both teachers and rulers, or rulers only, provided they were placed over a parish, as inspectors or overt seers, were scriptural Bishops. Now this, I have no doubt, was the fact. When, therefore, the Apostle Paul, in writing to the Church at Philippi, addresses the Bishops and Deacons; and when in his conference with the Elders of the Church of Ephesus, at Miletus, he speaks of them all equally as Overseers, or, as it is in the original, *Bishops* (επισκοπους) of that Church, I take for granted he included the rulers as well as the teachers, in both instances. In a word, I suppose that, in every truly primitive and apostolic Church, there was a bench of Elders, or Overseers, who presided over all the spiritual interests of the congregation; that, generally, a small part only of these, and perhaps seldom more than one, statedly preached; that the rest, though probably ordained in the same manner with their colleagues, very rarely, if ever, taught publicly, but were employed as inspectors and rulers, and it may be, also, in visiting, catechizing, and instructing from house to house. If this were the case, and every part of the New Testament history favours the supposition, then nothing can be more natural than the language of the inspired writers in reference to this whole subject. Then we readily understand why the Apostle should say to Titus: "For this cause left I thee in Crete, that thou shouldest set in order the things that are wanting, and ordain Elders in every city, as I had appointed thee. If any be blameless, &c.; for a Bishop must be blameless, as the steward of God, &c." We may then perceive, why he speaks of a number of Bishops at Philippi, and a number also at Ephesus; and, in the same breath, calls the latter alternately Bishops and Elders; and, on this principle, we may see, no less plainly why the Apostle Peter said: "The Elders which are among you I exhort, who am also an Elder, and a witness of the sufferings of Christ, and also a partaker of the glory that shall be revealed. Feed the flock of God that is among you, taking the oversight thereof, *acting as bishops επισκοπουντες* among them, not by constraint but willingly; not for filthy lucre, but of a ready mind; neither as being lords over God's heritage, but being ensamples to the flock." And accordingly, it is remarkable that the word ποιμανατε, used in the second verse of the last quotation, is derived from a word signifying a shepherd, and carries with it the ideas of guiding, protecting, and ruling, as well as feeding in appropriate spiritual pastures. See Matthew ii. 6, and Revelation ii. 27.

This view of the subject takes away all embarrassment and difficulty in reference to the titles given to the primitive officers of the Church. There is abundant evidence that every class of Elders, as well those who commonly officiated as rulers only, as those who both ruled and taught, bore the names of Bishops, Inspectors, Overseers, during the apostolic age, and for some time afterwards. This was a name most significantly expressive of their appropriate function, which was to overlook, direct, and rule each particular Church, for its edification. How long this title continued to be applied to all the Elders indiscriminately, it is not easy to say. It was probably in the Church, as it was known to have been in the Synagogue. All the rulers of the Synagogue were popularly called *Archi-synagogi*, as is evident from several passages in the New Testament; but sometimes, as we learn from the same source, this title was applied, by way of eminence, to the presiding or principal Ruler of each Synagogue. So with regard to the title of Inspector, Overseer, or Bishop, we know that all the Elders of Ephesus (Acts xx. 17, 28) were indiscriminately called Bishops by the inspired Paul. We know, too, that the same Apostle recognizes a plurality of Bishops, or Overseers, in the Church at Philippi (Philip. i. 1), who could not possibly have been Prelates, as Episcopalians themselves allow. We find, moreover, the same "chiefest of the Apostles," giving the titles of Bishop and Elder, without discrimination, to all the Church Rulers directed to be ordained in Ephesus and Crete, as the Epistles to Timothy and Titus plainly evince. In those pure and simple times no difficulty arose from this general application of a plain and expressive title. For more than a hundred years after the apostolic age, this title continued to be frequently applied in the same manner, as the writings of Clemens Romanus, Hermas, Irenæus, and others, amply testify. We find them not only speaking of the Elders as bearing rule in each Church; but also calling the same men, alternately, Bishops, and Elders, as was evidently done in apostolic times.

In process of time, however, this title, which was originally considered as expressive of duty and labour, rather than of honour, became gradually appropriated to the principal Elder, who usually presided in preaching and ordering the course of the public service. Not only so, but as a worldly and ambitious spirit gained ground, he who bore this title began to advance certain peculiar claims; – first those of a stated Chairman, President, or Moderator; and finally those of a new order, or grade of office. That there was an entire change in the application of the title of Bishop not long after the apostolic age, a majority of our Episcopal brethren themselves allow. They grant that in the New Testament this title is given indiscriminately to all who were intrusted with the instruction and care of the Church. But that, in the succeeding period, it was gradually reserved to the highest order. In other words, they grant that the title Bishop had a very different meaning in the second and third centuries from that which it had borne in the first. Now, even conceding to them that this change took place earlier than the best records give us reason to believe;

it may be asked, why make such a change at all? Why not continue to get along with the language which the inspired Apostles had authorized by their use? Why insidiously make an old title, which was familiar to the popular ear, signify something very different from what it had been wont to signify from the beginning; and thus palm a new office with an old name on the people? Were there no other fact established by the early writers than this, it would be quite sufficient to convince us that the apostolic government of the Church was early corrupted by human ambition.

CHAPTER FOUR

Testimony of the Christian Fathers

That which is not found in the Bible, however fully and strongly it may be enjoined elsewhere, cannot be considered as binding on the Church. On the other hand what is plainly found in the word of God, though it be no where else taught, we are bound to receive. Accordingly, if we find Ruling Elders in the New Testament – as it is firmly believed we have done – it matters not as to their substantial warrant, how soon after the apostolic age they fell into disuse. Still if we can discover traces of them in the early uninspired writings of the Christian Church, it will certainly add something to the chain of proof which we possess in their favour. It will add strong presumption to that which is our decisive rule. Let us, then, see whether the early Fathers say any thing which can be fairly considered as alluding to this class of Church officers.

But before we proceed to examine these witnesses in detail, it may not be improper to make two general remarks, which ought to be kept steadily in view through the whole of this branch of our subject.

The first is, that we must be on our guard against the ambiguous use of the title, *Elder*, as it is expressed in different languages. When we look into the writings of the Christian Fathers who lived during the first two hundred years after Christ, all of whom, if we except Tertullian, wrote in Greek, we find them generally using the word $πρεσβυτερος$ to designate an Elder. Now this is precisely the same word which the advocates of

Prelacy apply to the "second order," as they express it, of their "clergy," always called by them "Presbyters." And when Presbyterians translate this word by the term *Elder*,[1] and consider it as used, at least in many cases, to designate that class of officers which forms the subject of this Essay, they are considered and represented, by some illiterate and narrow minded persons, as chargeable with an unfair, if not a deceptive use of' a term. This charge is manifestly unjust. It will never be repeated by any candid individual who is acquainted with the Greek language. This is the very word which is almost invariably used by the translators of the Septuagint, all through the Old Testament, to designate Elders who confessedly had nothing to do with preaching. In truth, it was a general title of office among the early Christians, as any one will immediately perceive by a candid perusal of the New Testament. And the fact is, that if Presbyterians wrote in Greek, they would, of course, employ this very term to express their Ruling Elder. The word *Elder* is the natural, literal, and, we may almost say, the only proper term by which to express the meaning of the Greek title πρεσβυτερος. And even when we meet in some of the early Fathers with passages in which the officers of the Church are enumerated as consisting of Επισκοποι, Πρεσβυτερος και Διακονοι, it may be said, with perfect truth, that if Presbyterians at the present day were called upon to enumerate the standing officers in all their Churches, which are completely organized agreeably to their public standards – they would, beyond all doubt, if they used the Greek language, represent their regular ecclesiastical officers as every where consisting of Επισκοποι, Πρεσβυτερος και Διακονοι; meaning by επισκοπος, a parochial Pastor or Overseer, in which sense Prelatists themselves acknowledge the title to have been generally used in the apostolic age; and meaning by the title πρεσβυτερος, a Ruling Elder, which we have no doubt has been shown, and will be yet further shown to be, in many cases, the

---

1. It is worthy of notice that whenever the word πρεσβυτερος occurs in the New Testament, our translation, when an ecclesiastical officer is meant, always renders it *Elder*. So far as is recollected, this is invariably done.

proper interpretation of the word. When, therefore, we thus translate the word in some of the following quotations, let no one feel as if we were taking an unwarrantable liberty. No imputation of this kind, assuredly, will be made by any reader of competent learning to judge in the case.

The second preliminary remark is, that, perhaps, no class of Church officers would be, on the whole, so likely to fall into disrepute after the apostolic age, and be discontinued, as that which is now under consideration. We know that the purity of the Church began to decline immediately after the apostolic age. Nay, while the Apostles were still alive, "the mystery of iniquity" had already begun "to work." Corruption, both in faith and practice, had crept in, and, in some places, to an alarming and most distressing extent. And, after their departure, it soon "came in like a flood." The discipline of the Church became relaxed, and, after a while, in a great measure prostrated. The hints dropped by several writers in the second century, and the strongly coloured and revolting pictures given by Origen and Cyprian of the state of the Church in their own times, present a view of this subject which needs no comment. Now, in such a state of things, was it not natural that the office of those whose peculiar duty it was to inspect the members of the Church; to take cognizance of all their aberrations; and to maintain a pure and scriptural discipline, should be unpopular, and finally as much as possible crowded out of public view, discredited, and gradually laid aside?

But this is not all. Shortly after the apostolic age, several ecclesiastical offices, as is confessed on all hands, were either invented or modified, so as to suit the declining spirituality of the times. To mention but a single example: The Deacons began to claim higher dignity and powers. Sub-deacons were introduced to perform some of those functions which had originally belonged to Deacons, but which they had become too proud to perform. Was it either unnatural, then, or umprobable – since things of a similar kind actually took place – that in the course of the undeniable degeneracy which was now reigning, the Ruling Elders of the Church should find the employment to which they had been originally destined, irksome both to themselves and others; by no means adapted to gratify either the love of gain, or the love of pleasure, which seemed to be the order of the day; – and that both parties gradually united in dropping the inspection and discipline once committed to their hands, and turning their attention to objects more adapted to the taste of ambitious, wordly-minded Churchmen? And this result would be, at once, more likely to occur and might have occurred with less opposition and noise, if we suppose, as some learned men have done, that the Ruling and Teaching Elders, from the beginning, not only both bore the general name of Elders, but were both set apart to their office with the same formalities. If this were the case, then there was nothing to change, in virtually discarding the office of Ruling Elder, but gradually to neglect all their appropriate duties, and in an equally gradual manner to slide into the assumption of duties, and especially that of public preaching, which, in the primitive Church, they had not been expected to perform.

Keeping these things in mind, let us examine whether some, both of the early and the late Fathers, do not express themselves in a manner which renders it probable, or rather certain, that they had in view the class of Elders of which we are speaking.

In the Epistle of Clemens Romanus, who lived toward the close of the first century, to the Church at Corinth, we find the worthy Father remonstrating with the members of that Church for having risen up against their Elders, and thrust them out of office, perhaps for the very reason just hinted at, that they found their inspection and rule uncomfortable. Accordingly, Clemens addresses the Corinthian Christians in the following manner: "It is a shame, my beloved, yea, a very great shame, to hear that the most firm and ancient Church of the Corinthians should be led, by one or two persons, to rise up against their Elders" (πρεσβυτερους). Again: "Let the flock of Christ enjoy peace with the Elders (πρεσβυτερων) that are set over it." Again: "Do ye, therefore, who first laid the foundation of this sedition, submit yourselves to your Elders, and be instructed into repentance, bending the knee of your hearts;" Epist. 47. 54, 57.

In these extracts we find an entire coincidence with the language of the New Testament; a plain indication that in every Church there was a plurality of Elders; and a distinct recognition of the idea that these Elders were rulers, in other words, held a station of authority and government over "the flock" of which they were officers.

In the Epistles of Ignatius, who lived at the close of the first, and the beginning of the second century, we find much said about Elders ($\pi\rho\varepsilon\sigma\beta\upsilon\tau\varepsilon\rho oi$). The following is a specimen of the manner in which he speaks of them, in connexion with the other classes of Church officers. "Obey your Bishop and the Presbytery (the Eldership) with an entire affection;" *Epistle to the Ephesians*, 20. "I exhort you that you study to do all things in a divine concord: your Bishop presiding in the place of God, your Elders in the place of the council of the Apostles, and your Deacons, most dear to me, being intrusted with the ministry of Jesus Christ." Again: "Do nothing without your Bishop and Elders;" *Epistle to the Magnesians*, 6. 7. "It is, therefore, necessary, that, as ye do, so without your Bishop you should do nothing; also be ye subject to your Elders, as to the Apostles of Jesus Christ our hope." Again: "Let all reverence the Deacons as Jesus Christ, and the Bishop as the Father, and the Elders as the Sanhedrim of God, and the college of the Apostles." Again: "Fare ye well in Jesus Christ; being subject to your Bishop as to the command of God, and so likewise to the Presbytery, (or Eldership);" *Epistle to the Trallians*, 2. 3. 13. "Which also I salute in the blood of Jesus Christ, which is our eternal and undefiled joy; especially if they are at unity with the Bishop and Elders, who are with him, and the Deacons appointed according to the mind of Jesus Christ." Again: "There is one cup, and one altar, and also one Bishop, together with his Eldership, and the Deacons, my fellow-servants." Again: "I cried whilst I was among you; I spake with a loud voice, Attend to the Bishop, to the Eldership, and to the Deacons;" *Epistle to the Philadelphians*, Pref. 4. 7. "See that ye all follow your Bishop, as Jesus Christ, the Father, and the Presbytery (or Eldership) as the Apostles; and reverence the Deacons as the command of God." Again: "It is not lawful without the Bishop either to baptize, or to celebrate the holy communion." Again: "I salute your very worthy Bishop; and your venerable Eldership, and your Deacons, my fellow-servants;" *Epistle to the Smyrneans*, 8. 12. "My soul be security for them who submit to their Bishop, with their Elders and Deacons;" *Epistle to Polycarp*, 6.

The friends of Prelacy have long been in the habit of insisting much on these and similar quotations from Ignatius, as affording decisive support to their system. But I must think that their confidence in this witness has not the smallest solid ground.[2] For, let it be remembered that these several Epistles were directed, not to large, prelatical dioceses, but to single parishes, or congregations; that in each of these Churches there are represented as being, a Bishop, a Presbytery, or bench of Elders, and a plurality of Deacons; and, therefore, that it is parochial episcopacy, and not diocesan, or prelatical, that is here described. And, accordingly, we learn from different parts of these Epistles, that, in the time of Ignatius, each Bishop had under his pastoral charge, but "one altar," "one cup," "one loaf," i.e., one communion table, and that the people under his care habitually came together to "one place," in other words, formed "one assembly."

Agreeably to this view of the subject, it is worthy of notice that Ignatius calls the Presbyters, or Elders of each Church which he addresses, the συνεδριον θεου, that is, the Sanhedrim, or council of God. But with what propriety could he designate them by this title, the popular title of a well known Jewish ecclesiastical court, if they did not constitute a corresponding court in the Christian Church; and if the whole body of ecclesiastical officers which he addressed from time to time were not the rulers of a single flock? The truth is, the whole language of Ignatius, in reference to the officers of whom he speaks, is strictly Presbyterian, and cannot be considered as affording countenance to any

---

2. Intelligent readers are no doubt, aware that the genuineness of the Epistles of Ignatius has been called in question by a great majority of Protestant divines, and is not only really but deeply questionable. All inquiry, however, on this subject is waived for the present.

other system without doing violence to its natural import.

Accordingly, it is worthy of notice, that the learned Mr. Joseph Mede, a very able and zealous divine of the Church of England, and a decisive advocate of diocesan Episcopacy, gives a representation of the state of things in the time of Ignatius, which, in substance, falls in with our account of the character of the Churches addressed by that Father. "It should seem," says he, "that in those first times, before dioceses were divided into those lesser and subordinate Churches, which we call parishes, and Presbyters assigned to them, they had only one altar to a Church, taking Church for the company or corporation of the faithful, united under one Bishop or Pastor; and that was in the city or place where the Bishop had his see and residence. Unless this were so, whence came it else, that a schismatical Bishop was said, *constituere,* or *collocare aliud altare?* And that a Bishop and an Altar, are made correlatives?"[3]

The same fact is asserted by Bishop Stillingfleet, in his *Sermon Against Separation*: "Though, when the Churches increased," says he, "the occasional meetings were frequent in several places; yet still there was but one Church, and one Altar, and one Baptistery, and one Bishop, with many Presbyters attending him. Which is so plain in antiquity, as to the Churches planted by the Apostles themselves, that none but a great stranger to the history of the Church can call it in question. It is true, after some time, in the great cities, they had distinct places allotted, and Presbyters fixed among them; and such allotments were called *Tituli* at Rome, *Lauræ* at Alexandria, and *parishes* in other places. But these were never thought, then, to be new Churches, or to have any independent government in themselves; but were all in subjection to the Bishop, and his college of Presbyters; of which multitudes of examples might be brought from the most authentic testimonies of antiquity, if a thing so evident needed any proof at all. And yet this distribution, (into distinct *Tituli,*) even in cities, was looked on as so uncommon in those elder times, that Epiphanius takes notice of it as an extraordinary thing

---

3. *Discourse on Church Government*, p. 48.

at Alexandria; and, therefore, it is probably supposed that there was no such thing in all the cities of Crete in his time."

That the Elders spoken of so frequently by Ignatius, were all the officers of a single parish or congregation, is also evident, not only from the titles which he gives to the body of Elders; but also from the duties which he represents as incumbent on the Bishop with whom these Elders were connected. It is represented as the duty of the Bishop to be present with his flock whenever they came together; to conduct their prayers; and to preside in all their religious assemblies. He is spoken of as the only person who was authorized, in ordinary cases, to administer Baptism, and the Lord's Supper; as the person by whom all marriages among the people of his charge were celebrated; whose duty it was to be personally acquainted with all his flock; who was bound to take notice, with his own eye, of those who were absent from public worship; to attend to the wants of the widows and all the poor of his congregation; to seek out all by name, and not to overlook even the servant men and maids under his care; to instruct the children; to reconcile differences, and, in short, to attend to all those objects, in detail, which are considered as devolving on every faithful parish minister. Now, all these representations so plainly apply to the pastor of a single Church, and are so evidently impossible to be realized by any other person, that it would be a waste of time, and an insult to common sense, to attempt a more formal establishment of the position.

But if the Bishop of Ignatius, be a simple parochial Bishop – in other words, the ordinary pastor of a congregation; and if the Presbytery, or bench of Elders of which he so frequently speaks, are to be considered as all belonging to a single parish; then we can scarcely avoid the conclusion, that they were not all of them employed in public preaching but that their principal employment was, as assistants of the pastor, and in union with him, to discharge the duties of Inspectors and Rulers of the Church.

Again; Polycarp, writing to the Church of Philippi, most evidently and unequivocally conveys the idea, that there was a plurality of Presbyters (or Elders), not only in his own Church, but also in that to which he wrote; and that they were the regularly appointed ecclesiastical rulers. He addressed them thus: "Let the Elders be tender and merciful, compassionate towards all, reclaiming those which have fallen into errors; visiting all that are weak; not negligent of the widow and the orphan, and of him that is poor; but ever providing what is honest in the sight of God and men; abstaining from all wrath, respect of persons, and unrighteous judgment; avoiding covetousness; not hastily believing a report against any man; not rigid in judgment; knowing that we are all faulty, and obnoxious to judgment."[4]

Cyprian, in his 29th Epistle, directed "to his brethren, the Elders and Deacons," expresses himself in the following terms: "You are to take notice that I have ordained Saturus, a reader, and the confessor Optatus, a sub-deacon; whom we had all before agreed to place in the rank and degree next to that of the clergy. Upon Easter day, we made one or two trials of Saturus, in reading, when we were approving our readers before the teaching Presbyters; and then appointed Optatus from among the readers, to be a teacher of the hearers." On this passage, the Rev. Mr. Marshall, the Episcopal translator and commentator on Cyprian, remarks: "It is hence, I think, apparent that all Presbyters were not teachers, but assisted the Bishop in other parts of his office." And Bishop Fell, another editor and commentator on Cyprian, remarks on the same passage in the following words: *"Inter Presbyteros rectores et doctores olim distinxisse videtur divus Paulus;* 1 Tim. v. 17." i.e., Paul appears to have made a distinction, in ancient times, between teaching and ruling Elders, in 1 Timothy v. 17. Here two learned Episcopal divines explicitly acknowledge the distinction between teaching and ruling Elders in the primitive Church; and one of them an eminent Bishop, not only allows that Cyprian referred to this distinction but also quotes as an authority for it the principal text which Presbyterians adduce for the same purpose.

There is another passage in Cyprian's 40th Epistle, which the very learned authors of the *Jus Divinum Regiminis Ecclesi-*

---

4. *Epistle to the Philippians*, Sect. 6.

astici[5] consider as containing an allusion to the office in question, and which may not be unworthy of notice. At the time when Cyprian wrote this letter, he was in a state of exile from his Church. It is directed to the Elders, Deacons, and People at large, of his congregation; and contains an expression of his wish that one Numidicus should be reckoned, or have a place assigned him with the Presbyters, or Elders of that Church, and sit with the clergy. And yet it would appear that this was only as a ruling, and not as a teaching Elder that he was to be received by them, for Cyprian subjoins: "He shall be promoted, if God permit, to a more distinguished place in his religion, (or his religious function,) when, by the protection of Providence, I shall return." Here, it seems, the Presbytery, or Eldership in that Church were directed immediately to receive, or set apart, this man to the office of Elder among them; and their absent pastor, or Bishop, promises that, when he returns, Numidicus shall be promoted to a still higher office. Now the only supposable promotion in this case was to the office of a Teaching Elder. That the passage is very naturally susceptible of this construction, none will deny. At any rate, it is adopted by some of the most mature divines and scholars in England, of the seventeenth century; however unceremoniously it may have been since rejected by less competent judges.

Accordingly, it is worthy of notice, that the famous Henry Dodwell, one of the most learned and zealous Episcopal writers in the British empire, of the seventeenth century, notwithstanding his determined opposition to every thing peculiarly Presbyterian; yet, in his celebrated *Dissertations on Cyprian*, freely grants, that, in the days of that Father there were Elders or Presbyters in the Christian Church who did not preach. He represents this fact as undoubtedly taught by Cyprian, in his Epistles, and particularly refers, for proof, to the first of the passages cited in a preceding page. Nay, he expresses a full persuasion that a similar fact existed in the apostolic Church, and quotes 1 Timothy v. 17, as a decisive confir-

---

5. *Jus Divinum.* &c., pp. 171, 172.

mation of his opinion.[6] The notion, then, that all testimony supposed to be derived from Cyprian in favour of non-preaching Elders, is a dream of modern sectaries, for the purpose of carrying a favourite point in Church government, is plainly not tenable. Some of the best talents and most mature learning in the Christian Church, without any leaning to Presbyterian opinions, have decisively interpreted that Father as setting forth such a class of Elders.

Hippolytus, who was nearly contemporary with Cyprian, repeatedly speaks of these Elders as existing, and as exercising authority in his day. In his Tract "Against the heresy of a certain Noetus," he states, in the beginning of the work, that Noetus being charged with certain heretical opinions, the "Elders (πρεσβυτεροι) cited him to appear, and examined him in the presence of the Church;" that Noetus having at first denied, but afterwards openly avowed the opinions imputed to him: "the Elders summoned him a second time, condemned him, and cast him out of the Church." It seems then, that in the third century there were Elders, whose duty it was to examine, try, and excommunicate such members of the Church as were found delinquent with respect to either doctrine or morals. In this case, a part, at least, of the trial, seems to have been conducted "in the presence of the Church," of which they were rulers; but still the trial, conviction, and excommunication were by the Elders.

Origen, who, it is well known, flourished a little more than two hundred years after Christ, in the following passage, has a plain reference to the class of officers under consideration. "There are some Rulers appointed whose duty it is to inquire concerning the manners and conversation of those who are admitted, that they may debar from the congregation such as commit filthiness."[7] This passage is replete with important and conclusive testimony. It not only proves, that, in the time of Origen, there were Rulers in the Christian Church; but that the chief and peculiar business of these Rulers was precisely that which we as-

---

6. *Dissertationes Cyprianicæ*, vi. Sect. 4, 5, 6.
7. *Contra Celsum*. Lib. iii. p. 142. Edit. Cantab. 1677.

sign to Ruling Elders, viz.: inspecting the members of the Church; watching over all its spiritual interests; admitting to its communion those who, on inquiry, were found worthy; and debarring those who were in any way immoral. It is perfectly evident from this passage alone, that, in the days of this learned Father, the government and discipline of the Church were not conducted by the body of the communicants at large, but by a *Bench of Rulers.*

The same important fact is also indubitably implied in the language of Origen in another place. In his seventh *Homily on Joshua*, he speaks of one who, "having been thrice admonished, and being unwilling to repent, was cut off from the Church by its rulers." Those who cut off then, from the communion of the Church, and restored the penitent, in the time of Origen, were not the body of the communicants, but a bench of Elders. This great historical fact is, moreover, explicitly established, as having existed in the third century (the age of Origen), by the Magdeburgh Centuriators, a body of very learned Lutheran Divines, contemporary with Melancthon, and whose authority as ecclesiastical historians, is deservedly high. "The right," say they, "Of deciding respecting such as were to be excommunicated, or of receiving, upon their repentance, such as had fallen, was vested in the Elders of the Church."[8]

In the *Gesta Purgationis Cœciliani et Felicis,* preserved at the end of Optatus, and commonly referred to the beginning of the fourth century, we meet with the following enumeration of Church officers: *"Presbyteri, Diaconi et Seniores,"* i.e., "The Presbyters, the Deacons, and the Elders." And a little after is added: *"Adhibete conclericos, et Seniores plebis, ecclesiasticos viros, et inquirant diligenter quæ sint istæ dissensiones,"* i.e., "Call the fellow clergymen and Elders of the people, ecclesiastical men, and let them inquire diligently what are these dissensions." In that assembly, likewise, several letters were produced and read; one addressed, *Clero et Senioribus,* i.e., "to the clergy and the Elders;" and another, *Clericis et Senioiribus,* i.e., "to the

---

8. *Cent.* iii. Cap. vii. p. 151.

Clergymen and the Elders." Here, then, is a class of men expressly recognized as ecclesiastical men, or Church officers, who are styled Elders; who were constituent members of a solemn ecclesiastical assembly, or judicatory; who are expressly charged with inquiring into matters connected with the discipline of the Church; and yet carefully distinguished from the Clergy, with whom they met, and officially united in the transaction of business. If these be not the Elders of whom we are in search, we may give up all the rules of evidence.

Some, indeed, have said, that the phrase *ecclesiasticos viros,* in one of the passages last cited was not intended to designate Church officers at all; that this phrase was early introduced to distinguish "men of the Church," i.e., Christians from Pagans, and other enemies of Christ: and that it probably had some such meaning, and nothing more, in the ancient records from which the foregoing extracts are made. It is freely granted that the phrase, *ecclesiastici viri,* was, for a time employed, in the Christian Church, as well as by the surrounding heathen, in the sense, and for the purpose just mentioned. That is, when Christians were spoken of, as distinguished from Jews, Infidels, Heretics, &c., they were called ecclesiastical men, importing that they did not belong to Jewish Synagogues, or to heathen temples, or to heretical sects; but were adherents, or members of the Church of Christ. But it is well known, that this language was never employed in this sense among Christians themselves, when distinguishing one class of their own body from another. When used in this case, it always designated men in ecclesiastical office.[9] Besides, in the passage before us, there can be no doubt that the phrase under consideration was used in the latter sense, and not in the former. For the ecclesiastical men, in these passages are represented as joined with the clergy, in ecclesiastical functions; especially as directed to investigate and settle ecclesiastical dissensions. Surely this could neither be required nor expected of men who sustained no office, and were, of course, invested with no authority in the Church.

---

9. Bingham's *Origines Ecclesiasticæ*, Book i. chapter i. section 8.

Another objection which has been confidently urged against that construction which we have put upon the extracts from the *Gesta Purgationis*, is that the Seniors or Elders, of which they speak, are mentioned after Deacons, and, therefore, are to be considered as inferior to them. "Now," say these objectors, "the Ruling Elders of the Presbyterian Church are always considered and represented, by the advocates of that denomination, as above Deacons, rather than below them, on the scale of ecclesiastical precedence. Of course, the Seniors here spoken of, cannot belong to the class of officers for which they contend." To this objection it is, sufficient to reply, that the mere order in which titles are arranged, cannot be considered as decisive of the relative rank with which these titles are connected. At once to illustrate and confirm this remark, a single example will suffice In the Epistles of Ignatius, when he speaks of Bishops, or Pastors, Elders and Deacons, no intelligent reader supposes that he means to represent the second and third of these classes of offices as inferior to the first. Yet, in his *Epistle to the Trallians*, he speaks thus: "Let all reverence the Deacons as Jesus Christ; and the Bishop as the Father; and the Presbyters as the Sanhedrim of God, and the college of the Apostles." This may argue carelessness or haste in writing; or it may argue a mind in the writer, less intent on ecclesiastical precedence, than on more important matters; but it surely cannot be considered as deciding the relative standing of the different officers of whom he speaks.

Besides, let it be recollected, that the date of these *Gesta* was about the year of Christ, 303, when the office of Ruling Elder, if we may credit the very explicit testimony of Ambrose, which will be stated presently, was going gradually out of use. If so, nothing was more natural than that the writers and speakers of that day should be disposed to throw it on the back ground, and rather degrade than advance its appropriate rank in the scale of ecclesiastical honour.

There is also a passage in Optatus, of the African Church, who flourished a little after the middle of the fourth century, which corroborates the foregoing quotations. It is as follows:

"The Church had many ornaments of gold and silver, which she could neither bury in the earth, nor carry away with her, which she committed to the Elders (*Senioribus*), as to faithful persons."[10] There can scarcely be a doubt that these were not merely aged persons, but official men; and, especially, as we know, from the writings of Cyprian, who resided in the same country, that there were such officers in the African Church, a few years before.

Ambrose, who lived in the fourth century,[11] in his commentary on 1 Timothy v. 1, has the following passage: "For, indeed, among all nations old age is honourable. Hence it is that the Synagogue, and afterwards the Church, had Elders, without whose counsel nothing was done in the Church; which by what negligence it grew into disuse I know not, unless, perhaps, by the sloth, or rather by the pride of the Teachers, while they alone wished to appear something." The great body of the Prelatists, as well as some others, have laboured hard to divest this passage of its plain and pointed testimony in favour of the office of Ruling Elder. They insist upon it that the pious Father had no reference whatever to ecclesiastical officers, but only to aged persons, and that he meant to say nothing more than that, formerly, in the Synagogue, and afterwards in the Church, there were old men, whom it was customary to consult; which practice, however, at the time in which he wrote, was generally laid aside. This perversion of an obvious meaning, is really so strange and extravagant, that the formality of a serious refutation seems scarcely necessary. Can any reflecting man believe that Ambrose designed only to inform his readers that in the Jewish Synagogues, there were actually persons who had attained a considerable age; that this was also, afterwards the case in the Christian Church; and that these aged persons were generally consulted? This would have

---

10. *Optat. Lib.* i. p. 41, edit. Paris, 1631.

11. It is not forgotten that learned men have generally considered the real name of this writer as Hilary. Yet as the name of Ambrose is more frequently given to him, especially by many writers hereafter to be quoted, the latter name will be more intelligible, and, therefore more convenient.

been a sage remark indeed! Was there ever a community of any extent, either ecclesiastical or civil, which did not include some aged persons? Or was there ever a state of society, or an age of the world, in which the practice of consulting the aged and experienced had fallen into disuse? That thinking, candid minds, should be able to satisfy themselves with such a gloss, is truly wonderful. It is certainly no argument in favour of this construction of the language of Ambrose, that he prefaces his statement respecting the Synagogue and the Church, by remarking, that "among all nations old age is honourable." Surely no remark could be more natural or appropriate, when he was about to state, that from the earliest period of the Christian Church, and long before in the Synagogue, all their affairs had been managed by colleges of Elders (a title importing a kind of homage to age and experience), without whose counsel nothing was done.

But there is a clause in this extract from Ambrose, which precludes all doubt that he intended to allude to a class of Church officers, and not merely to old age. It is this: "Which by what negligence it grew into disuse, I know not, unless, perhaps, by the sloth, or rather by the pride of the Teachers, who wished alone to appear something." It is very conceivable and obvious that both the pride and the sloth of the Teachers, or teaching Elders, should render them willing to get rid of a bench of officers of equal power with themselves, as rulers in the Church, and, consequently, able to control their wishes in cases of discipline. But it cannot easily be conceived why either sloth or pride should render any so particularly averse to all consultation with the aged and experienced, in preference to the young, on the affairs of the Church; especially if these aged persons bore no office, and there was, of course, no official obligation to be governed by their advice, as the gloss under consideration supposes. It being evident, then, that a class of officers was here intended, the question arises, what class of Presbyters, or Elders, was that which had grown into disuse in the fourth century? Not teaching Presbyters, surely; for every one knows that that class of Presbyters had not become obsolete in Ambrose's time. His own writings amply attest the reverse. And every one also knows that this class of Church officers has never been laid aside, or even diminished in number, to the present day.

It is worthy of very particular notice here, also, as no small confirmation of the construction which we put upon the words of Ambrose, that all the most learned and able of the Reformers, and a great number of others, the most competent judges in such matters, from the Reformation to the present time, have concurred in adopting the same construction, and have considered the worthy Father as referring to a class of Elders who held the place of inspectors and rulers in the Church. Learned Lutherans, and Episcopalians, as well as Calvinists, almost without number, have united in the interpretation of this Father, which we have given with a degree of harmony truly wonderful, if that interpretation be entirely erroneous. Is it less likely that Luther, and Melancthon, and Bucer, and Whitgift, and Zanchius, and Peter Martyr, who had no sectarian or private views to serve, should be able correctly to read and understand Ambrose, than that modern and more superficial scholars should be betrayed into a mistaken construction, on the side in favour of which their feelings were strongly enlisted? No disrespect whatever is intended to the latter; but it cannot be doubted that a great preponderancy of testimony, both as to numbers and competency, is on the side of the former.

Augustine, Bishop of Hippo, who also lived toward the close of the fourth century, often refers to this class of officers in his writings. Thus, in his work, *Contra Cresconium Grammaticum,* Lib. iii. cap, 56, he speaks of *"Peregrinus, Presbyter, et Seniores Ecclesiæ Musticancæ regionis;"* i.e., Peregrine, the Presbyter, and the Elders of the Church, of the Mustican district." And again, he addresses one of his Epistles intended for his Church at Hippo, in the following manner: *"Dilectissmis Fratribus, Clero, Senioribus et universæ Plebi Ecclesiæ Hipponensis;" Epist.* 137; i.e., "To the beloved brethren, the Clergy, the Elders, and all the people of the Church at Hippo." There were some Elders, then, in the time of Augustine, whom he distinguishes from other Presbyters, and whom he also distinguishes from the Clergy. And, lest any should suppose that the

Elders here spoken of were not officers, but mere private members of the Church, he distinguishes them from the *plebs universa* of the Church. Augustine, also, in another place (*De Verb. Dom.* Serm. 19), speaks thus: *"Cum ob errorem aliquem a Senioribus arguuntur, et imputatur alicui de illis, cur ebrius fuerit? cur res alienas pervaserit?"* &c., i.e., "When they are reprehended for any error by the Elders, and are upbraided with having been drunk, or with having been guilty of theft, &c." Can any one doubt that Augustine is here speaking, not of mere aged persons, but of Church officers, whose duty it was to inspect the morals of the members of the Church, and to "upbraid," or reprove those who had been reprehensible in their deportment? It would be easy to produce, from the same Father, a number of other quotations equally to our purpose. But Bingham, in his *Origines Ecclesiasticæ,* Bishop Taylor, in his *Episcopacy Asserted*, and other learned Prelatists, have rendered this unnecessary, by making an explicit acknowledgment, that Augustine repeatedly mentions these Seniors or Elders as belonging to other Churches as well as his own, in his time; and that the same kind of Elders are frequently referred to by other writers, both before and after Augustine, as then existing in the Church; as holding in it some kind of official station, and yet as distinguished from clergymen. It is true, indeed, that Bingham insists upon it that these were not Ruling Elders, in our sense of the word; but that they held some kind of office in the Church, and yet were not public preachers, he explicitly grants. We ask nothing more. This is quite sufficient for our purpose.

The ancient work, entitled *Apostolical Constitutions*, although by no means of apostolical origin, was probably composed sometime between the second and fifth centuries. The following significant and pointed rule, extracted from that work, will be considered by the intelligent reader as by no means equivocal in its aspect: "To Presbyter also, when they labour assiduously in the word and doctrine, let a double portion be assigned."[12] Here is, obviously, a distinction between Presbyters

---

12. *Apostol Constit.* Lib. ii. Cap. 28.

who are employed in teaching, and those who are not so employed. To what duties the others devoted themselves is not stated; but it is evident that teaching made no part of their ordinary occupation. We may take for granted that their duty was to assist in the other spiritual concerns of the Church, viz.: in maintaining good order and discipline. This is precisely the distinction which Presbyterians make, and which they believe to have been made in the primitive Church. Accordingly the Presbyters, in the same relic of Christian antiquity, and in a subsequent part of the same chapter, are called "the Counsellors of the Bishop, or Pastor; and the Sanhedrim, or Senate of the Church:" expressions which entirely harmonize with our views of the office of Elder in the ancient Church.

To the same class of officers, Isodore of Hispala, who flourished in the sixth century, seems to allude, when, in giving directions as to the manner in which pastors should conduct their official instructions, he says: *"Prius docendi sunt Seniores plebis, ut per eos infra positi facilius doceantur;"* i.e., "The Elders of the people are first to be taught, that by them such as are placed under them, may be more easily instructed." Here again, these Seniores are evidently spoken of as Church officers, who were set over the people, and yet occupied a station inferior to that of the pastors, or public preachers.

Nor does this class of officers appear to have entirely ceased in the Church at as late a period as that of Gregory the Great, who wrote in the latter part of the sixth century. In one of his Epistles he gives the following direction: "If any thing should come to your ears concerning any clergyman, which may be justly considered as matter of offence, do not easily believe it; but let truth be diligently investigated by the Elders of the Church, who may be at hand, and then, if the character of the act demand it, let the proper punishment fall on the offender."[13]

Here there is evidently a very distinct reference to such a class of officers as that of which we are speaking. They are dis-

---

13. *Epistolæ*, Lib. ii. Epist. 19 – quoted from the *Politica Ecciesiastica* of Voetius, Par. ii. Lib. ii. Tract. iii.

tinguished from clergymen; and yet they are represented as ecclesiastical officers, to whom it properly pertained to investigate ecclesiastical offences; and to give advice and direction in peculiarly delicate cases of discipline. At an earlier period of the Church, indeed, these Elders, as well as all other classes of ecclesiastical men, were styled clergymen; as we shall have occasion more fully to show hereafter. But from the fourth century and onward, Elders of this class declined in numbers and in popularity, and not long afterwards were in a great measure laid aside, excepting by the humble and devoted witnesses of the truth, of whose testimony we shall speak in the next chapter.

There is another species of evidence here worthy of notice. The representation which the fathers give of the manner in which the Bishop or Pastor and his Elders were commonly seated, when the Church was assembled, and during the solemnities of public worship, affords very strong evidence that the mass of the Elders were such as it is the object of this Essay to establish. We are told by several of the early Fathers, that when the Church was convened for public worship, the Bishop, or Pastor, was commonly seated on the middle of a raised bench, or long semi-circular seat, at one end of the Church; that his Elders were seated on each side of him, on the same seat, or on seats immediately adjoining, and commonly a little lower; and that the Deacons commonly stood in front of this bench, ready to give any notice, to execute any order, or to perform any service which the Pastor or Elders might think proper to direct. This practice was evidently drawn from the Jewish Synagogue. And, indeed, the order of assembling, sitting, and worship in the Christian assemblies, for the first two or three centuries, so strikingly resembled that of the Synagogue, that Christian Churches were frequently contemned, and opposed as "Synagogues in disguise."[14]

This general fact is so well attested by the early Christian writers, that it is unnecessary to detain the reader by any formal proof of it. Now, if in every Church, when assembled in ordinary circumstances, there were present a Pastor, Overseer, or Bishop,

---

14. Thorndike's *Discourse on Religious Assemblies*, p. 57.

and a body of Elders, sitting with him, and counselling and aiding him in the inspection and discipline of the Church; it is hardly necessary to say, that these Elders could not all have been such Presbyters as the friends of Prelacy contend for, as their "second order of clergy." The supposition is absurd. They could only have been such a bench of pious and venerable men, as were chiefly employed in overseeing and ruling; and corresponding, substantially, with the Elders of the Presbyterian Church. It is true, indeed, the advocates of Prelacy endeavour to persuade us that these Presbyters were the stated preachers in the several congregations or worshipping assemblies which were, as they suppose, comprehended in the Bishop's charge. But this supposition is wholly unsupported. Nay, it is directly contrary to the whole current of early testimony on this subject. The very same writers who inform us that there were any Presbyters at all in the Christian Church within the first three hundred years, represent a plurality of them as sitting with the Bishop or Pastor, and present in every worshipping assembly. There is no system with which this statement can be made essentially to agree, but that which is received among Presbyterians.

Another strong argument in support of the doctrine of Ruling Elders, as drawn from the early Fathers, is found in the abundant evidence which their writings furnish, that, during the first three or four centuries after Christ, the great body of the Christian Presbyters did not ordinarily preach, indeed, never but by the special permission of the Bishop or Pastor. The following statement by the learned Bingham, in his *Origines Ecciesiasticæ*, Book ii. chapter iii. section 4, will be found conclusive on this point:

"The like observation may be made upon the office of preaching. This was in the first place the Bishop's office, which they commonly discharged themselves, especially in the African Churches. Which is the reason we so frequently meet with the phrase, *tracante Episcopo,* 'the Bishop preaching,' in the writings of Cyprian. For then it was so much the office and custom of Bishops to preach, that no Presbyter was permitted to preach in their presence, till the time of Austin, who, whilst he was a

Presbyter was authorized by Valerius, his Bishop, to preach before him. But that, as Possidius, the writer of his life observes, was so contrary to the use and custom of the African Churches, that many Bishops were highly offended at it, and spoke against it; till the consequences proved that such a permission was of good use and service to the Church; and then several other Bishops granted their Presbyters power and privilege to preach before them. So that it was then a favour for the Presbyters to preach in the presence of the Bishops, and wholly at the Bishop's discretion, whether they would permit them or not; and when they did preach, it was wholly *potestate accepta,* by the power and authority of the Bishops that appointed them. In the Eastern Churches Presbyters were more commonly employed to preach, as Possidius observes, when he says Valerius brought the custom into Africa from their example. And Jerome intimates as much, when he complains of it as an ill custom only in some Churches to forbid Presbyters to preach. Chrysostom preached several of his elaborate discourses at Antioch, while he was but a Presbyter; and so did Atticus at Constantinople: and the same is observed to have been granted to the Presbyters of Alexandria and Cæsarea, in Cappadocia, and Cyprus, and other places. But still it was but a grant of the Bishops; and Presbyters did it by their authority and commission. And whenever Bishops saw just reason to forbid them, they had power to limit or withdraw their commission again: as both Socrates and Sozomen testify, who say that at Alexandria Presbyters were forbidden to preach from the time that Arius raised a disturbance in the Church. Thus we see what a power Bishops anciently challenged and exercised over Presbyters in the common and ordinary offices of the Church: particularly for preaching, Bishops always esteemed it their office as much as any other." This statement is amply illustrated and confirmed by the learned author by numerous references to early writers of the highest reputation, which it is altogether unnecessary to recite, on account of the notoriety of the fact alleged.

    Can such a statement be contemplated a moment without perceiving, that the mass of the Presbyters or Elders, during the times here spoken of, were a very different class of officers from those commonly styled "Presbyters," in the Papacy afterwards, and in more modern Prelatical Churches? The very circumstance of preaching making no part of their ordinary function; nay, that, in ordinary cases, they were never allowed to do it, but in virtue of a special permission, which is evidently the import of the whole account, unless we make nonsense of it; places it beyond all doubt that the authority which they received at ordination, did not really commission them to preach at all; but that the Bishop only was the commissioned preacher. This is exactly what Presbyterians say. And if ever Ruling Elders or Deacons among us conduct social worship, and address the people in public, it is always under the direction of the Bishop or Pastor; who may encourage or arrest it as he pleases. It is vain to say, that Presbyters in the Protestant Episcopal Church at the present day cannot preach, or perform any ecclesiastical act without the Bishop's permission. This is an idle evasion. The fact is that every one knows, that their original ordination, as Presbyters, or "Priests," as they are called, conveys the full power to preach, administer sacraments, and perform every duty of the ordinary parochial ministration, statedly, and without any further let or impediment. The cases then, are wholly unlike. There were, evidently, in the days of Ignatius and Cyprian, of Chrysostom and Augustine, of Socrates and Sozomen, some Elders who did not ordinarily preach, and were not considered as authorized to engage in this part of the public service, without a special permission; and who stood, not exactly, indeed, but very much on the same ground, as to this matter, with the Elders of our denomination.

The truth is, some of the very same writers who inform us that Elders and Deacons were not ordinarily allowed to preach during the first three or four centuries, also inform us, that laymen, in cases of necessity, might preach by the Bishop's permission. This at once illustrates and strengthens the Presbyterian argument. For the same authority which might give a special permission in each case, or a general permission, for a time, to an Elder or Deacon to preach – which permission, it seems, might be revoked at pleasure, without touching the official standing of the individual, much less deposing him from office – might also authorize the merest layman in the whole parish to perform the same service, whenever it was judged expedient to give the license.

The truth of the matter seems to have been this: A large majority of the officers called Elders, in the first three centuries, were, no doubt, Ruling Elders, ordained, it is probable, in the same manner with the Teaching Elders, i.e., with "the laying on of hands," and the same external solemnity in every respect. They were not qualified, and were not expected, when ordained, to be preachers; but were selected, on account of their piety, gravity, prudence, and experience, to assist in inspection and government. When, however, the Bishop or Pastor, who was the stated preacher, was sick, or absent, he might direct a Ruling Elder to take his place, on a single occasion, or for a few Sabbaths. But this function made no part of their stated work; and they seldom engaged in it. After a while, however, these Elders, like the Bishops on the one hand, and the Deacons on the other, began to aspire; were more and more frequently permitted to preach; until, at length, non-preaching Elders were chiefly banished from the Church. As this was a gradual thing, they were, of course, retained in some Churches longer than others. They were, probably, first laid aside in large cities, where ambition was most prevalent, laxity of morals most indulged, and strict discipline most unpopular. In this way things proceeded, until this class of officers was almost wholly lost sight of in the Christian community.

One more testimony, by no means unimportant, of the existence of this office in the primitive Church, is to be found in the Rev. Dr. Buchanan's account of the Syrian Christians, contained in his *Asiatic Researches*. It will be borne in mind that the learned and pious author considers those Christians as having settled in the East, within the first three centuries after Christ, before the corruptions of the Church of Rome had been introduced, and when the original simplicity of Gospel order had been but in a small degree invaded. Separating from the Western Church at that early period, and remaining, for many centuries, almost wholly secluded from the rest of the world, they were found in a great measure free from the innovations and superstitions of the Papacy. Now, if Ruling Elders had any existence in the Christian Church within the first three hundred years, as Ambrose expressly declares they had, we might expect to find the Syrian Christians, in their seclusion, retaining some traces at least of this office in their Churches. Accordingly, Dr. Buchanan, in describing the circumstances of a visit which he paid one of the Churches of this simple and highly interesting people, speaks as follows: "When we arrived, I was received at the door of the Church by three Kasheeshas, that is Presbyters, or Priests, who were habited in like manner, in white vestments. Their names were Jesu, Zacharias, and Urias, which they wrote down in my journal, each of them adding to his name the title *Kasheesha.* There were also present two *Shumshanas,* or Deacons. The Elder Priest was a very intelligent man, of reverend appearance, having a long white beard, and of an affable and engaging deportment. The three principal Christians, or Lay-Elders, belonging to the Church, were named Abraham, Thomas, and Alexandros."[15]

This remarkable fact, it is believed belongs most properly to the present chapter. For if these simple Syrian Christians were really settled in the East, as early as Dr. Buchanan seems, with good reason, to suppose, and were, for many centuries entirely secluded from all foreign influence; we may consider them as having in operation among them, substantially, that ecclesiastical system which existed through the greater part of the Christian Church, at the close of the third, and the beginning of the fourth century; a kind of testimony which, of course, falls in with our purpose in examining the testimony of the early ages of the Church.

Such then, is the amount of the testimony from the Christian Fathers. They tell us, with a unanimity and frequency truly remarkable, that, in every Church, there was a bench or college of Elders: that they sat with the Bishop or Pastor, as an ecclesiastical judicatory, and with him ruled the Church: that this bench or body of rulers was called by various names in different parts

---

15. *Christian Researches in Asia*, p. 65. New York Edit. 12mo. 1812.

of the world; such as, *Ecclesiæ Consessus,* the Session or Consistory of the Church; των πρεσβυτερων συνεδριον, the court or Sanhedrim of the Elders; *Ecclesiæ Senatus,* the Senate of the Church; βουλη εκκλησιας, the Council of the Church, &c., &c.: that they were always present with the Bishop or Pastor when he presided in public worship: that he did nothing of importance without consulting them: that they seldom or never preached, unless in cases of necessity, or when specially requested to do so by the Pastor: that they were more frequently than otherwise called clergymen, like the Elders who "laboured in the word and doctrine," but sometimes distinguished from the clergy: that, however, whether called clergymen or not, they were "ecclesiastical men," that is, set apart for ecclesiastical purposes, devoted to the spiritual rule and edification of the Church: that all questions of discipline, such as admitting members into the Church, inspecting their Christian deportment, and censuring, suspending, and excommunicating, were decided by these Elders: and, finally, from all it is apparent, that as discipline became unpopular, and ecclesiastics more aspiring, the ruling part of the Elder's office was gradually laid aside, and the teaching part alone retained.

CHAPTER FIVE

Testimony of the Witnesses for the Truth During the Dark Ages

It has been the habit of zealous and high-toned Prelatists, for more than two centuries past, as well as of some Independents, to assert, that Ruling Elders were unknown in the Christian Church until about the year 1541; that then Calvin invented the order, and introduced it into the Church of Geneva. And some worthy men of other denominations have allowed themselves, with more haste than good advisement, to adopt and repeat the assertion. It is an assertion which, undoubtedly, cannot be made good; as the following testimonies will probably satisfy every impartial reader.

At how early a period the old Waldenses took their rise is uncertain. In some of their Confessions of Faith, and other ecclesiastical documents, dated at the commencement, or soon after the commencement, of the Reformation by Luther, they speak of their Doctrine and Order as having been handed down from father to son for more than five hundred years. But Reinerius, who himself lived about two hundred and fifty years before Luther, who had once resided among the Waldenses, but afterwards became one of their bitterest persecutors, seems to ascribe to that people a much earlier origin. "They are more pernicious," says he, "to the Church of Rome than any other sect of heretics, for three reasons: 1. Because they are older than any other sect; for some say that they have been ever since the time of Pope Sylvester (who was raised to the Papal chair in 314); and others say, from the time of the Apostles.[1] 2. Because they are more extensively spread than any other sect; there being scarcely a country into which they have not crept. 3. Because other sects are abominable to God for their blasphemies; but the Waldenses are more pious than any other heretics; they believe truly of God, live justly before men, and receive all the articles of the creed; only they hate the Church of Rome."

Now, John Paul Perrin, the well known historian of the Waldenses, and who was himself one of the ministers of that people, in a number of places recognizes the office of Elder, distinguished from that of Pastor, or Teacher, as retained in their Churches. He expressly and repeatedly represents their Synods as composed of Ministers and Elders. The same writer tells us that, in the year 1476, the Hussites, being engaged in separating and reforming their Churches from the Church of Rome, understood that there were some Churches of the ancient Waldenses in Austria, in which the purity of the Gospel was retained, and in which there were many eminent Pastors. In order to ascertain the truth of this account, they (the Hussites) sent two of their ministers, and two Elders, to inquire and ascertain what those flocks or congregations were.[2]

The same historian, in the same work, speaks of the Ministers, and Elders of the Bohemian Churches.[3] Now the Bohemian brethren, it is well known, were a branch of the same people called Waldenses.[4] They had removed from Picardy, in the north of France, about two hundred years before the time of Huss and Jerome, to Bohemia, and there, in conjunction with many natives of the country, whom they brought over to their opinions, established a number of pure Churches, which long maintained

---

1. Reinerius flourished about A. D. 1250, more than 250 years before the Reformation; and, at that time, he speaks of the Waldenses as an ancient people, of too remote an origin to be traced with distinctness and certainty.

2. *History of the Old Waldenses*, Part ii. Book 1, Chap. 10. Book 2, Chap. 4. Book 5, Chap. 7.

3. Part ii. Book 2. Chapter 9, 10.

4. *History of the Waldenses*, 4to. 1655, published by order of Cromwell.

the simplicity of the Gospel. The undoubted existence of Ruling Elders, then, among the Bohemian Brethren, affords in itself strong presumptive proof that the same class of officers existed in other branches of the same body. And, accordingly, a Synod, of which we have an account, as held in Piedmont, in Italy, in 1570, is represented, repeatedly, as made up of "Pastors and Elders." Again; in the Form of Government of the same people, in the chapter on Excommunication, we find the following direction respecting the disorderly, who refuse to listen to private admonition: "Tell it to the Church," that is, to the "Guides, whereby the Church is ruled;" and that we may be at no loss who these "Rulers" were, we are told, in a preceding chapter, that they were Elders chosen from among the people for the purpose of governing; and informed that they were distinct from the pastors.

The testimony of Perrin and others, is supported by that of M. Gilly, another historian of the Waldenses, and also one of their Pastors. In the Confession of Faith of that people, inserted at length in the "Addition" to this work, and stated by the historian to have been the Confession of the Ancient, as well as of the Modern Waldenses, it is declared that, "It is necessary for the Church to have Pastors, to preach God's word; to administer the sacraments, and to watch over the sheep of Jesus Christ; and also Elders and Deacons, according to the rules of good and holy Church discipline, and the practice of the primitive Church" (p. 90 – Art. 31).

Sir Samuel Moreland, who visited the Waldenses in the year 1656, and took unwearied pains to learn from themselves their History, as well as their Doctrine and Order; informs us that, besides their Synodical meetings, which took place once a year, when all candidates for the pastoral office were commonly ordained, they had also Consistories in their respective Churches, by means of which pure discipline was constantly maintained.[5]

Accordingly, the Rev. Dr. Ranke, in his laboriously learned *History of France*, gives the following account of the Wal-denses and Albigenses, whom he very properly represents

---

5. *History of the Evangelical Churches of Piedmont*, Book i. chapter viii.

as the same people. "Their government and discipline were extremely simple. The youth intended for the ministry among them, were placed under the inspection of some of the elder barbes, or pastors, who trained them chiefly to the knowledge of the Scriptures; and when, satisfied of their proficiency, they received them as preachers, with imposition of hands. Their pastors were maintained by the voluntary offerings of the people. The whole Church assembled once a year, to treat of their general affairs. Contributions were then obtained; and the common fund was divided for the year, among not only the fixed pastors, but such as were itinerant, and had no particular district or charge. If any of them had fallen into scandal or sin, they were prohibited from preaching, and thrown out of the society. The pastors were assisted in their inspection of the people's morals, by Elders, whom probably both pastors and people elected, and set apart for that purpose."[6]

Further; not only does Perrin speak of the Ministers and Elders of the Bohemian Churches, thereby plainly intimating that they had a class of Elders distinct from their Pastors, or Preachers; but the same thing is placed beyond the possibility of doubt or question by the Bohemian Brethren themselves, who, in the year 1535, presented a Confession of their Faith, to Ferdinand, king of Hungary and Bohemia, with a friendly and highly commendatory Preface by Luther; and who, a number of years afterward published their "Plan of Government and Discipline," which contains the following paragraph:

"Elders (*Presbyteri, seu Censores morum*) are honest, grave, pious men, chosen out of the whole congregation, that they may act as guardians of all the rest. To them authority is given, either alone, or in connexion with the Pastor, to admonish and rebuke those who transgress the prescribed rules, also to reconcile those who are at variance, and to restore to order whatever irregularity they may have noticed. Likewise in secular matters, relating to domestic concerns, the younger men and youths are in the habit of asking their counsel, and of being

---

6. *History of France*, Vol. iii. p. 203, 204.

faithfully advised by them. From the example and practice of the ancient Church, we believe that this ought always to be done; see Exodus xviii. 21. – Deut. i. 13. – 1 Cor. vi. 2, 4, 5. – 1 Tim. v. 17."

This, they say, at the close, "is the ecclesiastical order which they and their forefathers had had established among them for two hundred years;[7] which they derived from the word of God; which they maintained through much persecution, and with much patience, and which they had observed with much happy fruit to themselves, and to the people of God."[8]

And that all mistake might be precluded respecting the real import of the above stated clauses, the Bohemian historian and commentator, Comenius, makes the following remarks on the Elders in question:

"Presbyter, a Greek term, signifying the same with Senior, in Latin, (an Elder,) is applied by the Apostles both to the Pastors of the Church, and to those who assisted them in taking care of the flock, 'who do not labour in the word and doctrine;' 1 Timothy v. 17. Such are our Elders; they are styled Judges of the congregation, or Censors of the people, and also Ruling Elders. I am not ignorant, indeed, that Hugo Grotius, has laboured hard to prove that, in the Apostles' days, there were no other Presbyters than Pastors; and that he assigns a different meaning to the passage in 1 Timothy v. 17. Yet, inasmuch as he finally confesses, that, although such Elders of the Church as sit with the Pastors in Ecclesiastical Judicatories, be an institution of human prudence, they are, nevertheless, very useful, and ought by all means to be retained, I hope no one will easily find any reasonable objection. To guard against abuses, he subjoins very

---

7. The "Plan of Government and Discipline," from which the above extracts are made, was drawn up by their "General Synod" in 1616, and printed in 1632. When, therefore, they declare that they and their forefathers had enjoyed the same order for two hundred years, it carries back the date of this system to 1416, that is, to the time of John Huss; and, of course, nearly a century before the birth of Calvin.

8. Jo. Amos, *Comenii Historia Fratrum Bohemorum. Ratio Disciplinæ Ordinisque*, &c., 11. 56. 68.

very judicious cautions, at the close of chapter xi. of the book which he entitled, *De Imperio Summarum Potestatum circa Sacra."*[9]

In precisely the same manner are both the theory and practice of the Bohemian Brethren understood by the celebrated Martin Bucer, a very learned Lutheran divine, whose fame, throughout Europe, induced Archbishop Crammer to invite him to England, during the progress of the Reformation in that country, where he received patronage and prefer, merit, and was held in high estimation. Bucer was a contemporary of the Bohemian worthies who published the exhibition of their faith and practice above quoted, and, of course, had every opportunity of knowing both its letter and spirit. He speaks of it in the following terms:

"The Bohemian Brethren (Picardi),[10] who published a Confession of their faith, in the year 1535, with a Preface by Luther, and who almost alone preserved in the world the purity of the doctrine, and the vigour of the discipline of Christ, observed an excellent rule for which we are compelled to give them credit, and especially to praise that God who thus wrought by them, notwithstanding those brethren are preposterously despised by some learned men. The rule which they observe was this: besides Ministers of the Word and Sacraments, they had, in each Church, a bench or college of men, excelling in gravity, and prudence, who performed the duties of admonishing and correcting offenders composing differences, and judicially deciding in cases of dispute. Of this kind of Elders, Hilary (Ambrose) wrote, when he said, "Therefore the Synagogue and afterwards the Church had Elders, without whose counsel nothing was done."[11]

---

9. *Annotationes ad Rationem Ordinis Fratrum Bohemorum*, ad Cap. i. p. 68.

10. Bucer styles these worthy people, *Fratres Picardi* in reference to their origin from the Waldenses, or rather the branch called Albigenses in France, to which those who migrated to Bohemia belonged. But the people to whom he refers are ascertained with unerring certainty by the "Confession of Faith" which he so precisely describes.

11. *Scripta duo Adversaria Latomi*, &c. in Cap. *De Ecclesiæ Auctoritate*, p. 159.

It would seem difficult to deny or resist this testimony that the Bohemian Brethren held to Ruling Elders, and actually maintained this class of officers in their Churches. Could Bucer, whom Mr. Middleton, in his *Biographia Evangelica*, represents as "a man of immense learning," and who is spoken of, by Bishop Burnet, as, "perhaps, inferior to none of all the Reformers for learning;" could he have been ignorant, either of the real meaning of a public document, put forth in his own time, or of the public and uniform practice of a body of pious people, whom he seems to have regarded with so much respect and affection, as witnesses for God in a dark world? It cannot be imagined. And what gives additional weight to the testimony of this illustrious man is that he seems to have had no interest whatever in vindicating this class of Church officers; for it is not known that he ever had any special inducement, from a sense of reputation, or any other cause, to exert himself in maintaining them; and the latter part of his life as spent in England in the service of the established Church of that kingdom, in the bosom of which he died.

As a further confirmation of Bucer's judgment in reference to the Bohemian Brethren, the celebrated John Francis Buddus, an eminently learned Lutheran divine of Germany, of the seventeenth century, who gave an edition, with a large preface, of the work of Comenius, in which the History of the Bohemian Brethren, and their Form of Government, are published, evidently understands their plan in reference to the office of Ruling Elder, precisely as Bucer and other learned men have understood it. He employs the greater part of his preface in recommending this office. And, although he does not seem prepared to allow that it existed, as a separate office, in the apostolic Church; yet he thinks that, virtually, and in substance, it did make part of the apostolic system of supervision and order. He thinks, moreover, that, without some such office, it is wholly impossible to maintain pure morals, and sound discipline in the Church of God; and that the Bohemian Brethren rendered a most important service to the cause of truth and piety in maintaining it in their ecclesiastical system.[12]

Luther, in some of his early writings, had expressed an unfavourable opinion of the Bohemian Brethren; but, upon being more fully informed of their Doctrine and Order, and more especially of their provision for maintaining sound discipline, by means of their Eldership in each congregation, he changed his opinion, and became willing both to speak and to write strongly in their favour. Hence, his highly commendatory Preface, to their "Confession of Faith," of which mention has been already made. And hence, at a still later period, the following strong expressions in favour of the same people: "There hath not arisen any people, since the times of the Apostles, whose Church hath come nearer to the apostolical doctrine and order, than the Brethren of Bohemia." And again: "Although these Brethren do not excel us in purity of doctrine, (all the articles of faith with us being sincerely and purely taken out of the word of God,) yet in the ordinary discipline of the Church which they use, and whereby they happily govern the Churches, they go far beyond us, and are, in this respect, far more praise-worthy. And we cannot but acknowledge and yield this to them, for the glory of God, and of his truth; whereas our people of Germany cannot be persuaded to be willing to take the yoke of discipline upon them."[13]

It is presumed that no one, after impartially weighing the foregoing testimonies, will listen, for one moment, with any respect to the allegation, that the plan of a Bench of Elders for ruling the Church and conducting its discipline, was invented by Calvin. But we may go further. The truth is that, instead of the Waldenses, or Bohemian Brethren taking this order of officers from Calvin, it may be affirmed, that precisely the reverse was the fact. We have satisfactory evidence that Calvin took the hint from the Bohemian Brethren; and that the system which he afterwards established in Geneva, was really suggested and prompted by the example of those pious sufferers and witnesses

---

12. Jo. Francisci Buddaei, *Praefatio de instauranda Disciplina Ecclesiastica* – Passim.

13. Joh. A. Comenii, *Historia Bohem.* Frat. Sect. 82.

for the truth, who had this class of officers in their Churches long before Calvin's day. This will be made clearly to appear from the following statement.

When Calvin first settled in Geneva, in 1536, he found the Reformed Religion already introduced, and to a considerable extent, supported, under the ministry of Farel and Viret, two bold and faithful advocates of evangelical truth. Such, however, was the opposition made to the doctrines which they preached, and especially to the purity of discipline which they struggled hard to establish, by the licentious part of the inhabitants, among whom were some of the leading Magistrates; that, in 1538, Calvin and his Colleagues were expelled from their places in the Genevan Church, because they refused to administer the Lord's Supper to the vilest of the population who chose to demand the privilege. In a paroxysm of popular fury, those faithful ministers of Christ were commanded to leave the city within two days. During this temporary triumph of error and profligacy, Calvin retired to Strasburg, where he was appointed Professor of Divinity and Pastor of a Church, and where he remained nearly four years.

In 1540, the year before he was recalled to Geneva, he corresponded with the Bohemian Brethren, and made himself particularly acquainted with their plan of Church government, which he regarded with deep interest; an interest, no doubt greatly augmented by the sufferings which he had recently undergone in fruitless efforts to maintain the purity of ecclesiastical discipline; in which efforts he had been baffled chiefly by the want of such an efficient system as the Bohemian Churches possessed. In the course of this correspondence, while yet in exile for his fidelity, Calvin addressed the Bohemian Pastors in the following pointed terms: "I heartily congratulate your Churches, upon which, besides sound doctrine, God hath, bestowed so many excellent gifts. Of these gifts, it is none of the least to have such Pastors to govern and order them; to have a people themselves so well affected and disposed; to be constituted under so noble a form of government; to be adorned with the most excellent discipline, which we justly call most excellent, and, indeed, the only bond by which obedience can be preserved. I am sure we find with us, by woful experience, what the worth of it is, by the want of it; nor yet can we by any means attain to it. On this account it is, that I am often faint in my mind, and feeble in the discharge of the duties of my office. Indeed I should quite despair, did not this comfort me, that the edification of the Church is always the work of the Lord, which He Himself will carry on by His own power, though all help beside should fail. Yet still it is a great and rare blessing to be aided by so necessary a help. Therefore, I shall not consider our Church as properly strengthened, until they can be bound together by that bond." And the pious historian, after giving this extract from the venerable Reformer, adds: "It so happened, in the course of divine providence, that, not long afterwards, this eminent man was recalled to minister in the Church of Geneva, where he established the very same kind of discipline, which is now famed throughout the world."[14]

Testimony more direct and conclusive could scarcely be desired. Comenius, himself a Bishop of the Bohemian Brethren, surely knew what kind of Eldership it was which was established among the Churches of his own denomination. He says it was the very same with that which Calvin afterwards established in Geneva. We know, too, that this venerable man, before he was expelled from Geneva, in 1538, and while he was struggling and suffering so much for want of an efficient discipline, made no attempt to introduce the institution in question. But, during his painful exile his attention is forcibly turned to the Bohemian plan. He is greatly pleased with it; speaks in the strongest terms of its excellence; declares that he has no hope of any Church prospering until it is introduced; and the very next year, on his return, makes it one of the conditions of his resuming his pastoral charge, that this plan of conducting the discipline of the Church, by a bench of Elders, shall be received with him, and thus causes it to be adopted in Geneva.

And yet the historian of the Waldenses, John Paul Perrin, has been reproached, and insinuations made unfavourable to his

---

14. Joh. A. *Comenii Historia Bohem. Frat.* Sect. 80.

honesty, because he has represented the Bohemian Brethren as having ecclesiastical Elders distinct from their Ministers of the Gospel. How utterly unjust such reproaches are, every one must now see. If there were ever Ruling Elders in Geneva, they were found in the Churches of Bohemia. Nor is it any solid objection to the fact, as we have stated it, that they had some other features in their system of Church order, which were not strictly Presbyterian. All that the historian has to do is with facts. Having stated these, he is answerable for nothing more. That those Churches gave the title of *Seniors,* but more frequently of *Antistites,* to certain elderly clergymen, who were peculiarly venerable in their character, and who chiefly took the lead in all ordinations, is, no doubt, true; that, in their plan of Church government, they distinguished their *Diaconi* from their *Eleemosynarii;* and that they include in the list of their ecclesiastical offices, some which are strictly secular, is also manifest. But surely none of these invalidate the fact that they had Ruling Elders; a fact stated in a manner which it is impossible either to doubt or mistake.

Thus we have good evidence, that all the most distinguished and faithful witnesses for the truth, during the dark ages, with whose faith and order we have any minute acquaintance, carefully maintained the office for which we are contending; that some of them, at least, considered it as of Divine appointment, and accordingly quote in its support scriptural authority; and that they appear, with good reason, to have regarded it as one of the most efficient means, under the Divine blessing, of promoting the spiritual order and edification of the Church.

CHAPTER SIX

Testimony of the Reformers, and Other Learned and Disinterested Witnesses, Nearly Contemporary With Them

We have seen how utterly groundless is the assertion, that Ruling Elders were invented and first introduced by Calvin at Geneva. If there be any truth in history, they were in use long before Calvin was born, and in the purest Churches on earth, to say nothing of their apostolical origin. Nor is this all. It may further be maintained, that a great majority of the Reformers, in organizing those Churches which separated from the Church of Rome, either actually introduced this class of officers, or, in their published writings, freely and fully declared in its favour. And this was the case, as we shall presently see, not merely on the part of those who followed Calvin, both as to time and opinion; but also on the part of those who either preceded, or had no ecclesiastical connexion whatever with that illustrious man; and who were far from agreeing with him in many other particulars. Now this is surely a marvelous fact, if, as some respectable writers would persuade us to believe, the office in question is a mere figment of Genevan contrivance, toward the middle of the sixteenth century.

The first Reformer whose testimony I shall adduce, in favour of this office, is Ulrick Zuingle, the celebrated leader in the work of Reformation in Switzerland. And I mention him first, because, as he never was connected with Calvin; nay, as he was removed by death, in 1531, five years before Calvin ever saw

Geneva, or appeared in the ranks of the Reformers, and ten years before the introduction of Ruling Elders into that city, he cannot be suspected of speaking as the humble imitator of that justly honoured individual.

On the subject of Ruling Elders, Zuingle speaks thus: "The title of Presbyter or Elder, as used in Scripture, is not rightly understood by those who consider it as applicable only to those who preside in preaching: for it is evident that the term is also sometimes used to designate Elders of another kind, that is, Senators, Leaders, or Counsellors. So we read Acts xv., where it is said, "the Apostles and Elders came together to consider of this matter." Here we see that the Elders spoken of are to be considered as Senators or Counsellors. It is evident that the πρεσβυτεροι mentioned in this place were not Ministers of the word; but that they were aged, prudent, and venerable men, who, in directing and managing the affairs of the Church, were the same thing as the Senators in our cities. And the title Elder is used in the same sense, in many other places in the Acts of the Apostles."[1]

Again; Oecolampadius, who also died before Calvin appeared as an active Reformer, and of course before the introduction of Ruling Elders in the Church of Geneva, speaks thus, in an Oration which he pronounced before the Senate of Basil, in 1530, about a year before his death: "But it is evident that those which are here intended, are certain Seniors or Elders, such as were in the Apostles' days, and who of old time were called πρεσβυτεροι, whose judgment, being that of the most prudent part of the Church, was considered as the decision of the whole Church."

Here, again, is the testimony of a man, who could not have been influenced by any knowledge of the opinions of Calvin, for Calvin had, as yet, published no opinions on the subject;

---

1. This quotation from Zuingle, is taken from the *Politicæ Ecclesiasticæ* of Voetius, in which it is cited for the same purpose as here; a copy of the works of the Swiss Reformer not being at present within the reach of the writer of the Essay.

and who yet speaks in very unequivocal terms of a class of officers, as not only existing afterwards, but as of apostolical institution; which, according to some, were not known in the Church, either in theory or practice, for ten years after the decease of this distinguished reformer.

The testimony of Martin Bucer, as one of the most venerable and active of the Reformers, properly belongs to this branch of the subject. But as his sentiments were so fully detailed in the quotation from him, presented in the preceding chapter, it is not deemed necessary to repeat the statement here. From that extract it is evident, not only that he approved of the office of Ruling Elder, as of eminent use in the Church; but also that he considered Ambrose as asserting that officers of this class were found in the primitive Church, and that he agreed with the pious Father in maintaining this assertion. Here was another eminently learned man, and a contemporary of Calvin, who bears testimony, that Ruling Elders were in use, in the purest portion of the Christian Church, as a laudable and scriptural institution, centuries before the Reformer of Geneva was born.

The learned Peter Martyr, a celebrated Protestant divine of Italy, whose high reputation induced Edward VI., to invite him to England, where he was made Professor of Divinity at Oxford, and Canon of Christ Church, speaks of Ruling Elders in the following decisive terms: "The Church" (speaking of the Primitive Church) "had its Elders, or, if I may so speak, its Senate, who consulted about things which were for edification for the time being. Paul describes this kind of ministry; not only in the 12th chapter of the Epistle to the Romans, but also in the first Epistle to Timothy where he thus writes: 'Let the Elders that rule well, be counted worthy of double honour, especially those that labour in the word and doctrine.' Which words appear to me to signify, that there were then some Elders who taught and preached the word of God, and another class of Elders who did not teach, but only ruled in the Church. Concerning these, Ambrose speaks, when he expounds this passage in Timothy. Nay, he inquires whether it was owing to the pride or the sloth of the sacerdotal order that they had then almost ceased in the

Church."[2]

The celebrated John A Lasco, a devoted and eminently useful Reformer, is also a decisive witness on the same side. A Lasco was a Polish nobleman, of excellent education, and great learning. He was offered two Bishoprics – one in Poland, and another in Hungary – but he forsook his native country, and all the secular and ecclesiastical honours which awaited him, from love to the Reformed Religion. In his youth he enjoyed the special friendship of Erasmus, who speaks of him in one of his letters (*Erasmi Epist.* Lib. 28. Ep. 3), as a man of uncommon excellence and worth. The Protestant Churches in the Low Countries being scattered in consequence of the agitation produced by the celebrated ordinance called the Interim, published by Charles V., A Lasco was invited to England, by King Edward VI., at the instance of Archbishop Cranmer. He accepted the invitation, and was chosen Superintendent[3] of the German, French and Italian congregations erected in London, which are said to have consisted, in the aggregate, of more than three thousand souls. He afterwards published an account of the form of government and worship adopted in those congregations. The affairs of each, it is distinctly stated in that account, were managed by a Pastor, Ruling Elders, and Deacons, and each of these classes of officers was considered as of divine appointment. We also learn, from his statement, that the Ruling Elders and Deacons of these Churches, as well as the Pastors, were ordained by the imposition of hands. He further informs us, that, in the administration of the Lord's Supper, in the Churches under his superintendency, the communicants sat at the table; and he occupies a number of pages in showing that this posture ought to be preferred to kneeling. In short, he declares: "We have laid aside all the relics of Popery,

---

2. P. Martyris, *Loci Communes.* Class iv. Cap. 1. Sect. 2.

3. It is worthy of notice here that although a Superintendent was regarded by A Lasco as one who had the inspection of several congregations; yet "he was greater than his brethren only in respect of his greater trouble and care, not having more authority than the other Elders, either as to the ministry of the word and sacraments, or as to the exercise of ecclesiastical discipline, to which he was subject equally with the rest."

with its mummeries, and we have studied the greatest possible simplicity in ceremonies."

Notwithstanding the publication of these sentiments, and the establishment of these practices, marking so great a non-conformity with the Church of England, A Lasco was highly esteemed, and warmly patronized, by Archbishop Cranmer, and also by the King, who granted him Letters Patent, constituting him and the other ministers of the foreign congregations, a body corporate, and giving them important privileges and powers. These letters may be seen among the Original Records subjoined to Burnet's *History of the Reformation*, ii. 202. The following remarks by A Lasco himself will serve at once to explain the design of the King in granting his royal sanction to these people, and also his own view of the principles upon which he and his brethren acted in founding the Churches in question:

"When I was called by the King, and when certain laws of the country stood in the way, so that the public rites of divine worship used under the Papacy, could not be immediately purged out (which the King himself greatly desired), and when I was anxious and earnest in my solicitations for the foreign Churches, it was, at length, his plea sure, that the public rites of the English Churches shall be reformed by degrees, as far as could be accomplished by the laws of the country; but that strangers, who were not strictly and to the same extent bound by these laws, should have Churches granted to them, in which they should freely regulate all things, wholly according to apostolical doctrine and practice, without any regard to the rites of the country; that by this means the English Churches also might be excited to embrace apostolical purity, by the unanimous consent of all the estates of the kingdom. Of this project, the King himself, from his great piety, was both the chief author and the defender. For although it was almost universally acceptable to the King's Council, and the Archbishop of Canterbury promoted it with all his might, there were not wanting some, who took it ill, and would have opposed it, had not his majesty checked them by his authority, and by the reasons which he adduced in favour of the design."

Again, in the Appendix to the same book, p. 649, he says:

"The care of our Church was committed to us chiefly with this view, that in the ministration thereof we should follow the rules of the Divine Word, and apostolical observance, rather than any rites of other Churches. In fine, we were admonished, both by the King himself, and his chief nobility, to use this great liberty granted to us in our ministry, rightly and faithfully, not to please men, but for the glory of God, by promoting the reformation of his worship."[4]

On the whole, we have in this case a witness as unexceptionable and weighty as can well be desired; a man of eminent learning, piety, and devotedness; a man formed, not in the school of Calvin, but of Zuingle; a man who, when the transactions and publications above alluded to, occurred, lived in England, where Ruling Elders were unknown: and who, yet, in these circumstances, declared himself in favour of this class of officers, as of Divine appointment, and as important to the purity and edification of the Church. But there is a still more conclusive fact in reference to this stage of the Reformation in England. A Lasco, it will be observed, asserts, that both King Edward, and Archbishop Cranmer, were strongly favourable to the plan of discipline which he and others had introduced into the Churches of Foreign Protestants in England. In confirmation of this statement, there is evidence that Cranmer, and the rest of the Commissioners, in Edward's reign, did directly propose the introduction of Ruling Elders in the national Church. They drew up a body of laws, which, though not finally ratified, partly on account of opposing influence, and partly from the premature decease of the monarch; yet clearly show the opinion and wishes of Cranmer and his associates. One of the proposed laws is as follows: "After evening prayers, on which all shall attend in their own parish Churches, the principal minister or Parson, and the Deacon, if

---

4. See McCrie's *Life of Knox*, Vol. i. p. 392-396. See also Gisberti Voetii, *Politicæ Ecclesiasticæ*. Tom. i. 420-422. See also, *Forma et Ratio totius Ecciesiastici Ministerii Edvardi sexti in Peregrinorum, maxime Germanorum, Eccles.* Also, *De Ordinatione Ecclesiarum Peregrinarum* in Anglia. *Epist. Dedicat*, et p. 649.

they are present, or, in case of their absence, the Curate and the Elders, shall consider how the money given for pious uses had best be laid out; and then let discipline be exercised. For, those whose sin has been public, and given offence to the whole Church, should be brought to a sense of it and publicly undergo the punishment of it, that so the Church may be the better for their correction. After that the minister shall withdraw, with some of the Elders, and consult how all other persons who are disorderly in their life and conversation may be conversed with; first by some sober and good men in a brotherly manner according to the direction or Christ in the Gospel; and if they hearken to their advice, God is to be praised for it; but if they go on in their wickedness, they are to be restrained by that severe punishment, which is in the Gospel prescribed for such obstinacy."[5]

The testimony of Calvin will next be introduced. As he is charged with being the inventor of this class of officers, the weight of his opinion as a witness in its favour, will probably be deemed small by its opposers. But there is one point of view in which his testimony will surely be regarded with deep respect, and, may I not add, as decisive? That he was a man of mature and profound learning, no one can doubt. Joseph Scaliger, himself a prodigy of erudition, pronounced him to have been the most learned man in Europe in his day; and, particularly, "that no man understood ecclesiastical history so well." Now, it is certain that Calvin did not consider the office of Ruling Elder as originating with himself; but that he regarded it as an apostolical institution; that he refers to Scripture for its support; and that he quotes Ambrose (whose testimony has been so often referred to), as an unquestionable witness for the existence of the office under consideration in the primitive Church. The following extracts from his *Commentary* and his *Institutes*, will fully establish what is here asserted.

In his exposition of 1 Tim. v. 17, he speaks thus: "From

---

5. Peirce's *Vindication of the Dissenters*, p. 23. Baxter's *Treatise of Episcopacy*, part ii. p. 112. *Reformatio Legum Ecclesiasticarum*, ex authoritate Regis. Hen. viii. et. Edv. vi. 4to. 1640.

this passage we may gather that there were then two kinds of Presbyters, because they were not all ordained to the work of teaching. For the words plainly mean that some ruled well, to whom no part of the public instruction was committed. And verily there were chosen from among the people, grave and approved men, who, in common council, and joint authority with the Pastors, administered the discipline of the Church, and acted the part of censors for the correction of morals. This practice Ambrose complains, had fallen into disuse, through the indolence, or rather the pride of the teaching elders, who wished alone to be distinguished."

In his *Institutes* (Book iv. Chapter iii), he has the following passage, equally explicit: "In calling those who preside over Churches by the appellations of 'Bishops,' 'Elders,' and 'Pastors,' without any distinction, I have followed the usages of the Scriptures, which apply all these terms to express the same meaning. For to all who discharge the ministry of the word, they give the title of 'Bishops.' So when Paul enjoins Titus to 'ordain Elders in every city,' he immediately adds, 'For a Bishop must be blameless.' So, in another place, he salutes more Bishops than one in one Church. And in the Acts of the Apostle, he is declared to have sent for the Elders of the Church of Ephesus, whom, in his address to them, he calls 'Bishops.' Here it must be observed, that we have enumerated only those offices which consist in the ministry of the word; nor does Paul mention any other in the fourth chapter of the Epistle to the Ephesians which we have quoted. But in the Epistle to the Romans, and the first Epistle to the Corinthians, he enumerates others, as 'powers,' 'gifts or healing,' 'interpretation of tongues,' 'governments,' 'care of the poor.' Those functions which are merely temporary, I omit, as foreign to our present subject. But there are two which perpetually remain, 'governments,' and 'the care of the poor.' 'Governors,' I apprehend to have been persons of advanced years, selected from the people, to unite with the Bishops in giving admonitions, and exercising discipline. For no other interpretation can be given of that injunction, 'He that ruleth, let him do it with diligence.' For from the beginning, every Church has had its senate, or council composed of pious, grave, and holy men, who were invested with that jurisdiction, for the correction of vices, of which we shall soon treat. Now, that this was not the regulation of a single age, experience itself demonstrates. This office of government is necessary, therefore, in every age."

I ask, was Calvin honest, or dishonest, in these declarations? If he had invented and introduced the office himself, could he have been ignorant of the fact? And whether it was so or not, who may reasonably be considered as best able to judge – HIMSELF, or those who live nearly three hundred years after him? And who would be most likely to know whether it were of ancient or modern origin; – the most learned man then, perhaps, in the world, or men with not a tenth part of his erudition, at the present day? The truth is, these passages, considered in connexion with that quoted in a former chapter, in which he speaks of himself, in reference to this office, as following the example of the pious Witnesses of the truth who preceded him; prove, either, that Calvin did not consider himself as the inventor of the office, but believed that it had been in the Church in all ages; or that he was gratuitously and profligately regardless of the truth to a degree never laid to his charge.

Nor is the testimony to the primitive existence of this class of officers confined to those of the Reformers who were favourable to their continuance in the Church. Some by no means friendly to their restoration, were yet constrained to acknowledge their early origin.

That there were Ruling Elders in the primitive Church, is explicitly granted by Archbishop Whitgift, a warm and learned friend of diocesan Episcopacy. "I know," says he, "that in the Primitive Church, they and in every Church certain Seniors, to whom the government of the Congregation was committed; but that was before there was any Christian Prince or Magistrate that openly professed the Gospel; and before there was any Church by public authority established."

And again: "Both the name and office of Seniors were extinguished before Ambrose's time, as he himself doth testify, writing upon the fifth of the first Epistle to Timothy. Indeed, as

Ambrose saith, the Synagogue, and afterwards the Church, had Seniors, without whose counsel nothing was done in the Church; but that was before his time, and before there was any Christian Magistrate, or any Church established."[6] The learned and acute Archbishop, it seems, was not only convinced that there were Ruling Elders, distinct from Preaching Elders, in the Primitive Church, but with all his erudition and discernment, he understood Ambrose just as the friends of this class of officers now understand him.

There is another testimony on this subject, from one of the most conspicuous and active friends of the Reformation in England, which is worthy of particular notice. I refer to that of the Rev. Dean Nowell, who flourished in the reign of Queen Elizabeth, and whose celebrated Catechism, drawn up in 1562, obtained, perhaps, as much currency and respect as any publication of that period. Nor are we to consider it as expressing the sentiments of the illustrious divine whose name it bears, alone; for it was unanimously approved and sanctioned by the same lower house of Convocation which passed the 39 Articles of the Church of England, and directed to be published and used as containing the true doctrine of that Church. In this Catechism, toward the close, when speaking of the evils of retaining unworthy members in the Church, the following questions and answers occur:

"Q. What remedy for this evil can be devised and applied?"

"A. In Churches well constituted and governed, there was, as I before said, a certain plan and order of government appointed and observed. Elders were chosen, that is, ecclesiastical rulers, who conducted and maintained the discipline of the Church. To these pertained authority, reproof, and chastisement; and they, with the concurrence of the Pastor, if they knew any who, by false opinions, troublesome errors, foolish superstitions, or vicious and profligate lives, were likely to bring a great public scandal on the Church of God, and who could not approach the

---

6. *Defence Against Cartwright*, pp. 638, 651.

Lord's Supper without a manifest profanation, repelled them from the communion, and no more admitted them until, by public penitence, they gave satisfaction to the Church."

"Q. What is to be done?" (when those who have been excluded from the Church, repent, and desire to be restored to its communion.)

"A. That they may be received again into the Church, and to the enjoyment of its holy mysteries, from which they have been deservedly cast out, they ought humbly to supplicate and pray. And, on the whole, there ought to be such moderation used in administering public penance, that neither by too much severity the offender may be reduced to despondency; nor by too much lenity, the discipline of the Church relaxed, its authority diminished, and others encouraged and incited to similar offences. But when, in the judgment of the Elders and of the Pastor, proper satisfaction shall be made, by the chastisement of the offender, for an example to others, he may be admitted again to the communion of the Church."[7]

Nothing can be more unequivocal or decisive than this testimony. In the opinion not only of the writer of the Catechism before us, but also of the leading clergy of the Church of England, who sanctioned it, and enjoined its general use, there ought to be, in every Church, besides the Pastor, a bench of Elders, or ecclesiastical Rulers, whose duty it should be to preside over the discipline, and, in conjunction with the Pastor, to receive, admonish, suspend, excommunicate, and restore members, – in a manner precisely agreeable to the well known practice of the Presbyterian Church. In truth, Dr. Nowell could scarcely have expressed in more distinct and unqualified terms his approbation of this part of our system, than in telling us, what, in his judgment, and that of his brethren, every well regulated Church ought to have.

Ursinus, a learned German divine, contemporary with Luther and Melancthon, speaks a language still more to our pur-

---

7. See Bishop Randolph's *Enchiridion Theologicum*. Vol. i. 326, 327. Third Edition.

pose. "Ministers," says he, "are either *immediately* called of God, or *mediately,* through the instrumentality of the Church. Of the former class, were Prophets and Apostles. Of the latter class there are five kinds, viz. Evangelists, Bishops, or Pastors, Teachers, Ruling Elders, and Deacons. Evangelists are ministers appointed to go forth and preach the Gospel to a number of Churches. Bishops, are ministers ordained to preach the word of God, and administer the sacraments, in particular Churches. Teachers are ministers appointed merely to fulfil the function of teaching in particular Churches. Ruling Elders are ministers elected by the voice of the Church, to assist in conducting discipline, and to order a variety of necessary matters in the Church. Deacons are ministers elected by the Church, to take care of the poor, and distribute alms."[8]

In the Confession of Saxony, drawn up by Melancthon, in 1531, and subscribed by a large number of Lutheran divines and Churches, we find this class of officers recognized, and represented as in use in those Churches. Speaking of the exercise of discipline, in its various branches, they say: "That these things may be done orderly, there be also Consistories appointed in our Churches." Of these Consistories, a majority of members, it is well known, were Ruling Elders.

Szegeden, a very eminent Lutheran divine of Hungary, contemporary with Luther, also speaks very decisively of the apostolic institution or Ruling Elders. The following passage is sufficient to exhibit his sentiments: "The ancient Church had Presbyters, or Elders, of which the Apostle speaks, 1 Corinth. v. 4. And these Elders were of two kinds. One class of them preached the Gospel, administered the sacraments, and governed the Church, the same as Bishops; for Bishops and Presbyters are the same order. But another class of Elders consisted of grave and upright men, taken from among the laity, who, together with the preaching Elders before mentioned, consulted respecting the affairs of the Church, and devoted their labour to admonishing,

---

8. Ursini, *Corpus Doctrinæ*. Par, iii. p. 21.

correcting, and taking care of the flock of Christ."⁹

The Magdeburgh Centuriators, who were eminently learned Lutheran divines, contemporary with Melancthon, and who have been regarded, for three hundred years, as among the highest authorities on questions of ecclesiastical history, speak in the following decisive terms with regard to the office in question. And although the extract has been given in a former page; yet, as it is brief and pointed, it may not be improper to assign it a place in this connexion. Speaking of the third century, they say: "The right of deciding respecting such as were to be excommunicated, or of receiving, upon their repentance, such as had fallen, was vested in the Elders of the Church."¹⁰

The learned Francis Junius, a distinguished divine and professor of Theology of the Church of Holland, who lived at the commencement of the Reformation in that country, and was, of course, contemporary with Martyr, Bucer, Melancthon, &c., wrote very fully and explicitly in favour of the office of Ruling Elder. In his work entitled *Ecclesiastici,* he decisively, and with great learning, maintains, that Pastors, Ruling Elders, and Deacons, are the only three spiritual orders of Church officers; that Pastors, or ministers of the word and sacraments, are the highest order, and, of course, are invested with the power of ordaining; that the second class, are men of distinguished piety and prudence, chosen from among the members of the Church, to assist the Pastor in the government of the Church; and that the Deacons are appointed to collect and distribute the alms of the Church. He affirms that these three orders are set forth in Scripture, and existed in the primitive Church: and that the disuse of Ruling Elders, as well as the introduction of Prelacy, is a departure from the primitive model.¹¹

The Protestant Churches of Hungary and Transylvania, although, in organizing their Churches, they did not actually

---

9. Szegedeni, *Loci Communes,* p. 197. Edit. quint, folio – Basil, 1608.

10. Cent. iii. cap. vii. p. 151.

11. *Ecclesiastici, sive de flat. et administrat. Ecclesiæ,* &c. bib. ii. Cap. 2, 3, 4.

adopt and introduce the office of Ruling Elder; yet in the Preface, and other statements, published with their ecclesiastical Formularies, they spoke, in the most unequivocal terms, both of the value, and the early origin of this class of officers. The following extract may be considered as a fair specimen of their testimony on this subject: "Most other nations, belonging to the Evangelical Confession, have been in the habit of choosing and constituting Elders, in every village and city, agreeably to the practice of the Old Church, and also of the New Testament: men sound in the faith, blameless, the husbands of one wife, having faithful children, chargeable with no crime, grave, prudent, &c. – It is made the official duty of these men diligently to watch over the lives and conversation of all the members of the Church, to rebuke the dissolute, and, if need be, to refer their cases to the Pastors and to the whole Eldership, &c." Here they make a clear distinction between these Elders, and Pastors of the Churches, and represent the former as assistants to the latter in the spiritual concerns of the Church. They then proceed to state why a class of officers so useful, in most cases so necessary, and which they also considered as having existed in the Apostolic Church, was not received among them.[12]

The character of Jerome Zanchius, a learned divine of Italy, of the sixteenth century, who greatly distinguished himself among the Reformers, is so well known, that a detailed account of his great accomplishments and reputation is unnecessary. On the subject before us, he speaks thus: "The whole ministry of the Christian Church may be divided into three classes. The first consists of those who dispense the word and sacraments, corresponding with those who, under the Old Testament, were called Priests and Levites; and under the New Testament, Apostles, Pastors, and Teachers. The second consists of those whose peculiar office it is to take care of the discipline of the Church, to inspect the lives and conversation of all, and to take care that all live in a manner becoming Christians; and also, if at any time there should be a necessity for it, in the absence of the Pastor, to

---

12. See G. Voetii, *Polit. Eccles.* Par.ii. Lib. ii. Tract. iii.

instruct the people. There were such under the Old Testament in the Synagogue; and such also were the Senators who were added to the Bishop in the administration of the New Testament Church. These officers are styled Presbyters (*Presbyteri*), and Elders (*Seniores*), of which the Apostle speaks, besides other places, in 1 Timothy v. 17: 'Let the Elders that rule well be accounted worthy of double honour, especially those who labour in the word and doctrine.' In this passage the Apostle manifestly speaks of two sorts or classes of Elders, as he was understood by Ambrose and others, among the ancients, and by almost all our modern Protestant Divines, as Bullinger, Peter Martyr, &c., &c."[13]

The most cursory reader of this extract will not fail to take notice, not only that Zanchius evidently approved of this office, but that he thought it of Divine appointment; that he interpreted as we do the famous passage in Ambrose, which the opposers of Ruling Elders have expended so much ingenuity in labouring to explain away; and that he considered almost all the Reformed Divines as being of the same opinion with himself.

The high reputation of Paræus, a learned and pious German divine, contemporary with Melancthon and Zanchius, is also well known. His testimony respecting the office under consideration is very explicit. In his Commentary on Romans xii. 8, he observes: "Here the Apostle understands the function of that class of Elders, who, united with the Pastors, watch over and correct the morals and discipline of the Church. For there were two classes of Elders, as may be gathered from 1 Timothy v. 17; – some who laboured in the word and doctrine, who were to be accounted worthy of double honour; such as Teachers, Pastors, or Bishops; the others, such as laboured in conducting discipline, who are here called governments." And in his Commentary on 1 Corinthians xii. 28, he says: "The Apostle here, undoubtedly speaks of the Elders who presided in the administration of discipline. For the primitive Church had its Senate, who attended to the morals of the congregation, while the Apostles and Teach-

---

13. Zanchii, *Opera*. Tom. iv. In *Quartum Præceptum*, p. 727.

ers were left at leisure to preach. This the Apostle indicates very clearly in the first Epistle to Timothy v. 17, where two classes of Presbyters are represented as constituted. The governments here spoken of were not of Princes or Proctors, armed with the sword, but grave, experienced men, exercising authority over others, chosen out of the Church, by the consent of the Church, to assist the Pastors in conducting discipline, and to alleviate their burdens."

The celebrated Piscator, who held a distinguished place among the divines who adorned Germany, and maintained the Protestant cause in the sixteenth century, is equally decisive, as an advocate of the office under consideration. In his Commentary on 1 Tim. v. 17, he says: "The Apostle distributes Elders into two classes, those who presided in maintaining ecclesiastical discipline, but did not publicly teach; and those who both taught, and co-operated in ruling, and were, therefore, worthy of a greater honour, and a more liberal support than the others."

Few ministers of the Church of England, during the reign of Queen Elizabeth, were more distinguished for talents, learning, and piety, than Thomas Cartwright, Professor of Divinity in the University of Cambridge, the opponent of the high prelatical claims of Archbishop Whitgift, and concerning whom the celebrated Beza pronounced, that he thought "the sun did not shine upon a more learned man." This eminent divine, commenting on Matthew xviii. 17, "Tell it unto the Church," &c., thus remarks: "Theophylact upon this place, interpreteth, Tell the Church, that is many, because this assembly taketh knowledge of this and other things, by their mouths, that is, their governors. Chrysostom also saith, that to tell the Church is to tell the governors thereof. It is, therefore, to be understood, that these governors of the Church, which were set over every several assembly in the time of the law, were of two sorts; for some had the handling of the word; some other watching against the offences of the Church, did, by common counsel with the ministers of the word, take order against the same. Those governing Elders are divers times in the story of the Gospel made mention of, under the title of 'Rulers of the Synagogue.' And this manner of government, because it was to be translated into the Church of Christ, under the Gospel, our Saviour, by the order at that time used among the Jews, declareth what after should be done in his Church. Agreeably hereunto the Apostle both declared the Lord's ordinance in his behalf, and put the same in practice, in ordaining to every several Church, beside the ministry of the word, certain of the chiefest men which should assist the work of the Lord's building. This was also faithfully practised of the Churches after the Apostle's times, as long as they remained in any good and allowable soundness of doctrine. And being fallen from the Churches, especially from certain of them, the want thereof is sharply and bitterly cast into the teeth of the Church's teachers, by whose ambition that came to pass."[14] And as proof of this, the author quotes in the margin that very passage of Ambrose, cited in the preceding section, and which has always given so much trouble to Prelatists and Independents.

The same writer, in his *Second Reply* to Whitgift, speaking of the class of Elders under consideration, expresses himself thus: "For proof of these Church Elders, which, being occupied in the government, had nothing to do with the Word, the testimony of Ambrose, is so clear and open, that he which doth not give place unto it, must needs be thought as a bat, or an owl, or some other night-bird, to delight in darkness. His saying is, that the Elders fell away by the ambition of the Doctors; whereby opposing the Elders to Doctors, which taught, he plainly declareth, that they had not to do with the Word: whereupon it is manifest that it was the use, in the best reformed Churches, certain hundred years after the times of the Apostles, to have an Eldership which meddled not with the word, nor administration of sacraments."[15]

The testimony of the Rev. Richard Greenham, a divine of the Church of England, who flourished in the reign of Queen Elizabeth, and who was greatly revered both for his learning and piety, is very unequivocal and pointed on this subject. It is in these

---

14. Cartwright's *Commentary on the New Testament – Against the Rhemists*.
15. *Second Reply*. Part Second, p. 44. 4to. 1577.

words: "The Apostle Paul doth notably amplify the honour due to the true and faithful minister. 'The Elders that rule well, (saith he,) let them be had in double honour, specially they which labour in the word and doctrine;' 1 Timothy v. 17. As if he should say, let those Elders which are appointed to watch and look to the manners and behaviour of the children of God, if they execute this charge faithfully, be had in double honour: but above all, let the faithful ministers, such as labour in the word, be honoured: for why? the other are overseers of your outward behaviour, but these have another manner of office they watch over your souls which tendeth to the salvation both of body and soul." And again: "The rulers of the Church are called the Church, to whom discipline appertaineth. Not the whole company of the Jews, but the rulers of the Synagogue, are called the Church of the Jews."[16]

The celebrated Estius, the learned Popish expositor and professor at Douay, in his Commentary on 1 Tim. v. 17, delivers the following opinion: "From this passage it may manifestly be gathered that, in the time of the Apostles, there were certain Presbyters in the Church who ruled well, and were worthy of double honour, and who yet did not labour in the word and doctrine; neither do the heretics of the present day (meaning the Protestants) deny this." And, in speaking of the establishment of this class of Elders in Geneva, about half a century before he wrote, he seems only to blame Calvin for considering and styling them laymen. He expresses a decisive opinion, that the Elders spoken of by Paul, in this place, were ecclesiastical men, set apart by ecclesiastical rites, and devoted to ecclesiastical duties; but they did not preach. And he explicitly acknowledges that Ambrose, in the fourth century, speaks of such Elders as having existed long before his day. It is worthy of remark, that the same learned Romanist in another work, not only avows, in the most distinct manner, his belief in the apostolic appointment of non-preaching Elders, and quotes 1 Tim. v. 17, in support of his opinion; but also refers to Jerome and Augustine, as witnesses to

---

16. *Works*, pp. 352, 842. fol. 1612.

the same fact.[17]

The opinion of the learned Professor Whitaker, a divine of the Church of England, who flourished in the reign of Queen Elizabeth, as to the true meaning of 1 Timothy v. 17, was given, at length, in a preceding page. The same distinguished divine, in writing against Dury, expresses himself thus, concerning the office under consideration: "Art thou so ignorant as not to know that in the Church of Christ there ought to be Elders who should devote themselves to the work of government alone, and not to the administration of the word or sacraments, as we are taught in 1 Tim. v. 17?"[18]

To these testimonies might be added many more, from learned men of the same distinguished character with those already mentioned, and to the same effect. Chemnitius, of Germany; Salmasius, of Holland; Marloratus, and Danaus, of France; Hemmingius, of Denmark[19] – with a long list of similar names, might all be cited as warm advocates of the class of Elders under consideration, and almost all of them decisive advocates of its divine authority.

Nor are these individual suffrages, though numerous and unequivocal, all that can be alleged in favour of our cause. The great body of the Protestant Churches, when they came to organize their several systems in a state of separation from the Papacy, and from each other differing, as they did, in many other respects, were almost unanimous in adopting and maintaining the office of Ruling Elder. Instead of this office being confined; as many appear to suppose, to the ecclesiastical establishments of Geneva and Scotland, it was generally introduced, with the Reformation, by Lutherans as well as Calvinists: and is generally retained to the present day, in almost all the Protestant Churches, excepting that of England. Those of France, Germany, Holland, Switzerland, &c., received this class of Elders early, and express-

---

17. Estii, *Sententiarum Commentaria*. Lib. iv. Par. 2. Sect, 21.

18. *Contra Duræum*, Lib. ix. p. 807.

19. See these writers, as well as a number of others, referred to in the *Politicæ Ecclesiasticæ* of Voetius: Par. ii. Lib. ii. Tract. iii.

ly represented them in their public Confessions, as founded on the word of God. It is probably safe to affirm, that, at the period of the Reformation, more than three-fourths of the whole Protestant world declared in favour of this office, not merely as expedient but as warranted by Scripture, and as necessary to the order and edification of the Church.

Does all this, it may be confidently asked, look like the office in question being a mere Genevan innovation? How shall we reconcile with this extraordinary position, the undoubted fact, that Lutherans and Reformed, in every part of Europe – those who never saw Calvin as well as those who were within the sphere of his acquaintance and influence; nay, some of those who died before the illustrious Reformer of Geneva ever appeared at all, either as a writer or preacher; – are found among the decisive, zealous advocates of the office in question, and quoting, as of conclusive authority, in its favour, the principal passages of Scripture, and the principal Father, relied on by Presbyterians to establish its apostolical warrant, and its actual existence in the early ages of the ancient Church? Truly, it is difficult to conceive how any one, who seriously and impartially weighs these facts, can resist the impression, that an Institution, in behalf of which so many eminently learned and pious men, of different and distant countries, without concert with each other, and without any common interest to serve, in reference to this matter, have so remarkably concurred in opinion, must have some solid foundation, both in the inspired volume, and in the nature and necessities of the Church.

CHAPTER SEVEN

Testimony of Eminent Divines Since the Time of the Reformers

While we justly attach so much importance to the persons and services of the Reformers, and recur with the deepest reverence to their opinions, we owe scarcely less respect to the judgment of a number of other men, who have lived since their time, and of whom the world was not worthy; – men whose testimony can never be quoted but with veneration, and whose characters give an ample pledge of research at once profound and honest. To the decision of a few of these illustrious men on the subject before us, the attention of the reader is respectfully requested.

The decisive opinion of Dr. Owen, undoubtedly one of the greatest divines that ever adorned the British nation, in favour of the scriptural warrant of the office of Ruling Elder, was given in a preceding section, and need not now be repeated. I may, however, add, that the more weight ought to be attached to this opinion, on account of Dr. Owen's ecclesiastical connexions, which, as is well known, were by no means adapted to give him a bias on the side of Presbyterian order.

The venerable and eminently pious Richard Baxter was no Presbyterian. Yet he expresses himself in the following very unequivocal language, on the subject under consideration: "When I plead, that the order of subject Presbyters (or lay-Elders), was not instituted in Scripture times, and consequently that it is not of divine institution, I mean, that, as a distinct office, or species of Church ministers, it is not a divine institution, nor a lawful institution of man; but that, among men in the same office, some might, prudentially, be chosen to an eminency of degree, as to the exercise; and that according to the difference of their advantages, there might be a disparity in the use of their authority and gifts, I think was done in Scripture times, and might have been after, if it had not then. And my judgment is, that, ordinarily, every particular Church (such as our parish Churches are) had more Elders than one, but not such store of men of eminent gifts, as that all these Elders could be such. But as if half a dozen of the most judicious persons of this parish were ordained to be Elders, of the same office with myself; but because they are not equally fit for public preaching, should most employ themselves in the rest of the oversight, consenting that the public preaching lie most upon me, and that I be the moderator of them, for order in circumstantials. This I think was the true Episcopacy and Presbytery of the first times."[1]

Although it may be doubted whether this venerable man be correct in his whole view of this subject; yet it will be observed by every attentive reader, that in maintaining the existence of a plurality of Elders in each Church, in primitive times, and that a great part of these Elders were not, in fact, employed in preaching, but in inspecting and ruling, he concedes every thing that can be deemed essential in relation to the office which we are considering.

The Puritan Congregationalists of England, about the year 1605, in the summary of their Faith and Order, entitled *English Puritanism*, drawn up by the venerable Mr. Bradshaw, translated into Latin for the benefit of the foreign Protestants, by the learned Dr. Ames, and intended to express the sense of the general body of the Puritans, speak thus on the subject of Ruling Elders: "Since even in the best constituted Churches, they know that not a few enormous offences will arise, which, if not timely met, will do injury both to those who believe, and those who are inquiring; while, at the same time, they see that the authority of a single person in a parish, resembling the papal,

---

1. *Disputations of Church Government.* – Advertisement, pp. 4, 5. 4to. 1659.

a single person in a parish, resembling the papal, is contrary to the will of Christ: they think, as the case itself requires, and as appointed of God, that others also should be selected from the Church, as officers, who may be associated with the ministers in the spiritual government.

"These are inspectors, επιτιμηται, a kind of censors, whose duty it is, together with the ministers of the word, as well to watch over the conduct of all the brethren, as to judge between them. And they think that this office is instituted, that each may take the more heed to himself and his ways, while the ministers enjoy more leisure for study and devotion, and obtain, through the assistance of their co-adjutors, a more accurate view of the state of the flock; since it is the peculiar duty of the inspectors to be always watchful over the manners and conduct of all the members of the Church.

"To this office they think that none should be preferred, but men very eminent for gravity and prudence, established in the faith; of tried integrity; whose sanctity of life and upright example are well known to the whole society.

"In the choice of these Elders, respect should always be had to their outward circumstances. They should be able to support themselves in some respectable manner; though it will not be an objection to them that they pursue some mechanical art, provided they be morally qualified."[2]

Nor were these venerable men the only Independents who declared, in the most decisive manner, in favour of this class of officers. The celebrated Dr. Thomas Goodwin, one of the Westminster Assembly of divines, and who is styled by Anthony A. Wood, a very "Atlas and Patriarch of Independency," is well known to have been one of the most learned and influential Independents of the seventeenth century, and one of the most voluminous and instructive writers of his class. In his *Church Order Explained, in a Way of Catechism*, the following passage occurs: "What sort of Bishops hath God set in his Church? Answer, Two; some Pastors and Teachers; some Ruling Elders, under two

---

2. Neal's *History of the Puritans*, Vol. i. p. 449. 4to. Edit.

heads; some labour in word and doctrine, and of those, some are Pastors, some Teachers; others *rule only,* and labour not in the word and doctrine." Again; "What is the office and work of the Ruling Elder? Answer: Seeing the kingdom of God is not of this world, but heavenly, and spiritual, and the government of his kingdom is not lordly, but stewardly and ministerial; and to labour in the ministry of exhortation and doctrine is the proper work of the Pastors and Teachers; it remaineth, therefore, to be the office and work of the Ruling Elders to assist the Pastors and Teachers in diligent attendance to all other aids of rule besides exhortation and doctrine, as becometh good stewards of the household of God. As, first, to open and shut the doors of God's house, by admission of members, by ordination of officers, by excommunication of notorious and obstinate offenders. Secondly, to see that none live in the Church inordinately, without a calling, or idle in their calling. Thirdly, to prevent and heal offences, whether in life or doctrine, that might corrupt their own Church, or other Churches. Fourthly, to prepare matters for the Church's consideration, and to moderate the carriage of all matters in the Church assemblies. Finally, to feed the flock of God, by a word of admonition, and, as they shall be called, to visit and pray with their sick brethren. The ground of all this is laid down in Romans xii. 8, where the Apostle, besides him who exhorteth and teacheth, maketh mention of another officer, who ruleth with diligence, and is distinct from the Pastors and Teachers, and that is the sum of his work, to rule with diligence. Thus you see the whole duty of these Ruling Elders, and how they are to assist the Pastors and Teachers in all other acts of rule besides word and doctrine. *Use* 1. From hence observe the great bounty of God unto Pastors and Teachers, that God hath not left them alone in the Church, as Martha complains to Christ that Mary had left her alone to serve: the ministers of the Church have no such cause to complain: for, as he gave the Levites to the Priests, to help them in their service, so hath he given Ruling Elders to such as labour in the word and doctrine, that they might have assistance from them in ruling the Church of God. *Use* 2. It may serve to answer a cavil that some have against this office, who say, that, if God hath given these officers to the Church, he would then have set down the limits of these officers, and not have sent them forth with illimited power. To which it is answered, that their power is strongly limited, as a stewardly or ministerial power and office. It is the power of the keys, which Christ hath expressed in his word, and it consisteth in those things that have been spoken of God's house, to open and shut the doors of God's house, by admission of members, &c. This is such a rule as is no small help to the spirits and hearts of those who labour in doctrine; and no small help it is also to the whole Church of God; and when they are wanting, many evils will grow, and those without the possibility of redress and amendments much idleness, much confusion, many offences. Though other ministers have been in the Church, we may see how much, in the want of these officers, the Churches have been corrupted."[3]

The character of the Rev. Thomas Hooker, one of the most learned and pious Fathers of New England, and a distinguished advocate of Independency, is too well known to require remark. In his work, entitled *A Survey of Church Discipline*, he speaks thus of the office under consideration: "We begin with the Ruling Elder's place, for that carries a kind of simplicity with it. There be more ingredients required to make up the office of Pastor and Doctor, and therefore we shall take leave to trade in the first, *quo simplicius ac prius*. That there is such an office and officer appointed by Christ, as the Scriptures are plain to him, whose spirit and apprehension is not possessed and forestalled with prejudice. The first argument we have from Romans xii. 7, which gives in witness to this truth, where all these officers are numbered and named expressly. The second argument is taken from 1 Cor. xii. 28. The scope of the place, and Apostle's intendment is, to lay open the several offices and officers that the Lord hath set in his Church, and so many chief members, out of which the Church is constituted as an entire body." And, after making some other remarks for the right discovery of the Apostle's pro-

---

3. *Church Order Explained*, &c., page 16, 19, 22, to be found in the 4th Vol. of Coodwin's *Works*, four vols. fol. London, 1697.

ceeding and purpose, he adds: "From which premises, the dispute issues thus. As Apostles, Prophets, and Teachers are distinct, so are Helps and Governments distinct: for the Spirit puts them in the same ranks, as having a parity of reason which appertains to them all. But they were distinct offices, and found in persons as distinct officers, as verse 30, Are all Apostles? Are all Teachers? Therefore, the same is true of Governors. A third argument is taken from the famous place, 1 Timothy v. 17, which is full to our purpose in hand, and intended by the Holy Spirit of the Lord, to make evident the station and office of Ruling Elders, unto the end of the world."

The praise of the Rev. John Cotton, one of the most distinguished of the first ministers of New England, was in all the Churches, in his time. In a small work entitled *Questions and Answers on Church Government*, begun 25th November, 1634, the following passages occur: "*Quest.* What sorts of ministers or officers hath God set in his Church? *Answer.* The ministers and officers of the Church are some of them extraordinary, as Apostles, Prophets, Evangelists; some ordinary, as Bishops and Deacons. *Quest.* What sorts of Bishops hath God ordained in his Church? *Answer.* There are three sorts of them, according as there be three sorts of Elders in the Church, though under two heads; some Pastors, some Teachers, some Ruling Elders. That is to say, such Elders as labour in the word and doctrine, and such as rule in the Church of God; 1 Tim. i. 13; 1 Cor. xii. 28; Rom. xii. 7, 8; 1 Tim. v. 17. *Quest.* What is the work of a Ruling Elder? *Answer,* Seeing the kingdom of Christ is not of this world, but heavenly and spiritual; and the government of his kingdom is not lordly, but stewardly and ministerial: and to labour in the administration of exhortation and doctrine is the proper work of Pastor and Teacher, it remains to be the office of the Ruling Elder to assist the Pastor and Teacher in all other acts of rule besides, as becomes good stewards of the household of God. And, therefore, to put instances, as, *First,* To open and shut the doors of God's house, by admission of members, by ordination of officers, by excommunication of notorious and obstinate offenders. *Secondly,* To see that none live in the Church inordinately, without a calling, or idly in their calling. *Thirdly,* To prevent or heal offences. *Fourthly,* To prepare matters for the Church's consideration, and to moderate the carriage of all things in the Church assemblies. *Fifthly,* To feed the flock of God with the word of admonition, and, as they shall be called, to visit and pray over the sick brethren."[4]

The venerable John Davenport, it is well known, held a distinguished place among the early lights of the Massachusetts and Connecticut Churches. In a treatise entitled *The Power of Congregational Churches Asserted and Vindicated*, &c., although his plan did not require, or even admit, that he should treat expressly and at length on the officers of the Church; yet he repeatedly, and in the most unequivocal manner alludes to the office of Ruling Elder, as belonging to the Church by divine appointment; as altogether distinct from the office of both Teaching Elder and Deacon; and as being of indispensable importance to the edification of the Church.

Nor are these the sentiments of detached individuals merely. They were adopted and published, about the same time, by public bodies, in the most solemn manner. In a work entitled, *Church Government and Church Covenant Discussed*, in an answer of the Elders of the several Churches of New England, to two and thirty questions sent over to them by divers ministers in England, to declare their judgment thereon, Ruling Elders are spoken of, as of Divine institution, and as actually existing, at the time, in the Churches of New England. The fifteenth question is: "Whether do you give the exercise of all Church power of government, to the whole Church, or to the Presbyters thereof alone?" To which it is answered, "We do believe that Christ hath ordained that there should be a Presbytery or Eldership; 1 Tim. iv. 14; and that in every Church, Titus i. 5; Acts xiv. 28; 1 Cor. xi. 28, whose work is to teach and rule the Church by the word and laws of Christ, 1 Tim. v. 17, and unto whom, as teaching and

---

4. *A Treatise, 1. Of Faith. 2. Twelve Fundamental Articles of Christian Religion. 3. A Doctrinal Conclusion. 4. Questions and Answers on Church Government.* pp. 20, 21.

ruling, all the people ought to be obedient, and submit themselves; Heb. xiii. 17. And, therefore, a government merely popular, or democratical (which divines and orthodox writers do so much condemn, in Morillius, and such like), is far from the practice of these Churches, and, we believe, far from the mind of Christ." The twenty-third question is, "What authority or eminency have your preaching Elders above your sole Ruling Elders; or are they both equal? *Answer.* It is not the manner of Elders among us, whether Ruling only, or Ruling and Teaching also, to strive for authority or pre-eminence one above another. As for the people's duty toward their Elders, it is taught them plainly in that place, 1 Thess. v. 12, 13, as also in that of 1 Tim. v. 17; and this word (especially) shows them that, as they are to account all their Elders worthy of double honour, so in special manner their Teaching or Preaching Elders."[5]

But there is another testimony of the same class, of still higher authority. In a volume entitled, *The Result of Three Synods,* held by the Elders and Messengers of the Churches of Massachusetts Province, New England, there is abundant evidence to the same effect. These Synods met in 1648, 1662, and 1679: Each of them was called by the General Court, or Legislature of the Province, and the results published by the court, with their sanction.

The Synod of 1648, consisting of the divines of Massachusetts and Connecticut, and which drew up what is commonly known as the Cambridge Platform, distinctly recognized the office under consideration as of Divine appointment. It speaks as follows: "The Ruling Elder's office is distinct from the office of Pastor and Teacher. Ruling Elders are not so called to exclude the Pastors and Teachers from ruling; because ruling and government is common to these with the other: whereas attending to teach and preach the word, is peculiar unto the former; Romans xii. 7, 8, 9; 1 Timothy v. 17; 1 Corinthians xii. 27 Hebrews xiii. 17" (Chapter vii).

The Synod of 1679 gave its sanction, most unequivocally

---

5. *The Power of Congregational Churches*, &c. p. 47, 48-76.

to the same doctrine; not only by unanimously renewing their approbation of the Platform of 1648, but also by new acts of the most decisive character. Two questions proposed to the Synod of 1679 were; First, "What are the evils that have provoked the Lord to bring his judgments on New England?" Secondly, "What is to be done, that so many evils may be removed?" In their answer to the second question, the Synod say, "It is requisite that the utmost endeavours should be used, in order to a full supply of officers in the Church, according to Christ's institution. The defect of these Churches, on this account, is very lamentable; there being, in most of the Churches, only one Teaching officer for the burdens of the whole congregation to lie upon. The Lord Christ would not have instituted Pastors, Teachers, and Ruling Elders (nor the Apostles ordained Elders in every Church), if he had not seen that there was need of them for the good of his people. And, therefore, for men to think they can do well enough without them, is both to break ne second Commandment, and to reflect upon the wisdom of Christ, as if he did appoint unnecessary offices in his Church."[6] It may not be improper to add, that this Synod assembled in consequence of the General Court of the Colony having called upon all the Churches therein to send their Elders and Messengers, that they might meet in form of a Synod, in order to a most serious inquiry into the questions propounded to them; and that the result, when proposed, was read once and again, each paragraph being duly and distinctly weighed in 'the balance of the sanctuary,' and then, upon mature deliberation, the whole unanimously voted, as to the substance and scope thereof."[7]

It is well known that in the Westminster Assembly of divines there was a small number of learned and zealous Independents, who opposed some of the most prominent features in the Presbyterian form of government with much ardour and pertinacity, and who protracted the debates respecting them for many weeks. But it is equally well known, that all the most able

---

6. *Result of Three Synods*, &c., p. 109.
7. Preface, p. 5, 6.

of those divines were warm advocates of the office of Ruling Elder, not only as a useful office, but as of Divine institution. The recorded opinion of one of them, the Rev. Dr. Goodwin, has been already stated. No less pointed in maintaining the same opinion, were Messrs. Bridge, Burroughs, and Nye, forming with Dr. Goodwin, a majority of the whole number. And, accordingly, in their *Reasons Against the Third Proposition Concerning Presbyterial Government*, they admit, that "the Scripture says much of two sorts of Elders, Teaching and Ruling; and in some places so plain, as if of purpose to distinguish them; and, further, that the whole Reformed Churches had these different Elders."[8]

The following very explicit extract from the well known work of the learned Herbert Thorndike (a divine of the Church of England), on *Religious Assemblies*, chapter iv. p. 117, will show his opinion on the subject before us. Speaking of the language of the Apostle, in 1 Cor. xii. 28, he says: "There is no reason to doubt that the men whom the Apostle here calleth doctors, are those of the Presbyters which had the abilities of preaching and teaching the people at their assemblies; that those or the Presbyters that preached not, are here called by the Apostle governments."

The following remarks of the Rev. Cotton Mather, well known as an eminent Congregationalist of Massachusetts, and author of the *Magnalia Christi Americana*, have too much point, and convey too much instruction, to be omitted in this list of testimonies: "There are some who cannot see any such officer as what we call a Ruling Elder, directed and appointed in the word of God; and partly through a prejudice against the office; and partly, indeed chiefly, through a penury of men well qualified for the discharge of it, as it has been heretofore understood and applied, our Churches are now generally destitute of such helps in government. But unless a Church have divers Elders, the Church government must needs become either prelatic or popular. And that a Church's needing but one Elder, is an opinion, contrary not only to the sense of the faithful in all ages, but also to the law of

---

8. *Reasons*, &c. p. 3, 40.

the Scriptures, where there can be nothing plainer than Elders who rule well, and are worthy of double honour, though they do not labour in the word and doctrine; whereas, if there were any teaching Elders, who do not labour in the word and doctrine, they would be so far from worthy or double honour, that they would not be worthy of any honour at all. Towards the adjusting of the difference which has thus been in the judgments of judicious men, some essays have been made, and one particularly in such terms as these. Let it be first recognised, that all the other Church officers are the assistants of the Pastor, who was himself intrusted with the whole care of all, until the further pity and kindness of our Lord Jesus Christ, joined other officers unto him for his assistance in it. I suppose none will be so absurd as to deny this at least, that all the Church officers are to take the advice of the Pastor with them. Upon which I subjoin, that a man may be a distinct officer from his Pastor, and yet not have a distinct office from him. The Pastor may be the Ruling Elder, and yet he may have Elders to assist him in ruling, and in the actual discharge of some things which they are able and proper to be serviceable to him in. This consideration being laid, I will persuade myself, every Pastor among us will allow me, that there is much work to be done for God in preparing of what belongs to the admission and exclusion of Church members; in carefully inspecting the way and walk of them all, and the first appearance of evil with them; in preventing the very beginnings of ill blood among them, and instructing of all from house to house, more privately, and warning of all persons unto the things more peculiarly incumbent on them; in visiting all the afflicted, and informing of, and consulting with the ministers, for the welfare of the whole flock. And they must allow me, that this work is too heavy for any one man; and that more than one man, yea, all our Churches, do suffer beyond measure, because no more of this work is thoroughly performed. Moreover, they will acknowledge to me, that it is an usual thing with a prudent and faithful Pastor himself, to single out some of the more grave, solid, aged brethren in his congregation, to assist him in many parts of this work, on many occasions in a year; nor will such a Pastor, ordinarily, do any important thing in his government, without having first heard the counsels of such brethren. In short, there are few discreet Pastors, but what make many occasional Ruling Elders every year. I say, then, suppose the Church, by a vote, recommend some such brethren, the fittest they have, and always more than one, unto the stated assistance of their Pastor, in the Church rule, wherein they may be helps unto him. I do not propose that they should be biennial, or triennial only, though I know very famous Churches throughout Europe have them so. Yea, and what if they should by solemn lasting and prayer be commended unto the benediction of God in what service they have to do? What objection can be made against the lawfulness? I think none can be made against the usefulness of such a thing. Truly, for my part – if the fifth chapter of the first Epistle to Timothy would not bear me out, when conscience, both of my duty and my weakness made me desire such assistance, I would see whether the first chapter of Deuteronomy would not."[9]

After these strong attestations in favour of the office of Ruling Elder from the most pious and learned of the early Independents, or Congregationalists, of New England, it will naturally occur to every reader, as an interesting question, how it came to pass, that Churches which once unanimously held such opinions, laid so much stress on them, and practised accordingly, for about three-fourths of a century, should have, long since, as unanimously, discontinued the office? The first company of emigrants, in 1620, brought a Ruling Elder with them; and the office was universally retained for many years afterwards. Yet, in 1702, when Dr. Cotton Mather published the first edition of his *Magnalia*, it had been, as would seem, from the quotation just made, in a great measure, laid aside; and before the middle of the eighteenth century, it had entirely disappeared from the Churches of New England. A well informed and discerning friend has suggested, that the chief reason of this remarkable fact, is probably to be traced to another fact alluded to in the following extract. In a small volume, printed in Boston, in 1700, and entitled, *The Or-*

---

9. *Magnalia*, &c. Book v. Part ii. pp. 206, 207, octave edition, 1820.

der of the Gospel, Professed and Practised by the Churches of Christ in New England, &c; by Increase Mather, President of Harvard College, and Teacher of a Church in Boston. In this work, one of the questions discussed is: "Whether or not our Brethren, and not the Elders of the Churches only, are to judge concerning the qualifications and fitness of those who are admitted into their communion." In answering it, he says: "If only Elders have power to judge who are fit to come to the sacrament, or to join to the Churches; then, in case there is but one Elder in a Church, (as there are very few Churches in New England that have more Elders than one,) the sole power will reside in that one man's hands."[10] On this passage, the friend above referred to remarks, "I am inclined to think that he here means Ruling Elders; for, 1. Several Churches (whether in consequence of the recommendation of the Synod of 1679, I do not know) had then two ministers. 2. This question and answer of Dr. I. Mather's is annexed to a reprint in Boston (now lying before me) of *A Vindication of the Divine Authority of Ruling Elders in the Church of Christ*, asserted by the ministers and Elders met together in a Provincial Assembly, Nov. 2d, 1649, and printed in London, 1650. But whether this was his meaning or not, it is abundantly evident from various other sources, that the Churches of New England, while they retained the office of Ruling Elder, had but one such Elder at a time, and his business was especially to attend to discipline. The office was, of course, an unwelcome one; and it became more and more difficult to find men willing to assume it."

It appears, then, that our excellent brethren, the Puritan Independents, while they zealously maintained the Divine warrant, and the great importance of the Ruling Elder's office, misapprehended its real nature, and placed it under an aspect before the Churches evidently adapted to discredit and destroy it. Instead of appointing a plurality of those Ruling Elders, they seldom or never had more than one in each Church; and instead of uniting the Pastor with him, and forming a regular judicial bench

---

10. *Order of the Gospel*, &c., p. 25.

for regulating the affairs of the Church, they seemed to have placed each in a sphere entirely separate, and independent of each other; nay, to have made the offices of Teacher and Ruler, wear an appearance of being rivals for influence and power. Certain it is, that the views entertained by each, of his proper department of duty, often, in fact, brought them into collision, and made the situation of the Ruler both uncomfortable and useless. Can it be matter of surprise, that, in these circumstances, the office of Ruling Elder in the Congregational Churches of New England gained but little favour with the body of the people; that it came to be considered as, at once, odious and useless; would be undertaken by few; and, at length, fell into entire disuse?

The testimony of the Rev. Dr. John Edwards, an eminently pious and learned divine of the Church of England, who flourished during the latter half of the seventeenth century, is equally decisive in favour of this office. His language is as follows: "This office of a Ruling Elder is according to the practice of the Church of God among the Jews, his own people. It is certain that there was this kind of Elders under that economy. There were two sorts of Elders among the Jews the Ruling ones, who governed in their Assemblies and Synagogues, and the Teaching ones, who read and expounded the Scriptures."

Accordingly, Dr. Lightfoot, in his *Harmony of the New Testament*, inclines to interpret 1 Timothy v. 17, of the Elders in the Christian congregations, who answer to the lay-Elders in the Jewish Synagogue. For this learned writer, who was well versed in the Jewish customs and practices, tells us, that in every Synagogue among the Jews, there were Elders that ruled chiefly in the affairs of the Synagogue, and other Elders, that laboured "in the word and doctrine." "And so it was in the Christian Church; there was a mixture of Clergy and Laity in their consults about Church matters, as we see frequently in the Acts of the Apostles. The Christian Church retained this usage, for which they quote St. Augustine's 137th Epistle, where he mentions the Clergy and the Elders, and the people. So in his third book against Cresc60nius, he mentions Deacons and Seniors, that is lay-Elders, for he distinguishes them from other Presbyters. One of his Epistles to his Church in Hippo, is thus superscribed, 'To the Clergy and the Elders.' See chapter 56th, in the forenamed book against Cresconius, where he mentions Peregrinus, the Presbyter, and the Elders (Seniores).[11] And nothing can be plainer than that of St. Ambrose – 'Both the Synagogue and afterwards the Church, had their Elders, without whose counsel nothing was done in the Church, &c' Further, we read of these Seniors in the writings of Optatus, p. 41, and in the Epistles annexed to him, which the reader may consult. Thus it appears that this was an *ancient office* in the Church, and *not invented by Calvin,* as some have thought and writ."[12]

"And then as to the reason of the thing, there should be no ground of quarrelling with this office in the Church, seeing it is useful. It was instituted for the ease of the preaching Elders, that they might not be overburdened with business, and that they might more conveniently apply themselves to that employment which is purely ecclesiastical and spiritual. Truly if there was no such office mentioned in the Scripture, we might reasonably wish for such a one, it being so useful and serviceable to the great purposes of religion. What can be more desirable than that there should be one or more appointed to observe the conversation of the flock, in order to the exercising of discipline? The Pastor himself cannot be supposed to have an eye on every one of his charge; and, therefore, it is fitting, that out of those who are fellow-members, and daily converse with one another, and, therefore, are capable of acquainting themselves with their man-

---

11. It will not escape the notice of the discerning reader, that these testimonies from Augustine, Ambrose, and Optatus, which some have ventured, very unceremoniously, to treat with contempt, when brought forward on this subject, are regarded by this very learned Episcopalian, as evidence of the most conclusive character.

12. The old and hackneyed allegation, which has been the theme of high-toned Episcopalians and Independents, for more than two hundred years, that Calvin invented and first introduced Ruling Elders, it will be observed, is confidently rejected by this truly learned Episcopal divine, who, from his ecclesiastical connexion, cannot be supposed to have had any other inducement to adopt the opinion which he has expressed, than his love of truth.

ners and behaviour, there should be chosen these Elders I am speaking of, to inspect the carriage and deportment of the flock."[13]

The judgment of the Rev. Dr. Jerome Kromayer, a very learned Lutheran divine, and Professor of Divinity in the University of Leipsic, who lived in the seventeenth century, is very decisive in favour of the apostolical institution of Ruling Elders. "Of Presbyters, or Elders," says he, "there were formerly two kinds, those who taught, and those who exercised the office of rulers in the Church. This is taught in 1 Timothy v. 17; 'Let the Elders that rule well be accounted worthy of double honour, especially they who labour in the word and doctrine.' The latter were the same as our Ministers; the former, were like the members of our Consistories."[14]

A similar testimony may be adduced from Frederick Baldwin, another distinguished Lutheran divine and Professor, of the same century, who is no less decisive in favour of the class of offices under consideration.[15]

The celebrated John Casper Suicer, an eminently learned German divine and Professor, in his *Thesaurus Ecclesiasticus,* after speaking particularly of Teaching Presbyters or Elders, in the first place, proceeds to speak of another class of Elders, who, "chosen from among the people, (or laity,) are united with the Pastors, or Ministers of the Word, that they may be guardians of the discipline of the Church. To these the Apostle Paul refers in 1 Timothy v. 17, where, by the Elders who labour in the word and doctrine, he evidently understands that class of Elders of which we have spoken in the preceding section: and by those who rule well he plainly refers to the class of which we now speak. For if he had intended to speak of only one class, why did he add, especially those who labour in the word and doctrine? This class are also designated by the term προισταμενους, in Ro-

---

13. *Theologia Reformata*, Vol. i. Ninth Article of the Creed. p. 526, 528.

14. *Historia Ecciesiastica*, auctore Hieronymo Kromayero, D. D. S. S. T. D. in Acad. Leips. 4to. p. 59.

15. Fred. Balduini, *Institut. Ministrorum Verbi.* Cap. 10.

mans xii. 8, and by the term κυβερνησεις, in 1 Corinthians xii. 29."¹⁶

The very explicit testimony of Dr. Whitby, of the Church of England, was produced in a preceding chapter, when we were discussing the scriptural evidence in favour of the office under consideration. It need not, therefore, here be repeated, excepting simply to remind the reader of its decisive character. The concessions also of Bishop Fell, the Rev. Mr. Marshall, and the celebrated Mr. Dodwell, of the same Church, will also, in this connexion, be borne in mind. They may be found in the fourth chapter, in connexion with the testimony from the Fathers.

The pious and excellent Dr. Watts, though not a Presbyterian, must be considered as indirectly doing homage to this part of the Presbyterian system, when he says: "If it happens that there is but one Minister or Presbyter in a Church, or if the ministers are young men of small experience in the world, it is useful and proper that some of the eldest, gravest, and wisest members be deputed, by the Church, to join with and assist the ministers in the care and management of that affair" (the admission and exclusion of members).[17]

The Rev. Dr. Doddridge, universally known as an eminently learned and pious divine of England, of the Independent denomination, in reference to the office in question speaks thus: "It seems to be solidly argued, from 1 Timothy v. 17, that there were, in the primitive Church, some Elders, who did not use to preach. Nothing very express is said concerning them: only it seems to be intimated, James v. 14, that they prayed with the sick. It may be very expedient, even on the principles of human prudence, to appoint some of the more grave and honourable members of the society to join with the Pastor in the oversight of it, who may constitute a kind of council with him, to deliberate on affairs in which the society is concerned, and prepare them for being brought before the Church for its decision, to pray with the

---

16. Suiceri, *Thesaurus Ecclesiasticus*, Art. πρεσβυτερος.
17. *Treatise on the Foundation of the Christian Church*, p. 125.

sick, to reconcile differences, &c."[18]

The same distinguished writer, in his Commentary on 1 Timothy v. 17, has the following remark: "Especially they who labour, &c. This seems to intimate that there were some who, though they presided in the Church, were not employed in preaching. Limborch, indeed, is of opinion that κοπιωντες signifies those who did even fatigue themselves with their extradinary labours, which some might not do, who yet, in the general, presided well, supposing preaching to be a part of their work. But it seems to me much more natural to follow the former interpretation."

The celebrated Professor Neander, of Berlin, was mentioned in a preceding chapter, as probably the most profoundly learned Christian antiquarian now living. In addition to the quotation from him presented in that chapter, the following, from the same work, is worthy of notice: "That the name επισκοπος, was of the same signification with πρεσβυτερος, is manifest from those places in the New Testament where these words are exchanged the one for the other; Acts xx. 17. 28; Tit. i. 5. 7; and from those passages where, after the office of Bishop that of Deacon is mentioned; so that no other office can be imagined between them. If the name επισκοπος had been used to distinguish any of these Elders from the rest, as a ruler in the Church Senate, a *primus inter pares,* this use of it interchangeably with πρεσβυτερος would not have obtained."

"These Presbyters, or Bishops, had the oversight of the whole Church, in all its general concerns; but the office of teaching was not appropriated exclusively to them; for, as we have above remarked, all Christians had a right to speak in their meetings for the edification of the members. It does not follow from this, however, that all the Church members were capable of giving instruction: and it is important to distinguish a faculty for instruction which was under the command of an individual, from the miraculous and sudden impulses of inspiration, as in prophecy, and the gift of tongues; and which might be bestowed upon

---

18. *Lectures on Divinity*, Proposition 150, Scholium 5th.

those not remarkably favoured by natural gifts. The care of the Churches, the preservation and extension of pure evangelical truth, and the defence of it against the various forms of error, which early appeared, could not be left entirely to depend upon these extraordinary and often transient impulses. The weakness of human nature to which was committed the treasure of the Gospel, as in "earthen vessels," seemed to render it necessary that there should be, in every Church, some possessed of the natural endowments necessary to instruct their brethren in the truth, to warn and exhort them against error, and lead them forward in the way of life. Such endowments presuppose a previous course of instruction, clearness and acuteness of thought, and a power to communicate their ideas; and when these were present, and the Spirit of God was imparted to animate and sanctify, the man became possessed of the *"χαρισμα διδασκαλιας."* Those possessed of this *χαρισμα,* were, on this account, calculated for all the purposes above alluded to, without excluding the remainder from exercising the gift imparted to them, of whatever kind it might be. On this account, the *χαρισμα διδασκαλιας,* and the situation of teachers, (*διδασκαλοι,*) who were distinguished by this gift, was represented as something entirely distinct and peculiar. (1 Cor. xii. 28. xiv. 6; Ephes. iv. 11.) All members of a Church could, at times, speak before their brethren, either to call upon God, or to praise him, when so inclined; but only a few were *διδασκαλοι,* in the full sense of that term."

"It is very clear too, that this talent for teaching, was different from that of governing, (i.e., *χαρισμα κυβερνησεως,*) which was especially necessary for him who took his seat in the Council of the Church, that is for a *πρεσβυτερος* or *επισκοπος*. One might possess the knowledge of external matters, the tact, the Christian prudence necessary for this duty, without the mental qualities so peculiarly desirable in a teacher. In the first apostolic Church, from which every thing like mere arbitrary arrangements concerning rank was very distant, and all offices were looked upon only as they promised the attainment of the great end of the Christian faith, the offices of teacher and ruler, *διδασκαλος* and *ποιμην* were separated. For this distinction, see

Romans xii. 7, 8. In noticing this well defined distinction, we may be led to the opinion, that originally, those called, by way of preference, teachers, did not belong to the class of rulers, or overseers. Also, it is not clearly proved that they did always belong to the class of πρεσβυτεροι. Only this is certain, that it was considered as desirable that, among the rulers there should be those capable of teaching also. When it is enjoined upon the Presbyters in general, as in the farewell of Paul to the Church of Ephesus, (Acts xx.) to watch over the Church and preserve its doctrine pure, it does not necessarily follow that the duty of teaching, in its strict sense, was insisted on; but rather a general superintendence of the affairs of that body. But when, in the Epistle to Titus it is demanded in an επισκοπος that he not only 'hold fast the form of sound words' in his private capacity, but that he should be able to strengthen others therein; to overcome opposers, and 'convince gainsayers,' it seems to be implied that he should possess the 'gift of teaching.' This must have been, in many situations of the Churches, exposed as they were to errors of every kind, highly desirable. And on this account, in 1 Tim. v. 17, those among the πεσβυτεροι who united the gift of teaching (διδασκαλια) with that of governing, (κυβερνησις,) were to be especially honoured. This distinction of the two gifts shows that they were not constantly or necessarily united."[19]

The same writer says: "We find another office in the apostolic times – that of Deacons. The duties of this office were from the first only external, (Acts vi.,) as it seems to have taken its rise for the sole purpose of attending to the distribution of alms. The care of the poor, however, and of the sick, and many other external duties were, in process of time, imposed upon those in this station. Besides the Deacons, there were also Deaconesses appointed, who could have free access to the female part of the Church, which was, on account of the peculiar man-

---

19. It is worthy of notice that this profound ecclesiastical historian in another place, quotes Hilary (Ambrose) as speaking of the Ruling Elders, in the Synagogue, and in the Church, and interprets him as plainly teaching the distinction here made between Teaching and Ruling Elders, substantially as we have done in a preceding chapter.

ners of the East, denied, to a great extent, to men. Here the female had an opportunity of exercising her powers for the extension of the true faith, without overstepping the bounds of modesty and propriety, and in a field otherwise inaccessible. It was their duty, too, as experienced Christian mothers, to give advice and support to the younger women, as seems to have been the case from Tertullian, *De Virgin. Veland.*[20]

Only one authority more shall be adduced on this subject, and that shall be from the pen of our venerable and eloquent countryman, the Rev. Dr. Dwight, whose character for learning, talents, and piety, needs no attestation from the writer of this Essay. Though himself a Congregationalist, and without any other inducement to declare in favour of Ruling Elders, than that which the force of truth presented, he expresses himself concerning their office in the following unequivocal terms: "Ruling Elders are, in my apprehension, *scriptural officers of the Christian Church;* and I cannot but think our *defection,* with respect to these officers, from the practice of the first settlers of New England, *an error in ecclesiastical government.*"[21]

This array of witnesses might be greatly extended, were it proper to detain the reader with further extracts. But it is presumed that those which have been produced are abundantly sufficient. It will be observed that no Presbyterian has been cited as an authority in this case. The names, indeed, of multitudes of that denomination, might have been produced, equal to any others that can be shown on the catalogue of piety, talents, and learning. But the testimony of more impartial witnesses may be preferred. Recourse has been had, then, to those who could not possibly have been swayed by a Presbyterian bias. And a sufficiency of such has been produced, it is hoped, to make a deep impression on candid minds. Romanists, Protestant Episcopalians, Lutherans, and Independents, have all most remarkably concurred in vindicating an office, the due admission and scriptural use of which are, perhaps, of more importance to the best

---

20. Kirchengeschichte.
21. *Theology Explained and Defended*, Vol. iv. p. 399.

interests of the Church of God, than this, or any other single volume can fully display.

CHAPTER EIGHT

Ruling Elders Absolutely Necessary in the Church

By this is meant, that the laws which Christ has appointed for the government and edification of his people, cannot possibly be executed without such a class of officers in fact, whatever name they may bear. But that which is the necessary result of a Divine institution, is of equal authority with the institution itself. All powers or instruments really indispensable to the faithful and plenary execution of laws which an infinitely wise Governor has enacted, must be considered as implied in those laws, even should they not be formally specified.

Now, all serious impartial readers of the Bible believe, that, besides the preaching of the Gospel and the administration of the sacraments, there is very much to be done for promoting the order, purity, and edification of the Church, by the maintenance of a scriptural discipline. They believe that the best interest of every ecclesiastical community requires that there be a constant and faithful inspection of all the members and families of the Church; that the negligent be admonished; that wanderers be reclaimed; that scandals be removed; that irregularities be corrected; that differences be reconciled; and every proper measure adopted to bind the whole body together by the ties of Christian purity and charity. They consider it as vitally important that there be added to the labours of the pulpit, those of teaching "from house to house," visiting the sick, conversing with serious inquirers, catechizing children, learning as far as possible the character and state of every member, even the poorest and most obscure, of the flock and endeavouring, by all scriptural means, to promote the knowledge, holiness, comfort and spiritual welfare of every individual. They believe, in fine, that none ought to be admitted to the communion of the Church, without a careful examination in reference to their knowledge, orthodoxy, good moral character, and hopeful piety, that none ought to be permitted to remain in the bosom of the Church, without maintaining, in some tolerable degree, a character proper for professing Christians; that none ought to be suspended from the enjoyment of Church privileges but after a fair trial; and that none should be finally excommunicated from the covenanted family of Christ, without the most patient inquiry, and every suitable effort to bring them to repentance and reformation.

It is, no doubt, true, that the very suggestion of the necessity and importance of discipline in the Church is odious to many who bear the Christian name. The wordly and careless portion of every Church consider the interposition of ecclesiastical inspection and authority in reference to the lives and conversation of its members, as officious and offensive meddling with private concerns. They would much rather retain their external standing, as professors of religion, and, at the same time, pursue their unhallowed pleasures without control. They never wish to see a minister, as such, but in the pulpit; or any Church officer in any other place than his seat in the sanctuary. To such persons, the entire absence of the class of officers for which we are pleading, together with the exercise of all their appropriate functions, would be matter rather of felicitation than regret. Hence the violent opposition made to the introduction of Ruling Elders into the Church of Geneva, by the worldly and licentious part of her members. And hence the insuperable repugnance to the establishment of sound and scriptural discipline, manifested so repeatedly, and to this day, by some of the largest national Churches of Europe.

But I need not say to those who take their views of the Christian Church, and its real prosperity, from the Bible, and from the best experience, that enlightened, and faithful discipline is, not only important, but absolutely essential to the purity and edification of the Body of Christ. It ought to be regarded as one of the most precious means of grace, by which offenders are humbled, softened, and brought to repentance; the Church purged of unworthy members; offences removed; the honour of Christ promoted; real Christians stimulated and improved in their spiritual course; faithful testimony borne against error and crime; and the professing family of Christ made to appear holy and beautiful in the view of the world. Without wholesome discipline, for removing offences, and excluding the corrupt and profane, there may be an assembly; but there cannot be a Church. The truth is, the exercise of a faithful watch and care over the purity of each other in doctrine, worship, and life, is one of the principal purposes for which the Christian Church was established, and on account of which it is highly prized by every enlightened believer. And, I have no doubt, it may be safely affirmed, that a large part of all that is holy in the Church, at the present day, either in faith or practice, may be ascribed, under God, as much to sound ecclesiastical discipline, as to the faithful preaching of the Gospel.

And if the maintenance of discipline be all important to the interests of true religion, it is a matter of no less importance that it be conducted with mildness, prudence, and wisdom. Rashness, precipitancy, undue severity, malice, partiality, popular fury, and attempting to enforce rules which Christ never gave, are among the many evils which have too often marked the dispensation of authority in the Church, and not unfrequently defeated the great purpose of discipline.

To conduct it aright, is, undoubtedly, one of the most delicate and arduous parts of ecclesiastical administration; requiring all the piety, judgment, patience, gentleness, maturity of counsel, and prayerfulness which can be brought to bear upon the subject.

Now the question is, by whom shall all these multiplied, weighty and indispensable services be performed? Besides the arduous work of public instruction and exhortation, who shall attend to all the numberless and ever-recurring details of inspection, warning and visitation, which are so needful in every Christian community? Will any say, it is the duty of the Pastor of each Church to perform them all? The very suggestion is absurd. It is physically impossible for him to do it. He cannot be every where, and know every thing. He cannot perform what is expected from him, and at the same time so watch over his whole flock as to fulfil every duty which the interest of the Church demands. He must "give himself to reading;" he must prepare for the services of the pulpit; he must discharge his various public labours; he must employ much time in private, in instructing and counselling those who apply to him for instruction and advice; and he must act his part in the concerns of the whole Church with which he is connected. Now, is it practicable for any man, however diligent and active, to do all this, and at the same time to perform the whole work of inspection and government over a congregation of the ordinary size? We might as well expect and demand any impossibility; and impossibilities the great and merciful Head of the Church requires of no man.

But even if it were reasonable or possible, that a pastor should, alone, perform all these duties, ought he to be willing to undertake them; or ought the Church to be willing to commit them to him alone? We know that ministers are subject to the same frailties and imperfections with other men. We know, too, that a love of pre-eminence and of power is not only natural to them, in common with others; but that this principle, very early after the days of the Apostles, began to manifest itself as the reigning sin of ecclesiastics, and produced, first Prelacy, and afterwards Popery, which has so long and so ignobly enslaved the Church of Christ. Does not this plainly show the folly and danger of yielding undefined power to pastors alone? Is it wise or safe to constitute one man a despot over a whole Church? Is it proper to intrust to a single individual the weighty and complicated work of inspecting, trying, judging, admitting, condemning, excluding, and restoring, without control? Ought the members of a Church to consent that all their rights and privileges in reference to Christian communion, should be subject to the will of a single man, as his partiality, kindness, and favouritism, on the one hand; or his caprice, prejudice, or passion, on the other, might indicate? Such a mode of conducting the government of the Church, to say nothing of its unscriptural character, is, in the highest degree, unreasonable and dangerous. It can hardly fail to exert an influence of the most injurious character, both on the clergy and laity. It tends to nurture in the former, a spirit of selfishness, pride and ambition; and instead of ministers of holiness, love, and mercy, to transform them into ecclesiastical tyrants. While its tendency, with regard to the latter, is gradually to beget in them a blind, implicit submission to clerical domination. The ecclesiastical encroachments and despotism of former times, already alluded to, read us a most instructive lesson on this subject. The fact is, committing the whole government of the Church to the hands of Pastors alone, may be affirmed to carry in it some of the worst seeds of Popery; which, though under the administration of good men, they may not at once lead to palpable mischief, will seldom fail in producing, in the end, the most serious evils, both to those who govern, and those who obey.

Accordingly, as was intimated in a preceding chapter, we have no example in Scripture of a Church being committed to the government of a single individual. Such a thing was unknown in the Jewish Synagogue. It was unknown in the apostolic age. And it continued to be unknown, until ecclesiastical pride and ambition introduced it, and with it a host of mischiefs to the body of Christ. In all the primitive Churches we find a plurality of "Elders," and we read enough in the early records, in some particular cases, to perceive that these "Elders" were not only chosen by the members of the Church, out of their own number, as their representatives, to exercise over them the functions of inspection and ruling; but that, whenever they ceased to discharge the duties of their office acceptably, they might be removed from its actual exercise at the pleasure of those by whom they were chosen; thus plainly evincing, that the constitution of the primitive Church was eminently adapted to guard against ecclesiastical tyranny; and that if that constitution had been preserved, the evils of clerical encroachment would have been avoided. Accordingly, it is remarkable that the pious Ambrose, a venerable Father of the fourth century, quoted in a former chapter, expressly conveys an intimation of this kind, when speaking of the gradual disuse of the office of Ruling Elder. "Which order," says he, "by what negligence it grew into disuse, I know not, unless, perhaps, by the sloth, or rather by the pride of the teachers, who alone wished to appear something."

"It is a vain apprehension," says the venerable Dr. Owen, "to suppose that one or two teaching officers in a Church, who are obliged to give themselves unto the word and prayer, to labour in the word and doctrine, to preach in and out of season, would be able to take care of, and attend with diligence unto, all those things that do evidently belong unto the rule of the Church. And hence it is, that Churches at this day do live on the preaching of the word, and are very little sensible of the wisdom, goodness, love, and care of Christ in the institution of this rule in the Church, nor are partakers of the benefits of it unto their edification. And the supply which many have hitherto made herein, by persons either unacquainted with their duty, or insensible of their own authority, or cold, if not negligent in their work, doth not answer the end of their institution. And hence it is, that the authority of government, and the benefit of it, are ready to be lost in most Churches. And it is both vainly and presumptuously pleaded, to give countenance unto a neglect of their order, that some Churches do walk in love and peace, and are edified without it; supplying some defects by the prudent aid of some members of them. For it is nothing but a preference of our own wisdom, unto the wisdom and authority of Christ; or at best an unwillingness to make a venture on the warranty of his rule, for fear of some disadvantages that may ensue thereon."[1]

If, in order to avoid the evils of the pastor standing alone in the inspection and government of his Church, it be alleged that the whole body of the Church members may be his auxiliaries in this arduous work; still the difficulties are neither removed nor diminished. For, in the first place, a great majority of all Church members, we may confidently say, are altogether unqualified for

---

1. *True Nature of a Gospel Church*, pp. 177, 178.

rendering the aid to the Pastor which is here contemplated. They have neither the knowledge, the wisdom, nor the prudence necessary for the purpose; and to imagine a case of ecclesiastical regimen, in which every weak, childish, and indiscreet individual, who, though serious and well-meaning enough to enjoy the privilege of Christian communion, is wholly unfit to be an inspector and ruler of others, should be associated with the Pastor, in conducting the delicate and arduous work of parochial regulation, is too preposterous to be regarded with favour, by any judicious mind. Can it be believed for a moment, that the all-wise Head of the Church has appointed a form of government for his people in which ignorance, weakness, and total unfitness for the duty assigned them, should always, and almost necessarily, characterize a great majority of those to whom the oversight and guidance of the Church were committed? Surely this is altogether incredible.

And if this consideration possess weight in regard to old and settled Churches, established in countries which have been long favoured with the light and order of the Gospel; how much more to Pagan lands, and to Churches recently gathered from the wilds of Africa, the degraded inhabitants of the Sandwich Islands, or the miserable devotees of Hindoo idolatry? If in the best instructed and best regulated Churches in Christendom, a majority of the members are utterly unqualified to participate in the government of the sacred family; what can be expected of those recent, and necessarily dubious converts from blind heathenism, who must, of course, be babes in knowledge and experience, who are surrounded with ignorance and brutality, and have just been snatched themselves from the same degradation? Surely, if we may say, with propriety, of some nations, who have recently thrown off the chains of slavery, to which they had long been accustomed, that they were not prepared for a republican form of government; with still more confidence can we maintain, that, whoever may be prepared to take part in the government of the Church, the poor novices, in the situation supposed, are totally unqualified. Even if the popular form of ecclesiastical polity could be considered as well adapted to the case of a people of more enlightened and elevated character, which may well be questioned; it must be pronounced altogether unfit for a Church made up of such materials. Now it is the glory of the Gospel, that it is adapted to all people, and all states of society. Of course, that form of ecclesiastical government which is not of a similar stamp, affords much ground of suspicion that it is not of God, and ought to be rejected.

But further; if the greater part of the members of the Church were much better qualified than they commonly are, for co-operating in its government, would their co-operation be likely to be really obtained in a prompt, steady, and faithful manner? All experience pronounces that it would not. We know that there are few things, in the government and regulation of the Church, more irksome to our natural feelings, than doing what fidelity requires in cases of discipline. When the ministers of religion are called upon to dispense truth, to instruct, to exhort, and to administer sacraments, they engage in that in which we may suppose pious men habitually to delight, and to be always ready to proceed with alacrity. But we may say of the business of ecclesiastical discipline, that it is the "strange work," even of the pious and faithful. It is, in its own nature, an unacceptable and unwelcome employment. To take cognizance of delinquencies in faith or practice; to admonish offenders; to call them, when necessary, before the proper tribunal; to seek out and array proof with fidelity; to drag insidious error, and artful wickedness from their hiding places; and to suspend, or excommunicate from the privileges of the Church, when the honour of religion, and the best interests of the body of Christ, call for these measures; – is painful work to every benevolent mind. It is work in which no man is willing to engage, unless constrained by a sense of duty. Even those who are bound by official obligation to undertake the task, are too apt to shrink from it; but where there is no particular obligation lying on any one member of the Church more than another to take an active interest in this work – the consequence will probably be, that few will be disposed to engage in the self-denying duty. Where all are equally bound, all may be equally backward, or negligent, without feeling themselves chargeable with any special delinquency. And, what is worthy of notice, those who will be most apt to go forward in this work, and proffer their aid with most readiness, will generally be the bold, the vain, the ardent, the rash, the impetuous; precisely those who are, of all persons living, the most unfit for such an employment. But even if it were otherwise; if all the members of the Church were equally forward and active, what might be expected in a religious community, when every member of that community was equally a ruler; and when the most ignorant and childish busy-body among them, might be continually tampering with its government, and fomenting disturbances, with as much potency as the most intelligent and wise? The truth is, in such a community, tranquility, order, and peace, could scarcely be expected, long together, to have any place.

We could scarcely have a more instructive comment on these remarks than the practice of those Churches which reject Ruling Elders. Our Episcopal brethren reject them. But they are obliged to have their vestrymen and church wardens, who, though no divine warrant is claimed for them, and they are not set apart in the same manner, or formally invested with the same powers with our Ruling Elders, yet perform many of the same functions, in substance, and are, in fact, official counsellors and helps. True, indeed, these officers are not clothed with the power, and seldom perform any acts, of ecclesiastical discipline, properly so called, yet they may be, and sometimes, perhaps, are, consulted on subjects of this nature. And, where this is not the case, we may say, without impropriety, that, in Churches of that denomination, no discipline is exercised. In the Church of England, as is confessed on all hands, no scriptural discipline exists. The most profligate and vile are not excluded from the communion of the establishment. This is deeply lamented by many of the pious members of that establishment; and at an early period, after the commencement of the Reformation in that country, it was earnestly wished and proposed, as we have seen in a preceding chapter, to introduce Ruling Elders, as a principal means of restoring and maintaining discipline. And although the absence of discipline does not exist, to the same extent, in the Churches of the Protestant Episcopal denomination in the United States; yet, it may be altogether wanting, as to any pure and efficient exercise, in all those Episcopal Churches in which some leading, pious laymen are not habitually consulted and employed in maintaining it. A pious minister, indeed, of that denomination, may and does, conform to his rubrics, in giving the people proper instruction, and warning, as to a suitable approach to the communion which he dispenses. But here he is commonly obliged to stop; or, at any rate, does, in practice, usually stop. All efficient inspection of the moral condition or the whole Church, admonishing the careless, bringing back the wanderers, and causing those who persist in error or in vice, to feel the discipline of ecclesiastical correction, is, notoriously, almost unknown in the Churches of the denomination to which we refer. And this deficiency is, manifestly, not owing to the want of intelligent and conscientious piety in many of the ministers of those Churches; but, beyond all doubt, to the entire want of an organization which alone renders the exercise of a faithful and impartial discipline at all practicable.

Our Congregational brethren also reject Ruling Elders. Yet it is well known that, while they adopt a form of government which, in theory, allows to every member of the Church an equal share in the exercise of discipline; their most judicious pastors, warned by painful experience of the troublesome character, and uncertain issues, of popular management, in delicate and difficult cases which involve Christian character – are careful to have a committee of the most pious, intelligent, and prudent of their Church members, who consider each case of discipline beforehand in private, and prepare it for a public decision; and thus perform, in fact, some of the most important of the duties of Ruling Elders. This is what the venerable Dr. Cotton Mather, doubtless, means when he says, as quoted in a preceding chapter, that "there are few *discreet* pastors but what make many occasional Ruling Elders every year;" and when he gives it as his opinion, in the same connexion, that without something of this kind, Churches must suffer unspeakably with respect to discipline. And, where nothing of this kind is done, the experience of

Independent and Congregational Churches, in conducting discipline, it is well known, is often such as is calculated to give deep and lasting pain to those who love the peace and order of the Church. Strife, tumult, and division of the most distressing kind, are often the consequences of attempting to rid the Church of one corrupt member.

But perhaps it will be said, let the Pastor habitually call to his aid, in conducting the discipline of the Church, a few of the most judicious and pious of his communicants; those whom he knows to be most conscientious and wise in counsel. But neither is this an adequate remedy. The Pastor may consult such if he please. But he may choose to omit it, and be governed entirely by his own counsels. Or, if he consult any, he may always select his particular friends, who he knows will encourage and support him in his favourite measures; thus furnishing no real relief in the end. How much better to have a bench of assistant Rulers, regularly chosen by the people, and with whom he shall be bound to take counsel in all important measures!

Thus it is that those Churches which reject the class of officers which it is the object of this Essay to recommend, do practically bear witness that it is impossible to conduct discipline in a satisfactory manner, without having a set of individuals, virtually, if not formally, vested with similar powers. Where no such efficient substitute is employed, discipline is either in a great measure neglected; or its maintenance is attended with inconveniences of the most serious kind. In other words, the opponents of Ruling Elders are obliged either to neglect discipline altogether, or, for maintaining it, to have recourse to auxiliaries of similar character and power, while they deny that there is any divine warrant for them. Now, is it probable, is it credible, that our blessed Lord, and all-wise King and Head of his Church, and his Apostles, guided by his own Spirit, should entirely overlook this necessity, and make no provision for it? It is not credible. We must, then, either suppose, that some such officers as those in question were divinely appointed; or that means, acknow-ledged by the practice of all to be indispensable in conducting the best interests of the Church, were forgotten or neglected by her divine Head and Lord. Surely the latter cannot be imputed to infinite Wisdom.

There are some, however, who acknowledge that there ought to be, and must be, in every Church, in order to the efficient maintenance of discipline, a plurality of Elders. They confess that such a body or bench of Elders was found in the Jewish Synagogue; that a similar Eldership existed in the primitive Church; and that the scriptural government of a Christian congregation cannot be conducted to advantage without it. But they contend that these Presbyters, or Elders, ought all to be of the teaching class; that there is no ground for the distinction between Teaching and Ruling Elders; that every Church ought to be furnished with three or more ministers, all equally authorized to preach, to administer the sacraments, and to bear rule.

It requires little discernment to see that this plan is wholly impracticable; and that if attempted to be carried into execution, the effect must be, either to destroy the Church, or to degrade, and ultimately to prostrate the ministry. It is with no small difficulty that most Churches are enabled to procure and support one qualified and acceptable minister. Very few would be able to afford a suitable support to two; and none but those of extraordinary wealth, could think seriously of undertaking to sustain three or more. If, therefore, the principle of a plurality of Teaching Elders in each Church were deemed indispensable; and if a regular and adequate training for the sacred office were also, as now insisted on; and if it were, at the same time, considered as necessary that every minister should receive a competent pecuniary support; the consequence, as is perfectly manifest, would be, that nineteen out of twenty of our Churches would be utterly unable to maintain the requisite organization, and must, of course, become extinct. Nay, the regular establishment of Gospel ordinances in pastoral Churches would be physically possible only in a very few great cities, or wealthy neighbourhoods. Surely this cannot be the system enjoined by that Saviour who said, "to the poor the Gospel is preached."

The only remedy for this difficulty would be to reduce the preparation and acquirements for the ministry; to make choice of plain, illiterate men for this office; men of small intellectual and theological furniture; dependent on secular employments for a subsistence; and, therefore, needing little or no support from the Churches which they serve. This is the plan upon which several sects of Christians proceed; and it is easy to see that, upon this plan, the feeblest Churches may have a plurality of such ministers as these, and, indeed, any number of them without being burdened by their pecuniary support. But then, it is equally evident, that the execution of this plan must result in degrading the ministerial character, and in finally banishing all well qualified ministers from the Church. They could no longer be "able ministers of the New Testament, workmen that need not be ashamed." They could no longer "give themselves wholly" to the labours of the sacred office. They could no longer "give themselves to reading," as well as to exhortation and teaching. In short, the inevitable consequence of maintaining, as some do, that there must be a bench, that is, a plurality of Elders, in every Church, for the purpose of inspection and government, as well as of teaching; and, at the same time, that all these Elders must be of the same class, that is, that they must all be equally set apart for teaching and ruling, cannot fail to be, to bring the ministerial character, and, of course, ultimately, the religion which the ministry is destined to explain and recommend, into general contempt. The Sandemanians, and a few other sects, have substantially held the opinion, and made the experiment here stated: and invariably, it is believed, with the result which has been represented as unavoidable.

To obviate these difficulties, some have said, let Deacons, whom all agree to be scriptural officers, be employed to assist the Pastor in conducting the government and discipline of the Church. This proposal, together with some principles connected with it, will be considered in a subsequent chapter. All that it is deemed necessary or proper to say in this place, is, that an entirely different sphere of duty is assigned to Deacons in the New Testament. No hint is given of their being employed in the government of the Church. For this proposal, therefore, there is not the shadow of a divine warrant. Besides, if we assign to Deacons the real office, in other words, the appropriate functions of Ruling Elders, what is this but granting the thing, and only disputing about the title? If it Be granted, that there ought to be a plurality of officers in every Church, whose appropriate duty it is to assist the Pastor in inspecting and ruling the flock of Christ, it is the essence of what is contended for. Their proper title is not worth a contest, except so far as it may be proper to imitate the language of Scripture.

If, then, the maintenance of discipline be essential to the purity and edification of the Church; if enlightened, impartial, and efficient inspection and discipline, especially over a large congregation, cannot possibly be maintained by the Pastor alone; if it would be unsafe, and probably mischievous in its influence on all concerned, to devolve the whole authority and responsibility of conducting the government of a Church on a single individual; if it would, especially, in all probability, essentially injure the clerical character to be thus systematically made the depository of so much power, without control and without appeal; if every other mode of furnishing each Church with a plurality of rulers, besides that for which we contend, would either deprive a great majority of our Churches of the means of grace altogether; or, by bringing ministers within their reach, reduce and degrade the ministerial office far below the standard which the Scriptures require; if these things be so, then we are conducted unavoidably to the conclusion, that such officers as those for which we contend, are absolutely necessary: that, although a Church may exist, and, for a time, may flourish without them; yet, the best interests of the Church cannot be systematically and steadfastly pursued without those or some other officers of equivalent powers and duties.

But all the difficulties which have been supposed, are obviated, and all the advantages referred to, attained, by the plan of employing a judicious class of Ruling Elders in each Church, to assist in counsel and in government. In this plan we have provided a body of grave, pious, and prudent men, associated with the Pastor; chosen out of the body of the Church members; carrying with them, in some measure, the feelings and views of their constituents; capable of counselling the Pastor in all delicate and doubtful cases; counteracting any undue influence, or course of measures into which his partiality, prejudice, or want of information might betray him; exonerating him at once from the odium, and the temptation of having all the power of the Church in his own hands; conducting the difficult cases which often arise in the exercise of discipline with the intelligence, calmness, and wisdom, which cannot be expected to prevail in a promiscuous body of communicants; and, in a word, securing to each Church all the principal advantages which might be expected to result from being under the pastoral care of four or five ministers, vested with plenary preaching as well as ruling power; without, at the same time, burdening the Church with the pecuniary support of such a number of ordinary Pastors. In a word, the insuperable difficulty of doing without this class of officers, on the one hand; the great and manifest advantages of having them, on the other; and the perfect accordance of the plan which includes them, with that great representative system, which has pervaded all well regulated society, from its earliest existence, and received the stamp of Divine approbation – form a mass of testimony in favour of the office before us, which, independently of other considerations, seems amply sufficient to support its claims.

I shall close this chapter with the following extract from Dr. Owen, when speaking of the importance and necessity of the office of Ruling Elders in the Church. "It is evident," says he "that neither the purity nor the order, nor the beauty or glory of the Churches of Christ, nor the representation of his own majesty and authority in the government of them, can long be preserved without a multiplication of Elders in them, according to the proportion of their respective members, for their rule and guidance. And for want hereof have Churches of old, and of late, either degenerated into anarchy and confusion, their self-rule being managed with vain disputes and janglings, unto their division and ruin; or else given up themselves unto the domination of some prelatical teachers, to rule them at their pleasure, which proved the bane and poison of all the primitive Churches; and they will and must do so in the neglect of this order for the future."[2]

We have thus completed our view of the first part of the inquiry before us, viz. our warrant for the office of Ruling Elders. If this office was found in the Old Testament economy; – if it plainly had a place in the apostolic Church; – if a number of the early Fathers evidently recognize its existence in their day; – if the witnesses for the truth, in the darkest times, and the great body of the Reformers, sanctioned and retained it, as of Divine appointment; – if some of the most learned Episcopal and Independent divines, since the Reformation, have borne decisive testimony to this office, as of apostolical authority: – and if some such office be manifestly indispensable to the purity and order of the Church; – we may confidently conclude that our warrant for it is complete.

---

2. Owen's *True Nature of a Gospel Church*, Co. p. 178.

CHAPTER NINE

The Nature and Duties of the Office

Having considered, so much at large, the warrant for the office of Ruling Elder, chiefly because there is no part of the subject more contested; we now proceed to other points connected with the general inquiry. And the first of these which presents itself is, the nature and duties of the office in question.

The essential character of the officer of whom we speak is that of an Ecclesiastical Ruler. "He that ruleth, let him do it with diligence," is the summary of his appropriate functions, as laid down in Scripture. The Teaching Elder is, indeed, also a ruler. In addition to this, however, he is called to preach the Gospel, and administer sacraments. But the particular department assigned to the Ruling Elder is to co-operate with the Pastor in spiritual inspection and government. The Scriptures, as we have seen, speak not only of "Pastors and Teachers," but also of "governments;" – of "Elders that rule well, but do not labour in the word and doctrine."

There is an obvious analogy between the office of Ruler in the Church, and in the civil community. A Justice of the Peace in the latter, has a wide and important range of duties. Besides the function which he discharges when called to take his part on the bench of the judicial court in which he presides, he may be, and often is, employed every day, though less publicly, in correcting abuses, compelling the fraudulent to do justice, restraining, arresting, and punishing criminals, and, in general, carrying into execution the laws formed to promote public tranquility and order, which he has sworn to administer faithfully.

Strikingly analogous to this, are the duties of the ecclesiastical Ruler. He has no power, indeed, to employ the secular arm in restraining or punishing offenders against the laws of Christ. The kingdom under which he acts, and the authority which he administers, are not of this world. He has, of course, no right to fine, imprison, or externally to molest the most profligate offenders against the Church's purity or peace; unless they be guilty of what is technically called "breaking the peace," that is, violating the civil rights of others, and thus rendering themselves liable to the penalty of the civil law. And even when this occurs, the ecclesiastical Ruler, as such, has no right to proceed against the offender. He has no other than moral power. He must apply to the civil Magistrate for redress, who can only punish for breaking the civil law. Still there is an obvious analogy between his office and that of the civil Magistrate. Both are alike an ordinance of God. Both are necessary to social order and comfort. And both are regulated by principles which commend themselves to the good sense and the conscience of those who wish well to social happiness.

The Ruling Elder, no less than the Teaching Elder, or Pastor, is to be considered as acting under the authority of Christ, in all that he rightfully does. If the office of which we speak was appointed in the apostolic Church by infinite wisdom; if it is an ordinance of Jesus Christ, just as much as that of the minister of the Gospel; then the former, equally with the latter, is Christ's officer. He has a right to speak and act in his name; and though elected by the members of the Church, and representing them, in the exercise of ecclesiastical rule; yet he is not to be considered as deriving his authority to rule from them, any more than he who "labours in the word and doctrine" derives his authority to preach and administer other ordinances from the people who make choice of him as their teacher and guide. There is reason to believe that some, even in the Presbyterian Church, take a different view of this subject. They regard the Teaching Elder as an officer of Christ, and listen to his official instructions as to those of a man appointed by Him, and coming in His name. But with respect to the Ruling Elder, they are wont to regard him as one who holds an office instituted by human prudence alone, and, therefore, as standing on very different ground in the discharge of his official duties, from that which is occupied by the "ambassador of Christ." This is undoubtedly an erroneous view of the subject, and a view which, so far as it prevails, is adapted to exert the most mischievous influence. The truth is, if the office of which we speak is of apostolic authority, we are just as much bound to sustain, honour, and obey the individual who fills it, and discharges its duties according to the Scriptures, as we are to submit to any other officer or institution of our Divine Redeemer.

We are by no means, then, to consider Ruling Elders as a mere ecclesiastical convenience, or as a set of counsellors whom the wisdom of man alone has chosen, and who may, therefore, be reverenced and obeyed, as little, or as much, as human caprice may think proper; but as bearing an office of divine appointment – as the "ministers of God for good" to his Church – and whose lawful and regular acts ought to command our conscientious obedience.

The Ruling Elders of each Church are called to attend to a public and formal, or to a more private sphere of duty.

With regard to the first, or the public and formal duties of their office, they form, in the Church to which they belong, a bench or judicial Court, called among us the "Church Session," and in, some other Presbyterian denominations, the Consistory; both expressions importing a body of ecclesiastical men, sitting and acting together, as the representatives, and for the benefit of the Church. This body of Elders, with the Pastor at their head, and presiding at their meetings, form a judicial assembly, by which all the spiritual interests of the congregation are to be watched over, regulated, and authoritatively determined. Accordingly, it is declared in the ninth chapter of our Form of Government: "The Church Session is charged with maintaining the spiritual government of the congregation; for which purpose they have power to inquire into the knowledge and Christian conduct of the members of the Church; to call before them offenders and witnesses, being members of their own congregation, and to introduce other witnesses, where it may be necessary to bring the process to issue, and when they can be procured to attend; to receive members into the Church; to admonish, to rebuke, to suspend, or exclude from the sacraments, those who are found to deserve censure; to concert the best measures for promoting the spiritual interests of the congregation; and to appoint delegates to the higher judicatories of the Church."

The general statement of the powers and duties of the Church Session, it will be perceived, takes in a wide range; or rather, to speak more properly, it embraces the whole of that authority and duty with which the great Head of the Church has been pleased to invest the governing powers of each particular congregation, for the instruction, edification and comfort of the whole body. To the Church Session it belongs to bind and loose; to admit to the communion of the Church, with all its privileges; to take cognizance of all departure from the purity of faith or practice; to try, censure, acquit, or excommunicate those who are charged with offences; to consult and determine upon all matters relating to the time, place, and circumstances of worship, and other spiritual concerns; to take order about catechizing children, congregational fasts or thanksgiving days, and all other observances, stated or occasional; to correct, as far as possible, every thing that may tend to disorder, or is contrary to edification; and to digest and execute plans for promoting a spirit of inquiry, of reading, of prayer, of order, and of universal holiness among the members of the Church. It is also incumbent on them, when the Church over which they preside is destitute of a pastor, to take the lead in those measures which may conduce to the choice of a suitable candidate, by calling the people together for the purpose of an election, when they consider them as prepared to make it with advantage.

Although, in ordinary cases, the pastor of the Church may be considered as vested with the right to decide whom he will invite to occupy his pulpit, either when he is present, or occasionally, absent; yet, in cases of difficulty or delicacy, and especially when ministers of other denominations apply for the use of the pulpit, it is the prerogative of the Church Session, to consider and decide on the application. And if there be any fixed difference of opinion between the Pastor, and the other members of the Session, in reference to this matter, it is the privilege and duty of either party to request the advice of their Presbytery in the case.

In the Church Session, whether the Pastor be present and presiding or not, every member has an equal voice. The vote of the most humble and retiring Ruling Elder, is of the same avail as that of his Minister, so that no Pastor can carry any measure unless he can obtain the concurrence of a majority of the Eldership. And as the whole spiritual government of each Church is committed to its bench of Elders, the Session is competent to regulate every concern, and to correct every thing which they consider as amiss in the arrangements or affairs of the Church, which admits of correction. Every individual of the Session is, of course, competent to propose any new service, plan, or measure, which he believes will be for the benefit of the congregation, and if a majority of the Elders concur with him in opinion, it may be adopted. If, in any case, however, there should be a difference of opinion between the Pastor and the Elders, as to the propriety or practicability of any measure proposed, and insisted on by the latter, there is an obvious and effectual constitutional remedy; a remedy, however, which ought to be resorted to with prudence, caution, and prayer. The opinions and wishes of the Pastor ought, undoubtedly, to be treated with the most respectful delicacy. Still they ought not to be suffered, when it is possible to avoid it, to stand in the way of a great and manifest good. When such an alternative occurs, the remedy alluded to may be applied. On an amicable reference to the Presbytery, that body may decide the case between the parties.

And as the members of the Church Session, whether assembled in their judicial capacity or not, are the Pastor's counsellors and colleagues, in all matters relating to the spiritual rule of the Church; so it is their official duty to encourage, sustain, and defend him, in the faithful discharge of his duty. It is deplorable, when a minister is assailed for his fidelity, by the profane or the worldly, if any portion of the Eldership, either take part against him, or shrink from his active and determined defence. It is not meant, of course, that they are to consider themselves as bound to sustain him in every thing he may say or do, whether right or wrong; but that, when they really believe him to be faithful, both to truth and duty, they should feel it to be their duty to stand by him, to shield him from the arrows of the wicked, and to encourage him, as far as he obeys Christ.

But besides those duties which pertain to Ruling Elders, with the Pastor, in their collective capacity, as a judicatory of the Church; there are others which are incumbent on them at all times, in the intervals of their judicial meetings, and by the due discharge of which they may be constantly edifying the body of Christ. It is their duty to have an eye of inspection and care over all the members of the congregation; and, for this purpose, to cultivate a universal and intimate acquaintance, as far as may be, with every family in the flock of which they are made "overseers." They are bound to watch over the children and youth, and especially baptized children, with paternal vigilance, recognizing and affectionately addressing them on all proper occasions; giving them, and their parents in reference to them, seasonable counsel, and putting in the Lord's claim to their hearts and lives, as the children of the Church. It is their duty to attend to the case of those who are serious, and disposed to inquire concerning their eternal interests; to converse with them, and, from time to time, to give information concerning them to the Pastor. It is their duty to take notice of, and admonish in private, those who appear to be growing careless, or falling into habits in any respect criminal, suspicious, or unpromising. It is their duty to visit and pray with the sick, as far as their circumstances admit, and to request the attendance of the Pastor on the sick, and the dying, when it may be seasonable or desired. It is incumbent on them to assist the Pastor in maintaining meetings for social prayer, to take part in conducting the devotional exercises in those meetings; to preside in them when the Pastor is absent; and, if they are endowed with suitable gifts, under his direction, occasionally to drop a word of instruction and exhortation to the people in those social meetings. If the officers of the Church neglect these meetings (the importance of which cannot be estimated), there is every reason to apprehend that they will not be duly honoured or attended by the body of the people. It is the duty of Ruling Elders, also, to visit the members of the Church and their families, with the Pastor, if he request it; without him, if he do not; to converse with them; to instruct the ignorant; to confirm the wavering; to caution the unwary; to reclaim the wandering; to encourage the timid, and to excite and animate all classes to a faithful and exemplary discharge of duty. It is incumbent on them to consult frequently and freely with their Pastor, on the interests of the flock committed to their charge; to aid him in forming and executing plans for the welfare of the Church; to give him, from time to time, such information as he may need, to enable him to perform aright his various and momentous duties; to impart to him, with affectionate respect, their advice; to support him with their influence; to defend his reputation; to enforce his just admonitions; and, in a word, by every means in their power, to promote the comfort, and extend the usefulness of his labours.

Although the Church Session is not competent to try the Pastor, in case of his falling into any delinquency, either of doctrine or practice; yet if the members observe any such delinquency, it is not only their privilege, but their duty, to admonish him, tenderly and respectfully, yet faithfully, in private; and, if necessary, from time to time; and, if the admonition be without effect, and they think the edification or the Church admits and demands a public remedy, they ought to represent the case to the Presbytery, as before suggested in other cases, and request a redress of the grievance.

But the functions of the Ruling Elder are not confined to the congregation of which he is one of the rulers. It is his duty at such times, and in such order as the constitution of the Church requires, to take his seat in the higher judicatories of the Church, and there to exercise his official share of counsel and authority. In every Presbytery, Synod, and General Assembly of the Presbyterian Church, at least as many Ruling as Teaching Elders are entitled to a place; and in all the former, as well as the latter, have an opportunity of exerting an important influence in the great concerns of Zion. Every congregation, whether provided with a Pastor or vacant, is entitled, besides the Pastor (where there is one), to be represented by one Ruling Elder, in all meetings of the Presbytery and Synod; and, as in those bodies, vacant congregations, and those which are supplied with Pastors, are equally represented, each by an Elder, it is manifest that, if the theory of our ecclesiastical constitution be carried into effect, there will always be a greater number of Ruling Elders than of Pastors present. In the General Assembly, according to our constitutional plan, the numbers of each are precisely equal.

In these several Judicatories the Ruling Elder has an equal vote, and the same power, in every respect, with the Pastors. He has the same privilege of originating plans and measures, and of carrying them, provided he can induce a majority of the body to concur in his views; and thus may become the means of imparting his impressions, and producing an influence greatly beyond the particular congregation with which he is connected, and, indeed, throughout the bounds of the Presbyterian Church in the United States. This consideration serves to place the nature and the importance of the office in the strongest light. He who bears it, has the interest of the Church, as a spiritual trust, as really and solemnly, though not in all respects to the same extent, committed to him, as the Elder, who "labours in the word and doctrine." He not only has it in his power, but is daily called, in the discharge of his official duties, to watch over, inspect, regulate, and edify the body of Christ: to enlighten the ignorant; to admonish the disorderly; to reconcile differences; to correct every moral irregularity and abuse within the bounds of his charge; and to labour without ceasing for the promotion of the cause of truth, piety, and universal righteousness in the Church to which he belongs, and wherever else he has an opportunity of raising his voice, and exerting his influence.

But when it is considered that those who bear the office in question, are called upon, in their turn, to sit in the highest Judicatories of the Church; and there to take their part in deliberating and deciding on the most momentous questions which can arise in conducting ecclesiastical affairs: – when we reflect that they are called to deliberate and decide on the conformity of doctrines to the word of God: to assist, as judges, in the trial of heretics, and every class of offenders against the purity of the Gospel; and to take care in their respective spheres, that all the ordinances of Christ's house be preserved pure and entire when, in a word, we recollect that they are ordained for the express purpose of overseeing and guarding the most precious concerns of the Church on earth; – concerns which may have a bearing, not merely on the welfare of a single individual or congregation; but on the great interests of orthodoxy and piety among millions; – we may surely conclude without hesitation, that the office which they sustain is one, the importance of which can scarcely be overrated; and that the estimate which is commonly made of its nature, duties, and responsibility, is very far from being adequate.

If this view of the nature and importance of the office before us be admitted, the question very naturally arises, whether it be correct to call this class of Elders, *Lay*-Elders; or whether they have not such a strictly ecclesiastical character as should prevent the use of that language in speaking of them? This is one of the points in the present discussion, concerning which, the writer of this Essay frankly confesses that he has, in some measure, altered his opinion. Once he was disposed to confine the epithet *clerical* to Teaching Elders, and to designate those who ruled only, and did not teach, as *Lay*-Elders. But more mature inquiry and reflection have led him first to doubt the correctness of this opinion, and finally to be persuaded, that so far as the distinction between Clergy and Laity is proper at all, it ought not to be made the point of distinction between these two classes of Elders; and that, when we speak of the one as Clergymen, and the other as Laymen, we are apt to convey an idea altogether erroneous, if not seriously mischievous.

Some judicious and pious men have, indeed, expressed serious doubts whether the terms Clergy and Laity ought ever to have been introduced into our theological nomenclature. But it is not easy to see any solid reason for this doubt. Is it wise to contend about terms, when the things intended to be expressed by them are fully understood, and generally admitted? The only question, then, of real importance to be decided here, is this: Does the New Testament draw any distinct line between those who hold spiritual offices in the Church, and those who do not? Does it represent the functions pertaining to those offices as confined to them, or as common to all Christians? Now, it seems impossible to read the Acts of the Apostles, and the several Apostolical Epistles, especially those to Timothy and Titus; and to examine in connexion with these, the writings of the "Apostolical Fathers," without perceiving that the distinction between those who bore office in the Church, and private Christians, was clearly made, and uniformly maintained, from the very origin of the Church. That the terms, *Clergy* and *Laity*, are not found in the New Testament, nor in some of the earliest uninspired writers, is freely granted. But is not the distinction intended to be expressed by these terms evidently found in Scripture, and in all the early Fathers? Nothing can be more indubitably clear. The titles of "Rulers" in the house of God; – "Ambassadors of Christ;" – "Stewards of the mysteries of God;" – "Bishops, Leaders, Overseers, Elders, Shepherds, Guides, Ministers," &c., as distinguished from those to whom they ministered, are so familiar to all readers of the New Testament, that it would be a waste of time to attempt to illustrate or establish a point so unquestionable. If the inspired writers every where represent certain spiritual offices in the Church as appointed by God; if they represent those who sustain these offices, as alone authorized to perform certain sacred functions; and teach us to consider all others who attempt to perform them, as criminal invaders of a Divine ordinance; then surely the whole distinction intended to be expressed by the terms Clergy and Laity, is evidently, and most distinctly laid down by the same authority which founded the Church.

The word κληος properly signifies *a lot*. And as the land of Canaan – the inheritance of the Israelites – was divided among them by lot, the word, in process of time, came to signify an inheritance. In this figurative, or secondary sense, the term is evidently employed in 1 Peter v. 3. Under the Old Testament dispensation, the peculiar people of God were called (Septuagint translation) his κληος, or inheritance. Of this we have examples in Deuteronomy iv. 20, and ix. 29. The term in both these passages, is manifestly applied to the whole body of the nation of Israel, as God's inheritance, or peculiar people. Clemens Romanus, one of the "Apostolical Fathers," speaking of the Jewish economy, and having occasion to distinguish between the priests and the common people, calls the latter λαικοι. Clemens Alexandrinus, towards the close of the second century, speaks of the Apostle John as having set apart such persons for "clergymen" (κληροι) as were signified to him by the Holy Ghost. And in the writings of Tertullian, Origen, and Cyprian, the terms "clergy" and "laity" occur with a frequency which shows that they were then in general use. Jerome observes, that ministers are called *Clerici,* either because they are peculiarly the lot and portion of the Lord; or because the Lord is their lot, that is, their inheritance. Hence that learned and pious Father takes occasion to infer: "That he who is God's portion ought so to exhibit himself, that he may be truly said to possess God, and to be possessed by Him."[1]

And as we have abundant evidence that ecclesiastical men were familiarly called *Clerici,* or "Clergymen," from the second century; so we have the same evidence that this term was employed to designate all ecclesiastical men. That is, all persons who had any spiritual office in the Church, were called by the common name of *Clerici*, or "Clergymen." It was applied, continually to Elders and Deacons, as well as to Bishops or Pastors. Nay, in the third century, when not only the inceptive steps of Prelacy became visible, but when the same spirit of innovation had also brought in a number of inferior orders; such as sub-Deacons, Readers, Acolyths, &c., these inferior orders were all *Clerici.* Cyprian, speaking of a sub-Deacon, and also of a Reader, calls them both *Clerici.* The ordination of such persons

---

1. Epist. 2. ad Nepotian. 5.

(for it seems they were all formally ordained), he calls *Ordinationes Cleicæ*; and the letters which he transmitted by them, he styles *Literæ Clericæ*. The same fact may be clearly established from the writings of Ambrose, Hilary, and Epiphanius, and from the canons of the Council of Nice. Indeed there seems reason to believe, that in the fourth and fifth centuries, and subsequently, the title of *Clerici* was not only given to all the inferior orders of ecclesiastical men, but was more frequently and punctiliously applied to them, than to their superiors, who were generally addressed by their inure distinctive and honourable titles. Those who recollect that learning, during the dark ages, was chiefly confined to the ministers of religion; that few, excepting persons of that profession, were able to read and write; and that the whimsical privilege, commonly called "benefit of Clergy," grew out of the rare accomplishment of being able to read; will be at no loss to trace the etymology of the word clerk (*clericus*), or secretary, as used to designate one who officiates as the reader and writer of a public body.

To distinguish the mass of private Christians from those who bore office in the Church, they were designated by several names. They were sometimes called λαικοι, *laici*, laymen, from λαος, *populus;* sometimes ιδιωται, "private men," from ιδιος, *privatus* (Acts iv. 13); sometimes βιωτικοι, i.e., "seculars," from βιος, which signifies a secular life. Soon after the apostolical age, common Christians were frequently called ανδρες εκκλησιαστκοι, "men of the Church," i.e., persons not belonging either to Jewish Synagogues, or Pagan temples, or heretical bodies, but members of the Church of Christ. Afterwards, however, the title Ecclesiastics, became gradually appropriated to persons in office in the Church.[2]

The quotations made, in a former chapter, from Augustine, and the writings of some other Fathers about his time, in which they seem to distinguish between the Clergy and the Elders may seem to militate with the foregoing statement. But in reference to these passages, the learned Voetius, while he quotes

---

2. See Stephani, *Thesaurus*, and Bingham's *Origines Ecclesiasticæ*.

them, as decisive of the general fact of the early existence of the Elders under consideration, supposes that the office, in the fourth and fifth centuries, was beginning to fall into disuse; and that, of course, though it was still found in some Churches, it began to be spoken of with less respect and sometimes to be denied a place among the offices strictly clerical.[3]

But, after all, there is no real difficulty as to this point. For although the terms "clergy" and "clerical" were pretty generally applied to all classes of Church officers, even the lowest, in the third, fourth, and fifth centuries, yet this was not always the case. Thus in the Apostolical Canons, which were probably composed in the fourth or fifth centuries, there is an express distinction made between the Deacons and the Clergy. In the third and fourth Canons, having ordered what sorts of first fruits should be sent to the Church, and what to the home of the Bishop and Presbyters, it ordains as follows: "Now it is manifest that they are to be divided by them among the Deacons and the Clergy." From cases of this kind we may evidently infer that, although all kinds of ecclesiastical officers were generally ranked among the Clergy, during the period just mentioned, yet this was not invariably so; and, of course, no inference can be drawn from occasional diversity of expression as to this matter.

Now, if this historical deduction of the titles, Clergy and Laity, be correct, it is plain that, according to early and general usage, Ruling Elders ought not to be styled Laymen, or Lay-Elders. They are as really in office – they as really bear an office of Divine appointment, an office of a high and spiritual nature, and an office, the functions of which cannot be rightfully performed, but by those who are regularly set apart to it – as any other officer of the Christian Church. They are as really a portion of God's lot; as really set over the laity, or body of the people as the most distinguished and venerated minister of Jesus can be. Whether, therefore, we refer to early usage, or to strict philological import, Ruling Elders are as truly entitled to the name of Clergy, in the only legitimate sense of that term, that is, they are

---

3. *Politicæ Ecclesiasticæ*, par. ii. Lib. ii. Tract. iii.

as truly ecclesiastical officers as those who "labour in the word and doctrine."

The scope of the foregoing remarks will not, it is hoped, be mistaken. The author of this Essay has no zeal either for retaining or using the terms Clergy and Laity. So far as the former term has been heretofore used, or may now be intended, to convey the idea of a "privileged order" in the Church; a dignified body, lifted up, in rank and claim, above the mass of the Church members; in a word, as designating a set of men, claiming to be vicars of Christ, keepers of the human conscience, and the only channels of grace, he disclaims and abhors it. He is a believer in no such meaning or men. But so far as it is intended to designate those who are clothed with ecclesiastical office, under the authority of Christ, and authorized to discharge some important spiritual functions, which the body of the Church members are not authorized to perform, and to mark the distinction between these two classes, the writer is of the opinion that the language may be defended, and that either that, or some other of equivalent import, ought to be used, nay, must be used, if we would be faithful to the New Testament view of ecclesiastical office, as an ordinance of Jesus Christ. And if the term Clergy, in this humble, Christian, and only becoming sense, be applied to those who preside in the dispensation of public ordinances; it may with equal propriety, be applied to those who preside with Pastors, in the inspection and rule of the Church.

If any should be disposed to remark, on this subject, that the use of the term Clergy is so appropriated by long established public habit, to a particular class of ecclesiastical officers, that there can be no hope that the mass of the community will be reconciled to an extension of the title to Ruling Elders; the answer is – be it so. The writer of this volume is neither vain enough to expect, nor ambitious enough to attempt, a change in the popular language to the amount here supposed. But he protests against the continued use of the term Lay-Elder, as really adapted to make an erroneous impression. Let the class of officers in question be called Ruling Elders. Let all necessary distinction be made by saying: "Ministers, or Pastors, Ruling Elders, Deacons, and the Laity, or body of the people." This will be in conformity with ancient usage. This will be maintaining every important principle. This can offend none; and nothing more will be desired by any.

Were the foregoing views of the nature and duties of the Elder's office generally adopted, duly appreciated, and faithfully carried out into practice, what a mighty change would be effected in our Zion! With what a different estimate of the obligations and responsibilities which rest upon them, would the candidates for this office enter on their sacred work! And with what different feelings would the mass of the people, and especially all who love the cause of Christ, regard these spiritual Counsellors and Guides, in their daily walks, and particularly in their friendly and official visits! This is a change most devoutly to be desired. The interests of the Church are more involved in the prevalence of just opinions and practice in reference to this office, than almost any other that can be named. Were every congregation, besides a wise, pious and faithful Pastor, furnished with eight or ten Elders, to co-operate with him in all his parochial labours, on the plan which has been sketched; men of wisdom, faith, prayer, and Christian activity; men willing to deny and exert themselves for the welfare of Zion; men alive to the importance of every thing that relates to the orthodoxy, purity, order and spirituality of the Church, and ever on the watch for opportunities of doing good; men, in a word, willing to "take the oversight" of the flock in the Lord, and to labour without ceasing for the promotion of its best interests: – were every Church furnished with a body of such Elders, can any one doubt that knowledge, order, piety, and growth in grace, as well as in numbers, would be as common in our Churches, as the reverse is now the prevailing state of things, in consequence of the want of fidelity on the part of those who are nominally the overseers and guides of the flock?

While discussing the nature of this office, and the duties which pertain to it, it seems to be natural to offer a few remarks on the manner in which those who bear it ought to be treated by the members of the Church: in other words, on the duties which the Church owes to her Ruling Elders.

And here the discerning and pious mind will be at no loss to perceive that these duties are correlative to those which the Rulers owe to the Church. That is, if they are the spiritual Rulers of the Church, and bound to perform daily, and with fidelity and zeal, the duties which belong to this station, it is evident that the members of the Church are bound to recognize them in the same character, and to honour and treat them as their spiritual guides. Were it, then, in the power of the writer of this volume to address the members of every Presbyterian Church in the United States, he would speak to them in some such language as the following:

Christian Brethren.

Every consideration which has been urged to show the importance of and duties belonging to the office of Ruling Elders, ought to remind you of the important duties which you owe to them. Remember, at all times, that they are your ecclesiastical Rulers; Rulers of your own choice; yet by no means coming to you in virtue of mere human authority; but in the name and by the appointment of the great Head of the Church, and, of course, the "ministers of God to you for good."

In all your views and treatment of them, recognize this character. Obey them "in the Lord," that is, for his sake, and as far as they bear rule agreeably to his word. "Esteem them very highly in love for their work's sake." And follow them daily with your prayers, that God would bless them, and make them a blessing. Reverence them as your leaders. Bear in mind the importance of their office, the arduousness of their duties, and the difficulties with which they have to contend. Countenance, and sustain them in every act of fidelity; make allowance for their infirmities; and be not unreasonable in your expectations from them.

Many are ready to criminate the Elders of the Church, for not taking notice of particular offences, as speedily, or in such manner, as they expect. And this disposition to find fault is sometimes indulged by persons who have never been so faithful themselves as to give that information which they possessed, respecting the alleged offences; or who, when called upon publicly to substantiate that which they have privately disclosed, have drawn back, unwilling to encounter the odium or the pain of appearing as accusers, or even as witnesses. Such persons ought to be the last to criminate Church officers for supposed negligence of discipline. Can your Rulers take notice of that which never comes to their knowledge? Or can you expect them, as prudent men, rashly to set on foot a judicial and public investigation of things, concerning which many are ready to whisper in private, but none willing to speak with frankness before a court of Christ? Besides, let it be recollected, that the session of almost every Church is sometimes actually engaged in investigating charges, in removing offences, and in composing differences, which many suppose they are utterly neglecting, merely because they do not judge it to be for edification, in all cases, to proclaim what they have done, or are doing, to the congregation at large.

Your Elders will sometimes be called – God grant that it may seldom occur! – but they will sometimes be called to the painful exercise of discipline. Be not offended with them for the performance of this duty. Rather make the language of the Psalmist your own: "Let the righteous smite me, it shall be a kindness; and let him reprove me, it shall be an excellent oil, which shall not break my head." Add not to the bitterness of their official task, by discovering a resentful temper, or by indulging in reproachful language, in return for their fidelity. Surely the nature of the duty is sufficiently self-denying and distressing, without rendering it more so by unfriendly treatment. Receive their private warnings and admonitions with candour and affectionate submission. Treat their public acts, however contrary to your wishes, with respect and reverence. If they be honest and pious men, can they do less than exercise the discipline of Christ's house, against such of you as walk disorderly? Nay, if you be honest and pious yourselves, can you do less than approve of their faithfulness in exercising that discipline? If you were aware of all the difficulties which attend this part of the duty of your Eldership, you would feel for them more tenderly, and judge concerning them more candidly and indulgently than you are often disposed to do. Here you have it in your power, in a very important degree, to lessen their burdens, and to strengthen their hands.

When your Elders visit your families, for the purpose of becoming acquainted with them, and of aiding the Pastor in ascertaining the spiritual state of the flock, remember that it is not officious intrusion. It is nothing more than their duty. Receive them, not as if you suspected them of having come as spies or busy intruders, but with respect and cordiality. Convince them, by your treatment, that you are glad to see them; that you wish to encourage them in promoting the best interests of the Church; and that you honour them for their fidelity. Give them an opportunity of seeing your children, and of ascertaining whether your households are making progress in the Christian life. Nay, encourage your children to put themselves in the way of the Elders, that they may be personally known to them, and may become the objects of their affectionate notice, their occasional exhortation, and their pious prayers. Converse with the Elders freely, as with fathers, who "have no greater joy than to see you walking in the truth." And ever give them cause to retire under the pleasing persuasion, that their office is honoured, that their benevolent designs are duly appreciated, and that their labours "are not in vain in the Lord." In short, as every good citizen will make conscience of vindicating the fidelity, and holding up the hands of the faithful Magistrate, who firmly and impartially executes the law of the land: so every good Christian ought to feel himself bound in conscience and honour, as well as in duty to his Lord, to strengthen the hands, and encourage the heart of the spiritual Ruler, who evidently seeks, in the fear of God, to promote the purity and edification of the Church.

The nature of the office before us also leads to another remark, with which the present chapter will be closed. It is, that there seems to be a peculiar propriety in the Ruling Elders (and the same principle will apply to the Deacons, if there be any of this class of officers in a congregation) having a seat assigned them for sitting together, in a conspicuous part of the Church, near the Pulpit, during the public service, where they can overlook the whole worshipping assembly, and be seen by all. The considerations which recommend this are numerous. It was invariably so in the Jewish Synagogue. The same practice, as we have seen in a former chapter, was adopted in the early Church, as soon as Christians began to erect houses for public worship. This official and conspicuous accommodation for the Elders is constantly provided in the Dutch Reformed Church in this country, and it is believed by most of the Reformed Churches on the continent of Europe. It is adapted to keep the congregation habitually reminded who their Elders are, and of their official authority; and also to remind the Elders themselves of their functions and duties. And it furnishes a convenient opportunity for the Pastor to consult them on any question which may occur, either before he ascends the Pulpit, or at the close of the service.

CHAPTER TEN

Distinction Between the Offices of the Ruling Elder and Deacon

These offices have been so often confounded, and opinions attempted to be maintained, which tend to merge the former in the latter, that it is judged proper to make the difference between them the subject of distinct consideration.

The only account that we have in Scripture of the origin of the Deacon's office is found in the following passage, in the Acts of the Apostles vi. 1-6: "And in those days, when the number of the disciples was multiplied, there arose a murmuring of the Grecians against the Hebrews, because their widows were neglected in the daily ministration. Then the twelve called the multitude of the disciples unto them, and said: It is not reason that we should leave the word of God and serve tables. Wherefore, brethren, look ye out among you seven men, of honest report, full of the Holy Ghost and wisdom, whom we may appoint over this business. But we will give ourselves continually to prayer, and to the ministry of the word. And the saying pleased the whole multitude; and they chose Stephen, a man full of faith and of the Holy Ghost, and Philip, and Prochorus, and Nicanor, and Timon, and Parmenas, and Nicolas, a proselyte of Antioch: whom they set before the Apostles; and when they had prayed, they laid their hands on them."

On this plain passage various opinions have been entertained. It will be to our purpose to notice a few of them.

I. Some have doubted whether these were the first Deacons chosen by the direction of the inspired Apostles. The learned Dr. Mosheim supposed that the Church of Jerusalem, from its first organization, had its inferior ministers, in other words, its Deacons; and that there is a reference to these, in the fifth chapter, of the Acts of the Apostles, under the title of young men (νεωτεροι and νεανισκοι), who assisted in the interment of Ananias and Sapphira. He is confident that the Seven Deacons spoken of in the passage just cited, were added to the original number; and that they were intentionally selected from the foreign Jews, in order to silence the complaints on the part of the Grecians, of partiality in the distribution of the offerings made for the relief of the poor. To this opinion there seems to be no good reason for acceding. The objections to it are the following:

1. It is by no means probable that a class of officers of great importance to the comfort and prosperity of the Church, should have been instituted by Divine authority, and yet that the original institution should have been passed over by all the inspired writers in entire silence.

2. In this narrative of the election and ordination of the seven Deacons, there is not the most distant allusion to any pre-existing officers of the same character or functions. The murmuring spoken of, seems to have proceeded from the body of the Grecian, or foreign Christians, and to have been directed against the body of the native, or Hebrew Christians.

3. It is evident, from the spirit of the narrative, that the appointment of these Deacons was expressly designed to relieve the Apostles themselves of a laborious service, with which they had been before encumbered, but which interfered with their discharge of higher, and more important duties. Surely the address of the Apostles would have been strange, if not unmeaning, had there been already a body of officers who were intrusted with the whole of this business; and they had only been solicited to appoint an additional number, or to put a more impartial set in the place of the old incumbents.

4. It is plain that these officers were not chosen from among the young men of the Church, as Dr. Mosheim seems to imagine; nor was the office itself one of small trust or dignity. The

multitude were directed to "look out seven men of honest report," or established reputation, "full of the Holy Ghost and of wisdom;" and when the Apostle Paul afterwards writes to Timothy, and points out the character of those who ought to be selected for this office, he speaks of them as married men, fathers of families, distinguished for their gravity: men who had been "first proved," and found "blameless," as orthodox, just, temperate, holy men, regulating their own households with firmness and prudence.

5. Dr. Mosheim is not borne out by the best authorities in his interpretation of the words νεωτεροι, and νεανισκοι. The most skilful lexicographers assign to them no such official meaning. Besides, the nature and responsibility of the office, and the high qualifications for it pointed out by the Apostles at the time of this first choice, and required by the Apostle Paul afterwards, when writing to Timothy, respecting proper persons to be chosen and set apart as Deacons, by no means answer to the view which Dr. Mosheim takes of the inferiority of the office, or the propriety of bestowing it on young men as the Church's servants.

6. Finally; it may be doubted whether there had been any real need of the Deacon's office, until the time arrived, and the events occurred which are recorded in the sixth chapter of the Acts of the Apostles. But a short time had elapsed since the Church had been organized on the New Testament plan. At its first organization, the number of the poor connected with it was probably small. But very shortly after the day of Pentecost, the number of foreigners, who had come up to the feast, and had there been converted to the Christian faith, was so great, and the number of those who, at a distance from all their wonted pecuniary resources, and their friends, stood in need of pecuniary aid, had also become so considerable, that the task of "imparting to those who had need," became, suddenly, a most arduous employment. This had been accomplished, however, for a short time, under the direction of the Apostles, and without appointing a particular class of officers for the purpose. But, when the foreign Jews came forward, and made complaint of partiality in this business, the Apostles, under the direction of heavenly wisdom,

called upon the "multitude" to make choice of competent persons whom they might appoint over this branch of Christian ministration. This appears to be a plain history of the case, and to resort to Dr. Mosheim's supposition, is to throw a strange and perplexed aspect over the whole narrative.

II. There are others who have doubted whether the "seven," whose election and ordination are recorded in the 6th chapter of the Acts of the Apostles, were Deacons at all. They allege that the office to which they were chosen and set apart was a mere temporary function, not designed to be a permanent one in the Christian Church, and which, probably, did not last much if any longer than what is commonly called, "the community of goods," which existed sometime after the day of Pentecost.

Against this supposition, the following reasons are, in my view, conclusive.

1. If this supposition were admitted, then it would follow, that there is no account whatever in the Scriptures of the origin or nature of the Deacon's office. The office is mentioned again and again in the New Testament; but if the narrative in the beginning of the sixth chapter of the Acts of the Apostles be not a statement of its origin, nature, and duties, we have no account of them any where. Can this be considered as probable?

2. Is it likely, judging on the principles, and from the analogy of Scripture, that a short occasional trust, a mere temporary trusteeship, if I may so speak, would be appointed with so much formality and solemnity; – marked not only by a formal election of the people, but also by the prayers and "the laying on of the hands" of the Apostle? What greater solemnities attended an investiture with the highest and most permanent offices in the Christian Church?

3. It is a well known fact, that in the Jewish Synagogue which was assumed as the model of the primitive Church, there was a class of officers, to whom the collection and distribution of alms for the poor, were regularly committed. We may venture to presume, then, that the appointment of similar officers in the Church would be altogether likely.

4. When it is considered what an important and arduous

part of the Church's duty it was, in the apostolic age, and for some time afterwards, to provide for the very numerous poor who looked to her for aid, it is incredible that there should be no class of officers specifically set apart for this purpose. Yet if the "seven" are not of this class, there is no account of any such appointment in the New Testament.

5. The language of some of the earlier, as well as the later Christian Fathers on this subject, clearly evinces that they considered the appointment recorded in the chapter of the Acts of the Apostles, now under consideration, as the appointment of Christian Deacons – and as exhibiting the nature of that office, and the great purpose for which it was instituted. A small specimen of the manner in which they speak on the subject will be sufficient to establish this position. Hermas, one of the apostolical Fathers in his Similitude, 9-27, expresses himself thus: "For what concerns the tenth mountain, in which were the trees covering the cattle, they are such as have believed, and some of them have been Bishops, that is presidents of the Churches. Then such as have been set over inferior ministries, and have protected the poor and the widows." Origen (Tract. 16, in Matt.) evidently considered the Deacons as charged with the pecuniary concerns of the Church. "The Deacons," says he, "preside over the money tables of the Church." And again, "Those Deacons, who do not manage well the money of the Churches committed to their care, but act a fraudulent part, and dispense it, not according to justice, but for the purpose of enriching themselves; these act the part of money-changers, and keepers of those tables which our Lord overturned. For the Deacons were appointed to preside over the tables of the Church, as we are taught in the Acts of the Apostles." Cyprian speaks (Epist. 25) of a certain Deacon who had been deposed from his "sacred Diaconate, on account of his fraudulent and sacrilegious misapplication of the Church's money to his own private use; and for his denial of the widow's and orphan's pledges deposited with him." And, in another place (Epist. 3, ad Rogatianum), he refers the appointment of the first Deacons to his choice and ordination at Jerusalem. It seems, then, that the Deacons, in the

days of Cyprian, were intrusted with the care of widows and orphans, and the funds of the Church destined for their relief. It is incidentally stated in the account of the persecution under the emperor Decius, in the third century, that by order of the emperor, Laurentius, one of the Deacons of Rome, was seized, under the expectation of finding the money of the Church, collected for the use of the poor, in his possession. It is further stated, that this money had really been in his possession; but that, expecting the storm of persecution, he had distributed it before his seizure.

Eusebius (Lib. ii. cap. 1,) says; – There were also "seven approved men ordained deacons, through prayer and the imposition of the Apostles' hands," and he immediately afterwards speaks of Stephen as one of the number. Dorotheus, Bishop of Tyre, contemporary with Eusebius, also says (*Lives of the Prophets*, &c.): "Stephen, the first Martyr, and one of the seven Deacons, was stoned by the Jews at Jerusalem, as Luke testifieth in the Acts of the Apostles."

Ambrose, in speaking of the fourth century, the time in which he lived, says (Comment. in Ephes. iv.): "The Deacons do not publicly preach." Chrysostom, who lived in the same century, in his commentary on this very passage, in Acts vi., observes, that "the Deacons had need of great wisdom, although the preaching of the word was not committed to them;" and remarks further, that "it is absurd to suppose that they should have both the offices of preaching and taking care of the poor committed to them, seeing it is impossible for them to discharge both functions adequately." Sozomen, the ecclesiastical historian, who lived in the fifth century, says; (Lib. v. cap. 8,) that "the Deacon's office was to keep the Church goods." In the *Apostolical Constitutions*, which, though undoubtedly spurious as an apostolical work, may probably be referred to the fourth or fifth centuries, it is recorded (Lib. 8, cap. 28.): "It is not lawful for the Deacons to baptize, or to administer the Eucharist, or to pronounce the greater or smaller benediction." Jerome, in his letter to Evagrius, calls Deacons "ministers of tables and widows." Oecumenius, a learned commentator, who lived several centuries after Jerome, in his Commentary on Acts vi., expresses himself thus: "The Apostles laid their hands on those who were chosen Deacons, not to confer on them that rank which they now hold in the Church, but that they might, with all diligence and attention, distribute the necessaries of life to widows and orphans." And the Council of Constantinople, in the sixth century, expressly asserts (Can. 16), that the seven Deacons spoken of in the Acts of the Apostles, are not to be understood of such as ministered in divine service, or in sacred mysteries, but only of such as served tables, and attended the poor.

Another consideration, which shows beyond controversy that the early Christians universally considered the seven spoken of in the sixth chapter of the Acts of the Apostles, as the proper New Testament Deacons, is that, for several centuries, many of the largest and most respectable Churches in the world considered themselves as bound, in selecting their Deacons, to confine themselves to the exact number seven, whatever might be their extent and their exigencies, on the avowed principle of conformity to the number of this class of officers first appointed in the mother Church at Jerusalem. The Council of Neocæsarea enacted it into a canon, that there should be but seven Deacons in any city, however great, because this was according to the rule laid down in the Acts of the Apostles. And the Church of Rome, both before and after this Council, seems also to have looked upon that example as binding; for it is evident from the Epistles of Cornelius, written in the middle of the third century, that there were but seven Deacons in the Church of Rome at that time, though there were forty-six Presbyters. Prudentius intimates that it was so in the time of Sixtus, also in the year 261; for speaking of Laurentius, the Deacon, he terms him the chief of those "seven men," who had their station near the altar, meaning the Deacons of the Church. Nay, in the fourth and fifth centuries, the custom in that city continued the same, as we learn both from Sozomen and Hilary, the Roman Deacon, who wrote under the name of Ambrose.[1]

6. The current opinion of all the most learned and judi-

---

1. Bingham's *Origines Ecclesiasticæ*, B. ii. ch. 20, sect. 19.

cious Christian divines, of all denominations, for several centuries past, is decisively in favour of considering the passage in Acts vi., as recording the first appointment of the New Testament Deacons. Among all classes of theologians, Catholic and Protestant, Lutheran and Calvinistic, Presbyterian and Episcopal, this concurrence of opinion approaches so near to unanimity, that we may, without injustice to any other opinion, consider it as the deliberate and harmonious judgment of the Christian Church.

The very learned Suicer, a German Professor of the seventeenth century, in his *Thesaurus Ecclesiasticus* (Art. Διακονος), makes the following statement on this subject: "In the apostolic Church, Deacons were those who distributed alms to the poor, and took care of them: in other words, they were the treasurers of the Church's charity. The original institution of this class of officers is set forth in the sixth chapter of the Acts of the Apostles. With respect to them, the 16th canon of the Council of Constantinople (in Trullo) says: "They are those to whom the common administering to poverty is committed; not those who administer the sacraments." And Aristinus, in his Synopsis of the Canons of the same Council, Canon 18th, says: "Let him who alleges that the seven, of whom mention is made in the Acts of the Apostles, were Deacons, know that the account there given is not of those who administer the sacraments, but of such as 'served tables.' Zonaras, *ad Canon.* 16, Trullanum, p.145, says, those who by the Apostles were appointed to the Diaconate, were not ministers of spiritual things, but ministers and dispensers of meats. Oecumenius also, on the 6th chapter of the Acts of the Apostles, says: "They laid their hands on the Deacons who had been elected, which office was by no means the same with that which obtains at the present day in the Church (i.e., under the same name); but that with the utmost care and diligence, they might distribute what was necessary to the sustenance of orphans and widows."

From these considerations, I feel myself warranted in concluding with confidence, that the "seven" chosen at Jerusalem to "serve tables," were scriptural Deacons, and the first Deacons; and that, of course, every attempt to evade the necessary consequence of admitting this fact, is wholly destitute of support.

III. A third opinion held by some on this subject is, that, although the passage recorded in the beginning of the sixth chapter of the Acts of the Apostles, is an account of the first appointment of New Testament Deacons; and though their primary function was to take care of the poor, and "serve tables;" yet the appropriate duties of their office were afterwards enlarged. Thus the Prelatists say, that Philip, one of the "seven," is found, soon after his appointment as Deacon, preaching and baptizing. Hence they infer that these functions of right pertain to the Deacon's office, and have belonged to it from the beginning. On the other hand, some Independents say, that the word Deacon, according to its Greek etymology, means minister or servant; that this general term may cover a large field of ecclesiastical service; and that New Testament Deacons were, probably, at first intended, and now ought to be employed, to assist the Pastor in counsel and government, as well as in serving the Lord's table, and attending to the relief of the poor. And even some Presbyterians have expressed the opinion, that our Ruling Elders were a kind of Deacons in disguise, and ought so to be considered and called; and that there ought not to be, and cannot be, consistently with Scripture, any office bearer, charged with the duty of assisting the Pastor in counsel and rule, other than the Deacon.

I am fully persuaded that this is an erroneous opinion. It appears to me manifest, not only that it is inconsistent with the form of government of the Presbyterian Church; but what is a much more serious difficulty, that it is altogether irreconcilable with the New Testament. For,

1. An attentive and impartial perusal of the record of this first institution or Deacons, must convince any one, that preaching, baptizing, or partaking in the spiritual rule and government or the Church, were so far from being embraced in the original destination of the New Testament Deacon, that they were all absolutely precluded, by the very terms, and the whole spirit of the representation given by the inspired historian. The things complained of by the Grecian believers, are, not that the preaching was defective, or that the government and discipline of the

Church were badly managed. Not a hint of this kind is given. The only complaint was, that the poor "widows had been neglected;" in other words, had not had the due share of attention to their wants, and of relief from the Church's bounty. To remove all cause of complaint on this score, the "seven" were chosen and set apart. The sphere of duty to which they were appointed, was one which the Apostles declared they could not fulfil without "leaving the word of God to serve tables."[2] They say, therefore, to the members of the Church, "look ye out seven men of honest report, full of the Holy Ghost and of wisdom, whom we may appoint over this business," i.e., over the "serving of tables." "And we will give ourselves to prayer and the ministry of the word." Now, to suppose that these very Deacons were appointed to officiate in "the ministry of the word and prayer," is an inconsistency, nay, an absurdity, so glaring, that the only wonder is how any one can possibly adopt it after reading the passage in question. If the object had been to adopt a supposition fitted to exhibit the Apostles, and the "multitude" too, as acting like insane men, or children, one more directly adapted to answer the end, could not have been thought of.

2. The circumstance of Philip, sometime after his appointment as Deacon, being found preaching and baptizing, in Samaria and other places, does not afford the smallest presumptive evidence against this conclusion. Soon after his appointment to the deaconship in Jerusalem, the members of the Church in that city were chiefly "scattered abroad by persecution." Philip was, of course, driven from his residence. Now, the probability

---

2. It has been supposed by many that the phrase, "serving tables," in the history of the institution of the Deacon's office, had a reference either to the Lord's table, or to overseeing and supplying the tables of the poor, or perhaps both. But I am inclined to believe that this is an entire mistake. The word, τραπεα, signifies, indeed, a table; but, in this connexion, it seems obviously to mean a money-table, or a counter, on which money was laid. Hence τραπεζιτης, a money-changer, or a money merchant. See Matt. xxi. 12, xxv. 27; Mark xi. 15; Luke xix. 23. The plain meaning, then, of Acts vi. seems to be this: "It is not suitable that we should leave the word of God, and devote ourselves to pecuniary affairs."

is, that about this time, seeing he was a man "full of the Holy Ghost and of wisdom," and therefore, eminently qualified to be useful in preaching the Gospel, he received a new ordination as an Evangelist, and in this character went forth to preach and baptize. He is expressly called an "Evangelist" by the same inspired writer who gives us an account of his appointment as a Deacon (Acts xxi. 8). Until it can be proved, then, that he preached and baptized as a Deacon, and not as an Evangelist, the supposition is utterly improbable and altogether worthless. It is really an imposition on credulity to urge it. And that certainly never can be proved as long as the sixth chapter of the Acts of the Apostles remains a part of the inspired volume. As to Stephen, another of the "seven," disputing with gainsayers in private, and defending himself before the Council; it was not official preaching at all. It was nothing more than every professing Christian is at all times not only at liberty, but under obligation to do, when assailed by unbelievers, or when brought before an unjust tribunal.

The truth is, the practice of connecting the functions of preaching and baptizing with the Deacon's office, is one of the various human inventions which early begun to spring up in the Church, and which turned almost every ecclesiastical office which had been divinely instituted more or less from its primitive character. "But from the beginning it was not so." It is a departure from the apostolical model. We find, indeed, in several of the writers of the first three or four centuries, frequent intimations of Deacons being permitted to preach, and administer the ordinance of baptism. But in almost every instance, it is represented as done in virtue of a specific permission from the Pastor or Bishop in each case, and as entirely unlawful without such permission. A very different thing from a function inherent in an office, and always lawful when a proper occasion for its exercise occurred! In fact, ecclesiastical history, I believe, will bear me out in saying, that, within the first three centuries, it would be just as correct to assert that private Christians in general had a right to preach and baptize, as to maintain that Deacons, in virtue of their office as such, had this right, because we meet with some instances of their being both called upon to do so in cases of supposed necessity, or when specially permitted by superior ecclesiastics. Mr. Bingham, the learned Episcopal antiquary, explicitly tells us, on the authority of several early writers, that private Christians, who sustained no office whatever in the Church, were sometimes called upon to address the people, in the absence, or at the special request of him whose official duty it was to preach. The same learned author goes on to state, that, in the apostolic age, or as long as the special gifts of the Holy Spirit, enabling men to prophesy, continued, all who possessed such special gifts, whether in office or not, might use "the word of exhortation" in the Church. "But then," he adds, "as such extraordinary gifts of the Spirit of prophecy, were in a manner peculiar to the apostolical age, this could not be a rule to the following ages of the Church. And, therefore, when once these gifts were ceased, the Church went prudently by another rule, to allow none but such as were called by an ordinary commission to perform this office, except where some extraordinary natural endowments (such as were in Origen before his ordination) answering in some measure to those special gifts, made it proper to grant a license to laymen to exercise their talents for the benefit of the Church; or else, when necessity imposed the duty on Deacons, to perform the office of preaching, when the Bishop and Presbyters were by sickness, or other means debarred from it. For the aforesaid author (Ambrose) plainly says, that Deacons, in his time, were not ordinarily allowed *prædicare in populo,* i.e., preach to the people, as being an office to which they had no ordinary commission. And the same is said by the author of the Apostolical Constitutions, and many others. Therefore, since Deacons were not allowed this power, but only in some special cases; it is the less to be wondered at, that, after the ceasing of spiritual gifts, it should, generally, be denied to laymen."[3]

    A mistake on this point, in reference to the Deacon's office, has arisen from misinterpreting certain terms which are used by some of the early writers to express their public service. The words κηρυγμα, κηρυξ, κηρυσσω, &c., are frequently used in

---

3. Bingham's *Origines Ecclesiasticæ,* B. 14. Ch. 4. sect. 4.

the New Testament to express the public preacher, and preaching of the Gospel. Now when the same words are applied by some of the earlier Greek Fathers, and the corresponding words, *præco, prædicatio,* and *prædicare,* by the Latins, to the Deacon's office, it has been hastily concluded that they were, habitually, preachers in the New Testament sense of the term. But the truth is, as every one in the least degree acquainted with those writers knows, these terms when used by the Fathers, signify an entirely different thing. The Deacons, in the third, fourth, and fifth centuries, are every where represented as the common heralds or criers of the Church. That is, when any public notice was to be given; when the catechumens or the penitents were to be called upon aloud to come forward, or to withdraw; or when any public proclamation was to be made, in the course of the service in the Church; – it belonged to the Deacon's office to perform this duty. Hence he was called the *κηρυξ,* or crier, and was said *κηρυσσειν,* to cry aloud, or make proclamation. It belonged to the Deacons, also, to keep order at the doors, when the service was beginning; to see that the worshippers were seated in a quiet and orderly manner; to stand around the communion table, when it was spread, and with fans, made either of dried skins, or peacocks feathers, to keep off the flies from the consecrated elements; and, after the consecration of the sacramental elements, to bear them to the communicants. These, and a variety of subordinate duties, were considered as pertaining to their office, and hence they were regarded, not as having any part of the priesthood, according to the language of that day; but as being the "Church's servants." All this is so explicitly acknowledged, and so abundantly proved, by the learned Bingham,[4] that any further enlargement on the subject is altogether unnecessary. The original office of the Deacon was one of high trust and dignity; requiring much piety, wisdom, prudence, and diligence. But when the purity of the Church, both in doctrine and practice, declined, and especially, when the ardour of her charity to the poor had greatly slackened, that officer, having little to do in his ap-

---

4. *Origines Ecclesiasticæ,* Book ii. Chap. 20, and Book xiv. Chap. 4.

propriate department, sunk, for a time, into a kind of ecclesiastical menial.

3. The directions afterwards given by Paul to Timothy (1 Tim. iii.), respecting the proper qualifications of candidates for the Deacon's office, are decisively opposed to the view of the subject which I am now examining. When the Apostle speaks of the qualifications indispensable in a Teaching Elder, or Bishop, he says he must not only be grave, pious, and of good report, but also *"apt to teach,"* &c. But he prescribes no such condition in the choice of Deacons. He gives no intimation that teaching made any part of their official work. It is said, indeed, that they ought to be men "holding the mystery of the faith in a pure conscience." By which I understand to be meant, that they must be men holding the true faith in sincerity; in other words, that they must be orthodox, and pious; qualifications which ought to be found in all who bear office in the Church of God.

4. We have not the least evidence, from any source, that the function of government was ever connected with the Deacon's office. We read of Ruling Elders, but never of Ruling Deacons. Among all the multiplied witnesses drawn from the Synagogue and the Church, and from almost all denominations of Christians, ancient and modern, in favour of a bench of Elders in each congregation for conducting its government and discipline, I recollect no example of the members of that bench being called Deacons, or of Deacons having any place among them. Nay, it is perfectly manifest, that if, according to the scriptural model, there ought to be a bench or college made up of a plurality of Elders in each Church, to be intrusted with the inspection and rule of the whole body; then there is not a shadow of evidence to support the claim of the Deacons to a seat in that body. But if such a bench of Rulers, under the name of Elders, or Presbyters, be given up, then, I will venture to assert, there is not a shred of evidence, either in or out of the Bible, that similar powers were ever assigned to Deacons, as such. We may, indeed, call our Ruling Elders by the name of Deacons, if we please. And so we may call them Dervises, or Imams, with the Turks; and say that we mean by these titles, to designate the members of the par-

ochial Presbytery, or Consistory, in each Church. But the real questions which present themselves for solution are such as these: Is it agreeable to the New Testament model, that there be in every Christian congregation a plurality of pious and prudent men, invested with the office of inspection and government in the Church? Or, ought all ecclesiastical authority and discipline to be exercised by the Pastor alone? If the former be admitted, then, ought the body of spiritual rulers to be styled Elders or Deacons? If the latter name be contended for, as the more scriptural, then what passage of Scripture, or of early uninspired history, can be mentioned, which countenances the application of this title to ecclesiastical rulers as such? The truth is, it is not perceived how any can consistently maintain, that the officers whom Presbyterians are wont to call Ruling Elders, are really Deacons, and ought to be so designated, without abandoning the Church Session, as destitute of all scriptural warrant. He who does this, however, must hold, either that the Pastor of each Church has the whole government and discipline in his own hands, and that the persons called Elders, or Deacons, are only a set of convenient advisers, without any rightful judicial authority; or that all authority ought to be exercised by the body of the communicants, and every question of admission or discipline submitted to their vote. In the latter case, he may be a very pious and excellent Independent; but he has no claim to the character of a Presbyterian.

It is deeply to be regretted, that the office of Deacon, in its true nature, and its highly important and scriptural character, is not to be found in many Presbyterian Churches. In some, this office is wholly dropped. Neither the name nor the thing is to be found in them. In others, the Ruling Elders, or the members of the Church Session, are constantly styled Deacons, and scarcely ever designated by any other title; while the office really indicated in Scripture by that title is not retained. And in a third class of our Churches, those who are meant for real Deacons, that is, who are chosen and set apart as such, as well as called by that name, are employed in functions for which the office of Deacon was never instituted. The cases, it is feared, are few in which the offices of Elder and Deacon are both retained, and the appropriate functions of each distinctly maintained.

Perhaps in a majority of our Churches the office of Deacon, strictly so called, is entirely dropped. This, it is believed, is also virtually the case, to a considerable extent, in the Church of Scotland, and among the large and respectable body of Presbyterians in the North of Ireland. The origin of this extensive disuse of an unquestionable scriptural office, is probably to be traced to the peculiar form of the provision made in some countries for the support of the poor, which was supposed to render the deaconship, as a separate office, unnecessary. Deacons had a place in the original organization of the Protestant Church of Scotland; and, for many years after the Reformation, were universally retained and much employed in that Church, as a distinct class of officers. But, in later times the office has either been suffered to fall into desuetude altogether, or, as is more common, has been united with that of Ruling Elder, in the same individual. So that the Ruling Elders in the Church of Scotland, are generally expected, and undertake, to act as Deacons also. The same arrangement, it is believed, is also generally adopted among the Presbyterians in Ireland.

As to those Churches in our own country in which the office of Deacon has been suffered to fall into disuse altogether, this event is certainly, on a variety of accounts, to be regretted: – among others, for the following reasons:

1. Every scriptural precedent is worthy of serious regard. The office of Deacon was evidently brought into the Church by inspired men. And although it is not contended that it is essential to an organized Church to have officers of this class, inasmuch as the Church, undoubtedly, did without them, for a short time, after its first organization; yet as the office is an institution of infinite wisdom, and necessary to a full array of all the officers which belong to the visible Church, it seems expedient to retain it, in all cases in which it is possible.

2. We know that, in every Jewish Synagogue, before the coming of Christ, there was a class of officers whose peculiar duty it was to collect and dispense the moneys contributed for the

support of the poor. This seems to have been an invariable part of the Synagogue system. And as that system was evidently the model on which the Christian Church was formed, we may presume that a feature of it so strongly recommended by age and experience, is worthy of adoption.

3. Although some Churches may plead an excuse for discontinuing the use of this office, that they have no Church poor, and, therefore, no occasion for the appropriate services of Deacons; yet the question is, ought they to allow this to be the case? What though the laws of the State make provision of a decent kind for all the poor? Are there not within the bounds, and even among the communicants, of every Church of any extent, and of the ordinary standing in point of age, generally found a greater or less number of persons who have seen more comfortable days, but are now reduced; – aged widows; persons of delicate, retiring spirits, who are struggling with the most severe privations of poverty in secret, but cannot bring themselves to apply to the civil officer for aid as paupers; who, at the same time, would be made comparatively comfortable by a pittance now and then administered in the tender and affectionate spirit of the Gospel? Now, ought the Church to take no measures for searching out such members, who are not and cannot be reached by the legal provision, and kindly ministering to their comfort? But if there be no class of officers whose appropriate duty it is to make this whole concern an object of their attention, it will too often be neglected, and thus will the interest of Christian charity seriously suffer. It is not a sufficient answer to this argument to say, as those who philosophize on the subject of pauperism say, and, to a certain extent, with great truth, that this very provision would probably invite application, and perhaps, in some instances, induce improper reliance upon it, to the neglect of economy and diligence. Supposing this, in some degree, to be the case; would it not be better to relieve some portion of the poverty brought on by improvidence, than to allow humble, tender piety to pine in secret, unpitied, and unrelieved, under the pressure of that helpless penury, which was induced by the hand of a sovereign God? Nay, is no pity, no active sympathy due from the

Church even to indigence notoriously induced by sin? The considerations which have been suggested, furnish, indeed, a good argument for having Deacons of suitable character; – men of piety, wisdom, benevolence, practical acquaintance with the world, and with human nature, who would be likely to perform their duty with discernment, prudence, and unfeigned Christian charity, cautiously guarding against the evils to which the relief they are commissioned to bear is exposed; but no argument at all against affording such relief when really needed.

  4. It is a great error to suppose that Deacons cannot be appropriately and profitably employed in various other ways besides ministering to the poor of the Church. They might, with great propriety be made the managers of all the money-tables, or fiscal concerns of each congregation; and, for this purpose, might be incorporated, if it were thought necessary, by law, that they might be enabled regularly to hold and employ all the property, real and personal, of the Church. But, even if it were thought inexpedient that boards of Deacons should be allowed thus to supersede the boards of "Trustees," which are, at present, commonly employed to manage each ecclesiastical treasury; still there are very important services in reference to pecuniary concerns, which they might manage, and which, it is believed, would be greatly beneficial to the Church if they were considered as at all times bound to manage, and should actually manage with wisdom, energy, and zeal. I refer to the Church's contribution to the various great objects of Christian enterprise which distinguish the present day. That these contributions to the cause of the Bible; of Missions, foreign and. domestic; of Sabbath Schools; and of the various other Christian and benevolent undertakings for promoting knowledge, virtue, and happiness, temporal and eternal, among men, ought to be continued, and greatly increased, no one who looks into the Bible, or who knows any thing of the Christian spirit, can for a moment doubt. It is quite evident, too, that these contributions ought to be perfectly voluntary, and that any attempt to render them otherwise, would be both unscriptural and mischievous. But would it not tend to render the whole business of liberality to the cause of Christ more

regular, more easy, more abundant, and ultimately more productive, if it were placed under the enlightened advice, and wise management of six or eight Deacons in each Church? Suppose the Pastor and the Elders of every congregation to be animated with a proper spirit on this subject, and to be habitually uttering and diffusing proper sentiments; and suppose the whole business of collecting the contributions, and paying them over to the respective treasuries for which they were destined, were devolved on the Deacons, as an executive board, who might call to their aid, and would really confer, as well as receive a benefit, by calling to their aid, in the details of collection, a number of active, pious sub-agents. Can any one doubt that the contributions of the Churches would be more systematic, more regular, more conveniently received, better proportioned, and a part, at least, and, in some cases, a large part, of the expenses paid to travelling agents, saved for the cause of Christ? The truth is, an enlightened, active, pious board of Deacons might place this whole subject on such a footing, and when they had gotten it fairly arranged, and under way, might manage it in such a manner, as without adding in the least degree to the burdens of the people, would render their contributions more productive, as well as more easy and economical in every part of their management.

With respect to the mode of disposing of the Deacon's office adopted extensively in our sister Churches of Scotland and Ireland,[5] and in a few instances, in this country, namely, laying it on the Ruling Elders, and uniting both offices in the same individual – it is, undoubtedly, liable to very strong objections, as will appear from the following considerations.

1. One office is quite enough to be borne by the same person; especially an office so important, so responsible, so abundantly sufficient to employ the heart, the hands, and the time of the most active and zealous, as that of the Ruling Elder. However pious, wise, and unwearied he may be, he will find the work pertaining to his office as Elder, enough, and more than enough,

---

5. The same mixture of offices has also long existed, it is believed, in the Church of Geneva. See Le Mercier's *Ch. Hist. of Gen.*, p. 214.

especially in this day of enlarged Christian activity, to put in requisition all his powers. Why, then, add another office to one already occupied, if he be faithful, to the utmost extent of his faculties? Similar remarks may be made, to a considerable extent, concerning the Deacon's office. It is enough, when faithfully discharged, to occupy all the leisure time of the most active and faithful incumbent. Both certainly cannot be undertaken by the same individual, without some of the duties pertaining to one or the other being neglected.

2. Where there are suitable candidates for office among the communicants of a Church, it is commonly wise to distribute offices as extensively among them as circumstances will conveniently admit. If, indeed, there be a dearth of proper materials for making ecclesiastical officers, the difficulty must be surmounted in the best way that is practicable. But if there be individuals enough to sustain it, the diffusion of office power among a considerable number, is so far from being an evil, that it is manifestly, and may be highly, advantageous. It brings a greater number to take an interest in the affairs of the Church. It makes a greater number intimately acquainted with the concerns of the Church. And by calling a greater number to pray, and speak and act in behalf of the Church, it tends to promote the spiritual, and, it may be, the everlasting benefit of them and their children. Why, then, heap a plurality of offices upon a single person? It is depriving the Church of a manifest advantage; and may be the means of depriving the individuals themselves of both comfort and edification.

3. If there be not an absolute incompatibility between the offices of Ruling Elder and Deacon, there is at least, such an interference between their respective duties, as is certainly undesirable, and ought by all means to be avoided. There is a collision in this case analogous to that which takes place when a man visits the sick in the double character of a physician and a minister of the Gospel. For although, in many cases, the duties and services of each character may happily harmonize, and help one another; yet, perhaps, in many more, it will appear to the discerning eye that they had better be separated. When an Elder, as such,

goes forth to the discharge of his official duties, it is to promote the spiritual interest of the flock of which he is made one of the "overseers." To this purpose it is important that he should have the most unreserved and confidential access to all the members of the flock, and their children; and that nothing should be allowed to intervene which was adapted to disguise the feelings, to divide the attention, or to clog the operations of either party. But if, when this Elder visits the poor for the sake of benefitting their souls, they receive him with smiles, with apparent cordiality, and with much pious talk, chiefly for the concealed purpose of increasing the allowance which, as Deacon, he may be disposed to minister to them: or, when he visits them as a Deacon, they feel jealous, or alienated, on account of some supposed deficiency in that allowance, and of course, in some measure close their minds against him as their spiritual guide: or, when the mind of the Presbyter-Deacon himself becomes divided and perplexed between the rival claims of these two classes of duties, less good is done; less pure unmingled feeling exercised; and less comfort enjoyed on either side.[6]

On all these accounts, the two offices in question, as they are entirely different in their nature, ought undoubtedly, to be separated in practice, to be discharged by different persons, and to be carefully guarded against that interference which is adapted to render both less useful.

We are led, then, by the foregoing facts and arguments, to the following conclusions:

1. That the Deacon is a divinely instituted officer, and ought to be retained in the Church.

2. That the function to which the Deacon was appointed by the Apostles, was to manage the pecuniary affairs of the Church, and especially to preside over the collections and disbursements for the poor.

3. That Deacons, therefore, ought not only to be men of

---

[6]. See this subject treated in a striking manner, and at considerable length, in Dr. Chalmers' *Christian and Civic Economy of Large Towns*, Vol. i, Chapter vii.

piety, but also of judgment, prudence, knowledge of the world, and weight of character.

4. That preaching was not, in the primitive Church, any part of the Deacon's duty, but came in, among other human innovations, as corruption gained ground.

5. That there is no warrant whatever for assigning to Deacons the function of government in the Church; and that their undertaking any such function, is nothing less than ecclesiastical usurpation.

6. That confounding the office of Deacon with that of Ruling Elder, is all unwarranted confusion, both of names and offices, which are entirely distinct.

7. That even the uniting of these two offices in the same persons, is by no means advisable, and tends materially to impair the comfort and usefulness of both.

8. That Deacons ought to be ordained by the imposition of hands. In this ordination the hands of the Pastor and of the Eldership ought to be laid on. I know not the shadow of a reason why this solemnity should be omitted. The venerable Dr. Dwight, in his *System of Theology*, when treating on the office of Deacons, unequivocally declares his conviction that the laying on of hands ought always to be employed in setting them apart; and pronounces the omission of it to be "incapable, so far as he knows, of any defence." The disregard of scriptural example in the omission, is as painful, as it is obvious and unquestionable.

9. That the Deacons, although they ought always, if possible, to be present at the meetings of the Church Session, for the sake of giving information, and aiding in counsel, can have no vote as Church Rulers; and, therefore, cannot give their vote in the admission or exclusion of members, or in any case of ecclesiastical discipline.

CHAPTER ELEVEN

The Qualifications Proper For This Office

The account which has been given of the nature and duties of the office of Ruling Elder, is adapted to reflect much light on the qualifications by which he who bears it ought to be distinguished. Those who are called to such extensive, interesting, and highly important spiritual duties – duties which enter so deeply into the comfort and edification of the Church of God – it surely requires no formal argument to show, ought to possess a character in some degree corresponding with the sphere in which they are appointed to move. There cannot be a plainer dictate of common sense. Yet to attempt a brief sketch of the more important of the qualifications demanded for this office, may not be altogether unprofitable.

And here, it may be observed, in the outset, that it is by no means necessary that Ruling Elders should be aged persons. For although it cannot be doubted that the title is, literally, expressive of age; and although it is equally certain, that originally, the office was generally conferred on men somewhat advanced in life, as being most likely, other things being equal, to possess wisdom, prudence, experience, and weight of character; yet the term, from a very early period, came to be a mere title of office, without any respect to the years of the individual who bore it. This is evident, not only from the history of Jewish practice, but also from the statements of the New Testament. If Timothy was not merely a Ruling, but also a Teaching Elder, though so young a man, that the Apostle said to him, "let no man despise thy youth;" and if, in every age of the Church, young men have been considered as qualified on the score of age, to be Elders that labour in the word and doctrine, as well as rule; there can be no doubt that young men, if otherwise well qualified, may with propriety be appointed Elders to assist in ruling the Church of God. Nay, where such persons, with other suitable qualifications are to be found, it is expedient to introduce some in younger life into the Eldership of every Church, not only that there may be individuals in the body fitted for more active duties; but also that some of the number may have the kind of official training, and that familiarity with ecclesiastical business, which early experience, and long habit alone can give.

It may be remarked, however, that, although neither Scripture, nor the Constitution of the Presbyterian Church, prescribes any absolute rule with respect to the age of those who may be considered as candidates for the Eldership; yet it is very manifest, that those who are either minors in age, or "novices" in the Christian character and profession, ought by no means, in ordinary circumstances, to be elected to this office. In the Church of Scotland, the rule is, that no one can be chosen an Elder who is not twenty-one years of age. A similar regulation, it is believed, exists in some other foreign Churches; and it may be considered as a dictate of common prudence.

But, though the circumstance of age, as a general rule, does not enter into the essential qualifications of Ruling Elders, there are other qualifications which are highly important, and, indeed, indispensable. These are stated by the inspired Apostle, in writing to Timothy, in the following comprehensive, and pointed language: "An Elder must be blameless, the husband of one wife, having faithful children; one that ruleth well his own house, having his children in subjection with all gravity; not accused of riot, or unruly; not self-willed; not soon angry; not given to wine; no striker; not given to filthy lucre; but a lover of hospitality; a lover of good men; sober, just, holy, temperate, sound in the faith, in charity, in patience." See Timothy iii. compared with Titus i. 6-8, and ii. 2, which passages evidently appear, on tracing the connexion, to be equally applicable to Teaching and Ruling Elders.

The design of appointing persons to the office of Ruling Elder is not to pay them a compliment; not to give them an opportunity of figuring as speakers in judicatories; not to create the pageants of ecclesiastical ceremony; but to secure able, faithful, and truly devoted counsellors and rulers of the Church; to obtain wise and efficient guides, who shall not only go along with the flock in their journey heavenward, but go before them in every thing that pertains to Christian duty.

It cannot be doubted, indeed, that every member of the Christian Church is bound to exhibit a holy, devout, and exemplary life; to have his mind well stored with religious knowledge; to be able to give an answer to every one that asketh a reason of the hope that is in him; and to avoid every thing that is criminal in itself, that may be just cause of offence to his brethren, or that may have even the appearance of evil. But it is equally manifest that all these qualifications are still more important, and required in a still higher degree, in those who are intrusted with the spiritual inspection and regulation of the Church. As they occupy a place of more honour and authority than the other members of the Church; so they also occupy a station of greater responsibility. The eyes of hundreds will be upon them as Elders, which were not upon them as private Christians. Their brethren and sisters over whom they are placed in the Lord, will naturally look up to them for advice, for instruction, for aid in the spiritual life, and for a shining example. The expectation is reasonable, and ought not to be disappointed. The qualifications of Elders, therefore, ought, in some good measure, to correspond with it.

1. An Elder, then, ought, first of all, to be a man of unfeigned and approved piety. It is to be regretted when the piety of any member of the Church is doubtful, or evidently feeble and wavering. It is deplorable when any who name the name of Christ manifest so much indecision in their profession; so much timidity and unsteadiness in their resistance to error and sin; so much conformity to the world; and so little of that undaunted, ardent, and thorough adherence to their professed principles, as to leave it dubious with many, whether they are "on the Lord's

side" or not. But how much more deplorable when any thing of this kind appears in those who are appointed to watch, to preside, and to exert an extensive influence, over a portion of the family of Christ! What is to be expected, when "watchmen on the walls of Zion," – for such Ruling Elders are undoubtedly to be regarded – appear as beacons, to warn private Christians of what ought to be avoided, rather than as models, to guide, to attract, and to cheer them on to all that is spiritual, and holy, and becoming the Gospel?

Can he who is either destitute of piety, or who has but a small portion of it, engage in the arduous and deeply spiritual duties of the Ruling Elder with comfort to himself, or with any reasonable hope of success? It cannot be supposed. To fit ecclesiastical Rulers for acting in their appropriate character, and for performing the work which pertains to it, with cordial diligence, faithfulness, and perseverance, will require cordial and decisive attachment to the service of the Church – minds intent upon the work – hearts filled with love to Jesus, and to the souls of men, and preferring Jerusalem above their chief joy. Unless they are animated with this affectionate interest in their work; unless they are habitually impelled by an enlightened and cordial attachment to the great cause in which they are engaged, they will soon become weary of their arduous and self-denying labours; they will find waiting on the flock, visiting and praying with the sick, instructing the serious and inquiring, correcting the disorderly, watching over the spiritual interests of all, and attending the various judicatories of the Church, an irksome task. But with such a zeal as has been described, they will be ready to contend for the truth, to engage in the most self-denying duties, nay, to "spend and be spent," for Christ. To promote the best interests of Zion will be their "meat and drink." No labours, no trials, no difficulties will move them; neither will they count their lives dear unto themselves, so that they may finish their course with joy, and accomplish the work which they have received of the Lord Jesus. A few such Elders in every Church, would, with the divine blessing, do more to silence infidelity, to strike even the scorner dumb – to promote the triumph of Gospel truth – and to rouse, sustain, and bear forward the cause of vital piety, than hundreds of those Ministers and Elders, who act as if they supposed that supplying the little details of an ecclesiastical formality was the whole purpose of their official appointment. And, in truth, we have no reason to expect, in general, that the piety of the mass of members in any Church will rise much higher than that of their Rulers and Guides. Where the latter are either lifeless formalists, or, at best, but "babes in Christ," we shall rarely find many under their care of more vitality, or of superior stature.

2. Next to piety, it is important that a Ruling Elder be possessed of good sense and sound judgment. Without this he will be wholly unfit to act in the various difficult and delicate cases which may arise in the discharge of his duty. A man of weak and childish mind, however fervent his piety, is by no means adapted to the station of an ecclesiastical Ruler, counsellor, and guide. He who bears the office in question, is called to have intercourse with all classes of people; to engage in the most arduous and trying duties; and to deliberate and decide on some of the most perplexing questions that can come before the human mind. Can it be doubted that good sense, and solid judgment are indispensable to the due discharge of such official work as this? How would a Judge on the bench, or a Magistrate in his office, be likely to get along without this qualification? Much more important is it, if possible, that the ecclesiastical Ruler be enlightened and judicious; because he deliberates and decides on more momentous subjects; and because he has no other than moral power with which to enforce his decisions. Moses, therefore, spoke the language of good sense, as well as of inspired wisdom, when he said to the people of Israel, "Take ye wise men, and understanding, and known among your tribes, and I will make them Rulers over you" (Deut. i. 13). This point, indeed, it would seem, can scarcely be made more plain than common sense makes it; and might, therefore, be considered as foreclosing all illustration, did not some Churches appear posed to make the experiment, how far infinite Wisdom is to be believed, when it pronounces, by the prophet, a woe against those who make choice of babes to rule over them.

3. A Ruling Elder ought to be sound in the faith, and well informed in relation to Gospel truth. The Elder who is not orthodox in his creed, instead of contributing, as he ought, to build up the Church in the knowledge and love of the truth, will, of course, be the means of scattering error, as far as his influence extends. And he who is not well informed on the subject of Christian doctrine, will not know whether he is promoting the one or the other. Accordingly, when this class of officers is ordained in our Church, we call upon them to do what we do not require from the private members of the Church, viz.: solemnly and publicly to adopt the Confession of Faith, "as containing the system of doctrine taught in the Holy Scriptures." When this is considered; and also that they are expected to be, to a certain extent, instructers and guides in Divine things to many of those committed to their oversight; and, above all, that they will be often called to deliberate on charges of heresy, as well as immorality; and to sit in judgment on the doctrinal belief, not only of candidates for admission into the Church as private members; but also on cases of alleged aberration from the truth in ministers of the Gospel; the necessity of their being "sound in the faith," and of their having enlightened and clear views of the system of revealed truth, is too plain to need argument for its support.

The truth is, the Ruling Elder who is active, zealous, and faithful, will have occasion, almost every day, to discriminate between truth and error; to act as a guardian of the Church's orthodoxy; to pass his judgment, either privately or judicially, on real or supposed departures from it; and to instruct the inexperienced and the doubting in the great doctrines of our holy religion. And although all Elders are not expected to be profound theologians, any more than all ministers; yet that the former, as well as the latter, should have a general and accurate acquaintance with the Gospel system, and be ready to defend its leading doctrines, by a ready, pertinent, and conclusive reference to scriptural testimony, and thus be able to "separate between the precious and the vile," in theory as well as in practice, is surely as little as can possibly be demanded of those who are placed as leaders and guides in the house of God.

4. Again; an Elder ought to be a man of eminent prudence. By prudence here is, of course, not meant, that spurious characteristic, which calls itself by this name, but which ought rather to be called timidity, or a criminal shrinking from duty, on the plea that "there is a lion in the way." Yet, while we condemn this as unworthy of a Christian, and especially unworthy of a Christian Counsellor and Ruler; there is a prudence which is genuine, and greatly to be coveted. This is no other than practical Christian wisdom, which not only discerns what is right, but also adopts the best mode of doing it; which is not at all inconsistent with firmness, and the highest moral courage; but which happily regulates and directs it. It has been often observed, that there is a right and a wrong way of doing the best things. The thing done, may be excellent in itself; but may be done in a manner, at a time, and attended with circumstances, which will be likely to disgust and repel, and thus prevent all benefit. Hence a man who is characteristically eccentric, undignified, rash, precipitate, or indiscreetly talkative, ought by no means to be selected as an ecclesiastical ruler. He will, probably, do more mischief than good; will generally create more divisions than he heals; and will rather generate offences than remove them. Perhaps there is no situation in human society which more imperiously calls for delicacy, caution, reserve, and the most vigilant discretion, than that of an ecclesiastical Ruler. If popular rumour begin to charge a Church member with some delinquency, either in faith or practice, let one of the Elders, under the notion of being faithful, implicitly credit the story, go about making inquiries respecting its truth, winking and insinuating, and thus contributing to extend its circulation; and however pure his motives, he may before he is aware, implicate himself in the charge of slander, and become so situated in respect to the supposed culprit, as to render it altogether improper that he should sit in judgment on his case. The maxim of the wise man, "be swift to hear, slow to speak, slow to wrath," applies to every human being; especially to every professing Christian, but above all to every one who is appointed to maintain truth, order, purity, peace, and love in the Church of God.

It requires much prudence to judge when it is proper to commence the exercise of discipline against a supposed offender. Discipline is an important, nay, a vital matter, in the Christian Church. But it may be commenced indiscreetly; vexatiously; when that which is alleged cannot be shown to be an offence against the Divine law; or when, though a really censurable offence, there is no probability that it can be proved. To attempt the exercise of discipline in such cases, is to disgrace it; to convert it, from one of the most important means of grace, into an instrument of rashness, petulance, and childish precipitancy. Often, very often, has the very name of discipline been rendered odious, the peace of families and neighbourhoods grievously disturbed, the influence of ecclesiastical judicatories destroyed, and the cause of religion deeply wounded, by judicial proceedings which ought either never to have been commenced, or to which the smallest measure of prudence would have given a very different direction.

The importance of the subject constrains me to add, that prudence, much prudence is also imperiously demanded, in the exercise of a dignified and cautious reserve while ecclesiastical process is pending. One great reason why it is thought better by Presbyterians to exercise discipline rather by a bench of wise and pious ecclesiastical Senators than by the vote of the whole body of Church members, is, that the public discussion and decision of many things concerning personal character, which the exercise of discipline necessarily discloses, respecting others, as well as the culprit, is adapted in many cases, to do more harm than good, especially before the process is closed. To guard against this evil, it is very important that the Elders carefully avoid all unseasonable disclosures in respect to the business which may be at any time before the Session. Until they have done what shall be deemed proper in a delicate case, it is surely unwise, by thoughtless blabbing, to throw obstacles in their own way, and perhaps to defeat the whole purpose which they have in view. Yet how often, by one imprudent violation of this plain rule, has the discipline of the Church been degraded or frustrated, and the character of those who administered it exposed to ridicule?

These, and similar considerations, serve clearly to show, that no degree of piety can supersede the necessity of prudence in ecclesiastical rulers; and that, of all characters in a congregation, an indiscreet, meddling, garrulous, gossipping, tattling Elder, is one of the most pestiferous.

5. It is important that an Elder be *"of good report of them that are without."* The circumstance of his being chosen to the office by the members of the Church, does, indeed, afford strong presumption that he sustains among them an unexceptionable character. But it is also. of great importance that this class of officers, as well as those who "labour in the word and doctrine," should stand well with those who are without, as well as those who are within the pale of the Christian community. The ecclesiastical ruler may often be called, in discharging his official duties, to converse with the worldly and profane, who have no particular regard either for his Master, or his office. Nay, he must be, almost every day that he lives, the object of the scrutiny of such men. In this case, it is peculiarly desirable that his personal character be such as to command universal respect and confidence; that it be not liable to any particular suspicion or imputation; but that, on the contrary, it possess such weight and respectability in the community, as will render him an aid and a blessing to his ecclesiastical connexion. To this end, his unbending integrity in all the walks of life; his spotless probity and honour in every pecuniary transaction; his gravity and dignity in all the intercourse of society; his exemplary government of his own family; his abstraction from all unhallowed conformity to the world; – ought to present in some good measure, a pattern of Christian consistency. It is saying little in favour of a Church officer, to allege that his reputation is such that he does no harm to the ecclesiastical body with which he is connected. It is to be regretted, if he do not promote its benefit every day by his active services, and extend its influence by the lustre of his example.

6. A Ruling Elder ought to be a *man of public spirit and enlarged views*. He who is called by his official duty to plan and labour for the extension of the Redeemer's kingdom, surely ought not, of all men, to have a narrow and illiberal mind; to be

sparing of labour, parsimonious in feeling and habit, or contented with small attainments. It is eminently desirable, then, that a Ruling Elder be a man of expanded heart toward other denominations, as far as is consistent with entire fidelity to scriptural truth and order; that he aim high in spiritual attainment and progress; that he be willing to give much, to labour much, and to make sacrifices for the cause of Christ; and that he be continually looking and praying for the further enlargement and prosperity of Zion. Such a man will not be willing to see the Church fall asleep, or stagnate. Such a man's mind will be teeming with desires, plans, and prayers for the advancement of the Saviour's cause. Such a man will not content himself; nor be satisfied to see others contenting themselves, with a little round of frigid formalities, or with the interests of a single parish: – but the aspirations of his heart, and the active efforts of his life will be directed to the extension and prosperity of the Church in all its borders, and to the universal establishment and triumph of that Gospel which is "the power of God unto salvation to every one that believeth."

The qualification of which we speak has been, in all ages, and from the nature of the case, must ever be, of inestimable importance in every Ruler and Guide of the Church. But we may venture to pronounce that it never was so important to the Church that she should have such Rulers as it is at the present day. Now, that she is awaking from her slumber, and arousing to a sense of her long forgotten obligations: now that she is, as we hope, arising from the dust, and "putting on her beautiful garments," and looking abroad in the length and breadth of those conquests which have been promised her, by her Almighty Head – now that all her resources, physical and moral, are called for, in every direction, with an emphasis and a solemnity never before equalled – is it not manifest that all who, in such a stage of her course, undertake to be her counsellors and guides, ought to be neither drones nor cowards; neither parsimonious of labour and sacrifice, nor disposed to sit down contented with small acquisitions? Ruling Elders, at the present day, have, perhaps, an opportunity of serving the Church more extensively and effectually than ever before. How desirable and important, then, that they have a heart, in some measure, commensurate with the calls and opportunities of the flay in which their lot is cast! How desirable that they cherish those enlarged and liberal views, both of duty and of effort, which become those who are called to act a conspicuous and interesting part in a cause which is dear to all holy beings! So important is this, that it is probable we shall generally find that, in liberality of contribution to the various objects of Christian effort, and in enlargement of mind to desire and seek the extension of the Redeemer's kingdom, the mass of the members of any Church may commonly be graduated by the character of their Elders. If the leaders and guides of the Church be destitute of public spirit, and be not found taking the lead in large plans, labours, and sacrifices for extending the reign of knowledge, truth, and righteousness; it will be strange indeed if a more enlarged spirit be found prevailing among the generality of their fellow-members.

7. The last qualification on which I shall dwell, as important in the office before us, is ardent zeal, and a spirit of importunate prayer. Large views, and liberal plans and donations, will not answer without this. The truth is, the Church of God has the most serious and unceasing obstacles to encounter, in every step of her progress. As long as she is faithful, her course is never smooth or unobstructed. In maintaining truth; – in guarding the claims of gospel holiness; – and in sustaining discipline – the enmity of the human heart will not fail to manifest itself, and to offer more or less resistance to that which is good. The worldly and profane will ever be found in the ranks of determined opposition. And alas! that some who bear the name of Christ, are not unfrequently found in the same ranks; thus grieving the hearts, and trying the patience of those who are called to act as the representatives and leaders of the Church. To meet and overcome difficulties of this kind, requires all the fixedness of purpose, and all the zeal in the service of Christ, which his most devoted servants can bring to their work.

Besides all this, there is much in the daily duties of the Ruling Elder, which puts to a very serious test all his devotedness to the cause of his Master. He is called to live, like a minister of the Gospel, in the very atmosphere of prayer and religious conversation. In the chamber of the sick and dying; in conversing with the anxious inquirer, and the perplexed or desponding believer; in the private circle, and in the social meeting for prayer; abroad and at home, in the house, and by the way – it must be "his meat and drink" to be found ministering to the best interests of his fellow-men. So that if he have but little zeal; but little taste for prayer; but little anxiety for, the welfare of immortal souls; he will not, he cannot, enter with proper feeling into his appropriate employments. But if he be animated with a proper spirit, he will find it pleasant to be thus employed. Instead of shunning scenes and opportunities of usefulness, he will diligently seek them. And instead of finding them wearisome, he will feel no happiness more pure and rich than that which he experiences in such occupations as these.

It is evident, then, not only that the ecclesiastical Ruler ought to have unfeigned piety; but that his piety ought to be of that decisive character, and accompanied with that fervent zeal, which bears its possessor forward, without weariness in the discharge of self-denying duties. The higher the degree in which he possesses this characteristic, provided it be accompanied with wisdom, prudence, and a knowledge of human nature, the greater will probably be his usefulness in the Church which he serves; and the greater, assuredly, will be his own personal enjoyment in rendering that service.

It is more than possible that this view of the qualifications proper for the office which we are considering, may cause some, when solicited to undertake it, to draw back, under the conscientious impression, that they have not the characteristics which are essential to the faithful discharge of its duties. And it would be wrong to say that there are not some cases, in which such an impression ought to be admitted. There can be no doubt that there are those who bear this office, who ought never to have accepted it. To this class, unquestionably, belong all those who have no taste for the appropriate duties of the office, and who do not resolve sedulously and faithfully to perform them. But let no humble, devoted follower of Jesus Christ, who truly desires to serve and glorify Him, and who is willing, from the heart, to do all that God shall enable him, for the promotion of the Redeemer's kingdom, be deterred, by the representation which has been given, from accepting the office, if called to it by his Christian brethren. The deeper his sense of his own unfitness, the more likely will he be to apply unceasingly and importunately for heavenly aid; and the nearer he lives to the throne of grace, the more largely will he partake of that wisdom and strength which he needs. There are, no doubt, some, as was said, who are really unqualified for this office; but in general, it may be maintained, that those who have the deepest impression of the importance and arduousness of its duties, and of their own want of adequate qualifications, are far better prepared for those duties, than such as advance to the dis charge of them with unwavering confidence and self-complacency

CHAPTER TWELVE

On the Election of Ruling Elders

Under this general head, a variety of questions occurs, the solution of which is important.

I. In the first place, who are the proper electors of Ruling Elders? This question is not definitely resolved by the "Form of Government" of the Presbyterian Church in the United States. Its language is as follows: "Every congregation shall elect persons to the office of Ruling Elder, and to the office of Deacon, or either of them, in the mode most approved and in use in that congregation. But in all cases the persons elected must be male members in full communion in the Church in which they are to exercise their office."

When a new Church is to be organized, and when, of course, there are no Elders already in office, application ought to be made to the Presbytery, stating the wishes of those who contemplate forming the Church, requesting their sanction, and also the appointment of one or more of their number to preside in the election and ordination of the candidates for the respective offices of Elders and Deacons. The person or persons thus appointed by the Presbytery to act in the case, after causing due and regular notice of their appointment and its object, to be given, ought to meet with the members of the congregation; to preach on the subject which occasions the meeting; to explain the nature and importance of the office; and, having done this, to call upon those who may be qualified as electors, to give their votes for such of their number as they would wish to have as their spiritual rulers. Having done this openly, in the face of the congregation, the ordination of the Elders elect, may either take place on the spot, before the assembly shall separate; or may be postponed to a future time, as may be judged most expedient. By this is meant, that the election in this case, being made immediately by a popular vote of the members of the Church, there is no need of postponing the ordination, for the purpose of propounding the names of the persons elected, from the pulpit, as is necessary, and practised in other cases. In the case supposed, the full concurrence of the persons entitled to vote in the choice made, has been already ascertained by their suffrages.

In this choice, the votes may be given either *viva voce,* or by *ballot.* The latter method, however, is by far the most common, and, is evidently, the most proper, for a variety of reasons, some of which will readily occur to every enlightened and delicate mind.

Concerning the persons who are properly entitled to vote in such an election, there has been some diversity of opinion. That all the male members of the Church, in what is called "full communion," have this right, there can be no question. In this all are agreed. But it has been maintained, not, indeed, with the same unanimity, yet, it is believed, by a large majority of the most judicious and enlightened judges, and probably on the most correct principles, that all baptized members of the Church, who must be, of course, regarded as subject to the government and discipline administered by these Rulers, are entitled to a voice in their election. And when there are female heads of families, who bear the relation of membership to the Church, in either of the senses just mentioned, and who are not represented by some qualified male relative, on the occasion, it has been judged proper to allow them to vote in the choice of Ruling Elders, as is generally the case in the choice of a Pastor.

There seems, however, to be some good reason for restricting the right to vote for Ruling Elders within narrower bounds, than are commonly assigned in the choice of a Pastor. In that choice, in most congregations, all pew-holders, and all stated worshippers who are stated contributors to the support of the Pastor, in their just proportion, whether baptized or not, whether willing to submit to the exercise of discipline or not, and whether of fair moral character or not, are considered as entitled to a vote. But, in the election of a Pastor, there is one security against an improper choice, which does not exist in the case of a Ruling Elder; namely, that the call must be submitted to the Presbytery, and receive the sanction of that body before it can be prosecuted; whereas no such security exists in the case of a Ruling Elder. Of course, if all pew-holders, and pecuniary supporters, without any reference to membership or character, were allowed to vote in the election of the latter class of officers, they might choose persons to the last degree unsuitable for the office, and adapted to destroy rather than benefit the Church. Besides; every one, however heterodox or immoral, may be a stated attendant on public worship: and every stated attendant on the worship of any Church may be said to have an interest in the character of the Pastor, and a right, as far as may be, to be pleased in the choice. But no one can be said to have any part, or particular interest in the discipline of the Church, excepting those who are subject to its operation; which can be the case with none but those who are members of the Church.

Accordingly, the General Assembly of the Church which met in 1829, in answer to a question solemnly referred to it by one of the Western Presbyteries,[1] adopted and sent to the Churches the following judgment in relation to the subject before us: "It is the opinion of this General Assembly, that the office of Ruling Elder is an office in the Church of Christ; that Ruling Elders, as such, according to our Confession of Faith, Book i., on Government, Chapter v., are the representatives of the people, by whom they are chosen, for the purpose of exercising government and discipline in the kingdom of our Lord Jesus Christ; that the discipline lawfully exercised by them, is the discipline exercised through them by their constituents, in whose name, and by whose

---

1. The question submitted was in these words:– "Ought an unbaptized person, who yet pays his proportion for the support of a congregation, to be permitted to vote for Ruling Elders?"

authority they act in all that they do.[2] To suppose, therefore, that an unbaptized person, not belonging to the visible kingdom of the Redeemer, might vote at the election of Ruling Elders, would be to establish the principle, that the children of this world might, through their representatives, exercise discipline in the Church of God; which is manifestly unscriptural, and contrary to the standards of our Church. Resolved, therefore, that the question in the said overture be answered in the negative."

Where there is already an existing Church Session, and the object is to add to the number of its members, in this case the election of the new Elders may be made in any one of several methods: either by the vote of the members of the Church at large, as already stated; or by a nomination on the part of the existing Elders, proposed to the Church, and considered as their choice, if not objected to; or by the nomination of double the number proposed to be chosen, by the Session, and a choice by the members of the Church out of the list so nominated.

In the Church of Scotland, "new Elders are chosen by the voice of the Session.[3] After their election has been agreed upon, their names are read from the pulpit, in a paper called an Edict, appointing a day, at the distance of not less than ten days, for their ordination. If no member of the congregation offer any objection upon that day; or if the Session find the objections that

---

[2] It is well known that the General Assembly, in this clause of their judgment, did not mean to deny that Ruling Elders, in the rightful discharge of their duties, act in the name and by the authority of Christ. This great truth is plainly recognized in a preceding clause; but merely to say, that they act as the representatives, and on the behalf of the members of the Church at large; so that when a complaint is brought to the Eldership, it is, strictly speaking, according to ancient language, "telling it to the Church."

[3] In the infancy of the Reformed Church in Scotland, the mode of electing Ruling Elders was by no means uniform. In some Churches, the existing Session made a nomination to the Church members, out of which a choice was made by the latter. In other Churches, the choice was made immediately by the communicants at large. In some Churches, the Session appointed electors; and in others they acted as electors themselves. It was a number of years before the practice stated above as the prevalent one, became general. M'Crie's *Life of Melville*, ii. 477, 478.

are offered frivolous, or unsupported by evidence, the minister proceeds in the face of the congregation, to ordain the new Elders.[4]

The same method of adding new Elders to existing Church Sessions, is adopted, in substance, by many Presbyterian Churches in the United States. The Church Sessions, in these congregations, judge when it is proper to make an addition to the number of Elders;[5] deliberate on the proper candidates; ascertain privately whether they will serve if appointed; and after completing, with due consideration and care, their lists, cause them to be announced by their moderator, from the pulpit, on several successive Sabbaths; after which, at the proper time, their ordination takes place. This plan of choosing has some real advantages. When wisely executed, it may be supposed likely to lead to a more calm, judicious, and happy choice, than would probably result from a popular vote, especially where no consultation and understanding had taken place among the more grave, pious, and prudent of the Church members. And, therefore, where this plan has been long in use, and unanimously acquiesced in, it had, perhaps, better not be changed. Yet it seems to be more in harmony with the general spirit of Presbyterian Church government, and certainly with the prevailing character of our institutions, to refer the choice, where it can conveniently be done, after due consultation and care, to the suffrages of the members of the Church.

Accordingly, the General Assembly of our Church, which convened in 1827, in reply to a complaint made respecting the mode of electing Elders adopted in one of the Churches under the care of the Presbytery of Philadelphia, pronounced the following judgment:

---

4. Hill's *Institutes*, Part ii. Section 4th, 212, 213.

5. It is hardly necessary to say, that when the Church Session, in any such congregation shall be considered as unduly delaying to make a suitable addition of new Elders to their number, it is the privilege of the members of the Church, after due application and remonstrance to the Session, without effect, to apply to the Presbytery for the redress of their alleged grievance.

"While the Assembly would recognize the undoubted right of each congregation to elect their Elders in the mode most approved and in use among them, they would recommend that, in all cases where any dissatisfaction appears to exist, the congregation be promptly convened, to decide on their future mode of election. And they are inclined to believe that the spirit of our constitution would be most fully sustained by having, in all cases, a direct vote of the congregation in the appointment of their Elders."

In the Church of Holland, the following is the general rule in regard to the election of this class of officers: "The Elders shall be chosen by the suffrages of the Consistory, and of the Deacons. In making this choice, it shall be lawful, as shall best suit the situation of each Church, either to nominate as many Elders as shall be judged necessary for the approbation of the members in full communion, and upon their being approved, and found acceptable, to confirm them with public prayers and engagements; or, to propose a double number, that the one half of those nominated may be chosen by the members, and in the same manner confirmed in their office." Accordingly, in that country, although an election by the members of the Church sometimes takes place, yet the common method, it is believed, is for the Consistory, or Eldership of the Church, together with the Deacons, to make choice of new Elders and Deacons; in other words, to form a list of proper candidates for the office, to nominate them, agreeably to a certain rule, to the Church, and if no objection be made, to consider the person so nominated as the choice of the Church.

In the "Explanatory Articles" of government adopted by the Reformed Dutch Church in the United States, the following article explains the practice of that Church in this country: "The manner of choosing Elders and Deacons is not rigidly defined. A double number may be nominated by the Consistory, out of which the members of the Church may choose those who shall serve. Or, all the members of the Church may unite in nominating and choosing the whole number, without the interference of the Consistory. Or, the Consistory, for the time being, as representing all the members, may choose the whole, and refer the persons thus chosen, by publishing them in the Church, for the approbation of the people. The last method has been found most convenient, especially in large Churches, and has long been generally adopted. But where that, or either of the other modes, has for many years been followed in any Church, there shall be no variation or change, but by previous application to the Classis, and express leave first obtained for altering such custom."[6]

In the Church of Geneva, the choice of Elders and Deacons is made in the manner which the foregoing article declares to be most common in the Dutch Church in the United States, namely, by a selection and nomination by the consistorial assembly, which, if not opposed, is final, and followed by the usual ordination, without the "laying on of hands."[7]

The same method, also, of electing Elders and Deacons was early established in the Protestant Churches of France. The Consistory nominated, and the nomination was announced from the pulpit, for the approbation of the people.[8]

II. The next question which arises, is how often ought this election to be made? Is it for life, or for a limited time?

According to the original constitution of the Reformed Church of Scotland, the Elders and Deacons were chosen but for one year. This was the arrangement adopted in the "First Book of Discipline," formed in 1560, and also in the "Second Book of Discipline," drawn up in 1578, and which continued for a number of years in the Scottish Church. This plan seems to have been suggested by the earnest wish of the first elders themselves, who, finding the office burdensome, as it then involved much care and labour, begged permission to resign it to others after a single year. But although the election, at that time, was made annually, and a large portion of the incumbents of the office were actually changed every year; yet the same men might be elected from year to year, if they were willing to serve, and it sometimes happened

---

6. See the Constitution of the Reformed Dutch Church in the United States.

7. See Mercier's *Church History of Geneva*, p. 209. Quick's *Synodicon*, i. 27.

8. Quick's *Synodicon*, i. 27.

in fact, that a few, whose piety, and leisure rendered due attention to the duties of the office easy and pleasant, were re-elected for many successive years. The same form of ordination seems to have been repeated after every annual election, as well with respect to those who had often been ordained before, as to those who had never submitted to this solemnity.

This practice, however, has been long since laid aside in the Church of Scotland; and the office of the Ruling Elder been, for many years, regarded as an office for life, as much as that of the ministry of the Gospel.

In the Protestant Churches of France also, the office in question was, from the beginning, and it is believed still is, temporary. The rule on this subject, found in the Book of "Discipline of the Reformed Churches of France," as drawn up by the first National Synod, in 1559, is in these remarkable words: "The office of Elders and Deacons, as it is now in use among us, is not perpetual; yet because changes are not commodious, they shall be exhorted to continue in their offices as long as they can; and they shall not lay them down without having first obtained leave from their Churches."[9]

The Reformed Dutch Church in the United States, after the example of her parent Church in Europe, adopts the following plan for the election of Elders and Deacons: "In order to lessen the burden or a perpetual attendance upon ecclesiastical duties, and by a rotation in office to bring forward deserving members, it is the established custom in the Reformed Dutch Church, that Elders and Deacons remain only two years in service, after which they retire from their respective offices, and others are chosen in their places; the rotation being always conducted in such a manner, that only one half of the whole number retire each year (See Syn. Dord. Art. 27). But this does not forbid the liberty of immediately choosing the same persons again, if from any circumstances it may be judged expedient to continue them in office by a re-election."[10]

---

9. Quick's *Synodicon*, p. 28.
10. Constitution of the Reformed Dutch Church in the United States.

Yet, notwithstanding this annual election, those who have ever borne the office of Elder or Deacon in the Dutch Church, are still considered, though never re-elected, as bearing, while they live, a certain relation to the offices which they have sustained respectively. This appears from the following additional article, found in the same code: "When matters of peculiar importance occur, particularly in calling a Minister, building of Churches, or whatever relates immediately to the peace and welfare of the whole congregation, it is usual (and it is strongly recommended, upon such occasions, always) for the Consistory to call together all those who have ever served as Elders or Deacons, that by their advice and counsel they may assist the members of the Consistory. These, when assembled, constitute what is called the 'Great Consistory.' From the object or design of their assembling, the respective powers of each are easily ascertained. Those who are out of office, have only an advisory or couselling voice; and, as they are not actual members of the board or corporation, cannot have a decisive vote. After obtaining their advice, it rests with the members of the Consistory to follow the counsel given them, or not, as they shall judge proper."

But in the Presbyterian Church in the United States, the office of Ruling Elder is now, and has been from the beginning, perpetual. The election to it, is once for all. It, of course, continues through life, unless the individual be deposed from office. Like a minister of the Gospel, he cannot lay aside his office at pleasure.[11] He may, indeed, from ill health, or for other reasons,

---

11. The writer is here stating what is the actual constitution of the Presbyterian Church as to this point. He does not suppose, however, that there is any infringement of Presbyterian principle in the annual elections of Ruling Elders, formerly practised in the Church of Scotland, and still practised in the Dutch and French Churches. Where a Church is large, containing a sufficient number of grave, pious and prudent members, to furnish an advantageous rotation and where the duties of the office are many and arduous, it may not be without its advantages to keep up some change of incumbency in this office. But, in general, it seems manifest, that the spiritual interests of a congregation will be likely to be managed most steadily and to edification by per-

cease, if he think proper, to perform the active duties of the office. But he is still an Elder; and if he recover his health, or the reason which induced him to withdraw be removed, he may resume the duties of the office without a new ordination. Of this, however, more in a subsequent chapter.

III. A third question which arises under this head, is – How many Elders ought to be elected in each Church? In answer to this question little more than considerations of expediency can be suggested. No absolute rule can be laid down.

In the Jewish Synagogue, we are told, there were commonly at least three Ruling Elders found in each ecclesiastical Senate. In the time of Cyprian, in the third century, there were, in the single Church of Carthage, of which he was Bishop, or Pastor, eight Elders, of whom five were opposed to his being received as their Pastor. Soon after the opening of the Reformation in Scotland, and while there was only a single Protestant congregation in the city of Edinburgh, there were twelve Elders, and sixteen Deacons, belonging to that Church.[12] In the year 1560, four years before the decease of Calvin, there were twelve Ruling Elders in the Church of Geneva.[13]

The Form of Government of the Presbyterian Church in the United States, does not define the proper number of Elders in each Church. Speaking of the Church Session, it declares (Chapter 9. Sect. 2.) that of this Judicatory, "two Elders, if there be as many in the congregation, with the Pastor, shall be necessary to constitute a quorum." From this rule, it seems to be a legitimate inference, that if there be only one Elder in the congregation, he with the Pastor, may constitute a regular Session, for the transaction of business. The existence of so small a number as even two, however, is greatly to be regretted, and ought by no means to be submitted to, if proper candidates for the office can be found. In

---

manent officers, who are never even temporarily withdrawn from the sphere of duty in which they move, and who are daily gaining more knowledge of the Church, and more experience.

12. Dunlop, ii., 638.

13. Calv. Epist. Gaspari Olivetano.

the smallest Church it is desirable that there should be at least from five to seven Elders. Without some such number, there cannot be that weight in their judicial counsels, and that influence drawn from every part of the congregation in aid of the Pastor, and the best interests of the whole body, which a well selected bench of officers of that number, would be likely to impart. In large Churches, there ought to be at least ten or twelve: and in Churches much beyond the usual size, fourteen or fifteen would not be more than enough to gain all the advantages which the best arrangement with regard to this office might be expected to secure.

It ought to be borne in mind, however, that there is no advantage whatever to be gained by electing unsuitable men to this office, for the sake of adding mere numbers to the Church Session. It is much better to get along with three or four pious, wise and prudent Elders, than to add two or three dozens to their ranks of men of an opposite stamp, who, by their want of piety and wisdom, might be a nuisance instead of a comfort: a curse instead of a blessing. Pastors, then, and their Churches, instead of making haste to fill up the ranks of their congregational Senators with unsuitable members, had better wait patiently until the Head of the Church shall provide for them candidates in some measure "after his own heart."

IV. The last question which will be proposed for solution is, who may be considered as eligible to this office?

The proper personal qualifications for this office have been considered in a preceding chapter. These are not intended to be brought into view here. All that is designed is, a reference to two or three points of legal qualification which are necessary to render a candidate eligible in the view of the ecclesiastical casuist.

And first, no one can be elected an Elder in any Church, who is not a member in full communion in the Church of which he is to be chosen an officer. The extreme impropriety of choosing men who were not themselves in full communion with the body of Christ to represent the members of the Church, and to sit in judgment on the standing, deportment, and Church membership of others, is so glaring as to need no comment.

But the eligible candidate for this choice must be a male member. Some, indeed, have seriously doubted whether there were not in the apostolic Church, female Elders, or Elderesses; and also whether there ought not to be a similar class of Elders in every Church at the present day. A great majority, however, who have treated of this subject, believe, that the female officers apparently referred to in Titus ii. 3, and a few other passages in the New Testament, were intended to be merely a temporary appointment, arising out of that state of seclusion in which females lived, and do still live, in the Eastern world, and not at all necessary in those countries where females may be approached and instructed without the intervention of individuals of the other sex. The Presbyterian Church has judged and acted in conformity with this view of the subject.[14]

It has been queried, whether a person who is an acting Ruling Elder in one Church, may be chosen to the same office in another, and thus be an acting member of two Church Sessions at the same time. This question ought, undoubtedly, to be answered in the negative. An Elder can no more be a member of two different Sessions, and responsible, of course, to both, at the same time, than a private Christian can be enrolled as a member of two different Churches at the same time, and equally amenable to both; or than a minister of the Gospel can be a member of two Presbyteries, at the same time, and liable to be called to an account by both, simultaneously, and to have entirely inconsistent requisitions made by each. An Elder in one Church, then, is not eligible to the Eldership in another, unless on the principle of his taking a dismission from the former, for the purpose of forming a regular and official relation to the latter.

---

14. The Moravians, or United Brethren, and the society of Friends, or Quakers, are the only ecclesiastical bodies in Protestant Christendom, so far as is now recollected, in whose system of Church order Female Elders actually have a place.

CHAPTER THIRTEEN

Of the Ordination of Ruling Elders

By Ordination is meant that solemn rite, or act, by which a candidate for any office in the Church of Christ is authoritatively designated to that office, by those who are clothed with power for the purpose.

It cannot require formal argument to prove, that this rite, or something analogous and equivalent to it, is indispensable in conducting all regular ecclesiastical government. If certain officers have been appointed in the Church by Jesus Christ, her King and Head; – if certain qualifications have been declared by Him indispensable to fit men for serving the Church in these offices, without which they ought not to be permitted to occupy them and if an extraordinary and immediate designation to office by Jesus Christ Himself, be not now to be expected in any case; – if these things be so, it inevitably follows, that some person or persons must have power committed to them by the Head of the Church, to examine or try candidates for these offices; to judge of their qualifications; and if approved to invest them with office. The idea that, with such directions as the New Testament contains on this subject, men should be left at liberty to take these offices upon themselves, by their own act, and at their own pleasure, is full of absurdity; and, if realized, would undoubtedly lead to endless disorder and mischief. Only suppose the secular offices of a nation to be thus assumed by men at will; and by none more readily than the vain, the ignorant, the self-sufficient, and the ambitious; – as would inevitably be the case, if such were the path of access to office; – and there would be an end of all order. But if it be neither safe nor permitted for men to intrude into official stations uncalled; and if an immediate investiture by the Master Himself be out of the question; we are driven to the conclusion, that all regular and lawful introduction to office, must be through the medium of human ordainers, acting in the name of Christ, and governing themselves by His declared will.

Accordingly, while the Saviour Himself, in the days of His flesh, immediately invested with office the twelve Apostles, and all others whom He personally called and sent forth; no sooner had He ascended to heaven, than the practice of introducing to office by the instrumentality of men, began, and, so far as we are informed, was uniformly continued. Then the ministers of Christ began to act upon the principle afterwards so explicitly communicated to Timothy, and enjoined upon him: "That which thou hast heard of me, among many witnesses, the same commit thou to faithful men, who shall be able to teach others also." Here we are plainly taught that men are not to seize upon the sacred office themselves. It is to be "committed to them;" and that not by every one; but by those only who have regularly "received" it themselves. We find, too, that the method of ordination which had been in use in the Jewish Synagogue, and to which all the first Christians had been accustomed, was transferred to the Church, and became a stated part of ecclesiastical order. Paul and Barnabas were set apart to a particular service, by a plurality of ecclesiastical men, with prayer, imposition of hands, and fasting. When they, in their turn, went forth to execute the work to which they had been called, we find them, wherever they went, "ordaining Elders," and committing to them the care of the Church. Timothy was invested with office "by the laying on of the hands of the Presbytery;" and even the Deacons, were called to their office in the same manner. It was referred to the people to "look out" and elect the candidates; but having done so, they brought them to the Apostles, who "laid their hands upon them," and conferred on them the important office to which they were appointed.

It is no part of the belief of Presbyterians, that Ordination imparts any direct influence, either physical or moral, to him who receives it. They have no idea that, in this act, by a kind of *opus operatum*, according to the Romanists, an "indelible character" is communicated. They do not suppose that any hallowed energy proceeds from the hands of the ordainers to him on whose head they lay them, in the act of imposition. But they regard it simply as that official act by which a man is pronounced, declared, and manifested, to be actually put in possession of the office to which he has been chosen. It is, in one word, the actual induction into office of one elected to fill it. The case is precisely analogous to that of civil rulers. The man who is appointed to the office of Judge on a secular bench, has no real addition made either to his intellect, his learning, or his moral excellence, by taking the oath of office, and complying with those formalities which actually introduce him to his official station; and yet, so important are these formalities, that his power lawfully to act as Judge absolutely depends upon them. Before they take place, he is not really in office; and after they take place, he is clothed with that plenary power, which qualifies him for the regular discharge of every official duty. And so of every other civil officer in the land. Thus it is in the Church. Ordination is the essence of a lawful external call to ecclesiastical office. It is that act, before which, the ecclesiastical officer is not prepared, regularly, to discharge a single function appropriated to the station to which he is elected; but after which, he is prepared for their regular and valid performance.

That Ruling Elders, besides being regularly chosen to office, should be ordained; that is, publicly and solemnly designated and introduced to office by appropriate formalities; our ecclesiastical Constitution requires, and prescribes a Form for the purpose, concerning which I shall only say, that, as far as it goes, it is well devised, impressive, and excellent. I say, as far as it goes; for it has been, for many years, my settled conviction, that the Ordination service in question, in not making the imposition of hands a stated constituent part of it, is chargeable with an omission, which, though not essential, and, therefore, not a matter for which it is proper to interrupt the peace of the Church, yet appears to me incapable of a satisfactory defence; and which it is my earnest hope may not much longer continue to be, as I know it is with many, matter of serious lamentation.

The "imposition of hands," as a constituent part of Ordination, is an old and impressive rite. It was, notoriously, a familiar mode of designation to office through the whole of the Old Testament economy. It is, if I mistake not, universally acknowledged to have been employed in ordaining all the Elders of the Jewish Synagogue. We find it is used in every Ordination, without exception, the particulars of which are detailed in the New Testament history. And even in setting apart the Deacons, nothing can be more explicit than the statement, that it was done with the "imposition of hands." So far, then, as we are bound to reverence and follow ancient, primitive, and uniform usage, I know of no solid reason why it should be omitted in any case.

Some, indeed, have attempted to defend the omission of this rite, by alleging, that the imposition of hands, in the days of the Apostles, was connected with the supernatural gifts of the Holy Spirit, which were then common; and that with those special gifts, it ought to have ceased. In support of this allegation, they commonly adduce such passages as those recorded in Acts viii. 17, 18; xix. 6; Heb. vi. 2, &c. This argument, however, if it has any force, ought to banish the imposition of hands from all ordinations; but can never justify the omission of it in ordaining Ruling Elders and Deacons, while it is retained in the ordination of those who "labour in the word and doctrine." But the validity of the whole argument, it is believed, may be set aside without difficulty.

We read in the New Testament of four cases, or kinds of "laying on of hands." The first, by Christ Himself, to express an authoritative benediction (Matt. xix. 15; Mark x. 16); the second, in the healing of diseases (Mark xvi. 18; Acts xxviii. 8); the third, in conferring extraordinary gifts of the Spirit (Acts vii. 17; xix. 6); and the fourth, in setting apart persons to sacred office (Acts vi. 6; xiii. 3; 1 Tim. iv. 14). The venerable Dr. Owen, in his commentary on Heb. vi. 2, expresses the opinion, that the "laying on of hands," mentioned in that passage, is to be considered as belonging to the third kind or class of cases, and, of course, as referring to the extraordinary gifts of the Holy Spirit. Others have supposed, that it rather belongs to the fourth example here enumerated, and, therefore, applies to the ordination of ministers. On this point I decide nothing. But my reasons for supposing that the imposition of hands in the ordination of Church Officers, had no reference to the imparting of supernatural gifts, and consequently, ought not to be deemed an extraordinary and temporary rite, are such as these: 1. This rite has been employed in all ages of the Church in setting apart persons to ecclesiastical office. 2. It is one of the most natural and significant modes of designating a person who is intended to be consecrated or devoted to a particular service. 3. It was manifestly employed in a number of cases which occur in the sacred history, where no special gifts were intended to be conveyed; and therefore, though sometimes connected with those gifts, yet we are sure it was not in all cases thus connected.[1] 4. When hands were laid on Paul and Barnabas, at Antioch, it was not that they might receive these gifts, for they were possessed of them prior to this solemnity. 5. In this case, too, it is remarkable that they seem to have been ordinary pastors and teachers who laid their hands upon one, at least, of extraordinary gifts and character. 6. And, finally, in 1 Tim. v. 22, the whole rite of ordination seems to be comprehended in this act: "Lay hands suddenly on no man," &c. And if we consider the act of laying hands on the head of the candidate for sacred office, as intended, at once, solemnly to designate his person; to express an official benediction; and to indicate his entire consecration to the service of God; we could scarcely conceive of an act more sim-

---

1. "Imposition of hands was a Jewish ceremony, introduced, not by any Divine authority, but by custom; it being the practice among those people, whenever they prayed to God for any person, to lay their hands upon his head. Our Saviour observed the same custom, both when he conferred his blessings on children, and when he healed the sick, adding prayers to the ceremony. The Apostles likewise laid hands on those upon whom they bestowed the Holy Ghost. The priests observed the same custom when any one was received into their body. And the Apostles themselves underwent the imposition of hands afresh, when they entered upon any new design. In the ancient Church, imposition of hands was even practised on persons when they were married; which custom the Abyssinians still observe." – Burder's *Oriental Customs*, ii. 25.

ple, and yet more appropriate, and full of meaning. And although those who lay on hands in this transaction altogether disclaim, as was before stated, the power of conveying the Holy Ghost to the individual ordained; yet as an emblem of what he needs, and ought unceasingly to seek, and of what his brethren desire and pray for on his behalf, it is, surely, in a high degree expressive, and by no means open to the charge of either presumption or superstition. I would say, therefore, concerning this part of the solemnity of ordination, in the language of the venerable Calvin: "Although there is no express precept for the imposition of hands; yet since we find it to have been constantly used by the Apostles, such a punctual observance of it by them ought to have the force of precept with us. And certainly this ceremony is highly useful both to recommend to the people the dignity of the ministry, and to admonish the person ordained, that he is no longer his own master, but devoted to the service of God and the Church. Besides, it will not be an unmeaning sign. For if the Spirit of God institute nothing in the Church in vain, we shall perceive that this ceremony, which proceeded from Him, is not without its use, provided it be not perverted by a superstitious abuse."[2]

But if this rite be so reasonable, so scriptural, so expressive, and so generally adopted by almost all Christian denominations, in ordaining those Elders who "labour in the word and doctrine;" how comes it to pass that it should be so generally, not to say universally, omitted in the ordination of Ruling Elders? I have long deplored this omission;[3] and cannot help believing that

---

2. *Institutes*, Lib. iv, Cap. iii. 16.

3. Many years ago, the author of this volume, under the deep and unwavering conviction that he had scriptural authority to sustain him, when called upon to ordain Elders and Deacons in a vacant Church, added to the usual solemnity on such occasions, the act of "laying on of hands" in the ordaining prayer. Finding, however, that many of his brethren considered it as an innovation, and were by no means prepared to introduce the practice; believing that diversity of practice in relation to this matter would be very undesirable; and persuaded, moreover, that the act in question ought not to be deemed an essential in any ordination, he resolved not to repeat it, until it could be used

the restoration of so appropriate and impressive a part of the ordaining service would, in all probability, be attended with beneficial effects.

It is not easy to ascertain the origin of the omission in question. The apostolic office of Ruling Elder was preserved, as we have seen, by the witnesses of the truth, during the dark ages. Whether the pious Waldenses and Bohemian Brethren were in the habit of setting apart this class of officers with the imposition of hands, cannot now, so far as I know, be determined. The Reformers received the office under consideration from those pious Waldenses; and were well aware, as their writings evince, that all ordinations in the Synagogue, and in the primitive Church, had been accompanied with the laying on of hands. Still, however, while they with one accord, retained this rite in the ordination of Teaching Elders, they seem, quite as unanimously, to have discarded it in the ordination of Ruling Elders.[4] Of the cause of this, their writings give us no intimation; nor has it ever been my lot to hear, from any quarter, a single reason for the omission, which was in the least degree satisfactory. To be told, that the omission has "long been established;" that, while all the Protestant Churches in the world, except that of England, receive this class of officers, in one form or another, they are "no where ordained by the imposition of hands;" that this is "the custom of the Church;" that to depart from it would be "to innovate" and "give offence," &c., that this rite "may be omitted without injury, not being an essential part of ordination," &c. – is surely little adapted to satisfy an inquiring mind, desirous of receiving, as well as of being able to give a reason for every practice.

---

without offence, and with better prospects of edification to the Church.

4. It is worthy of remark that our Independent brethren, at early periods of their history, adhered more closely to the scriptural method of ordaining Ruling Elders and Deacons, than even Presbyterians. See the Cambridge Platform, chapters vii. and ix. See also a Confession of Faith, adopted by some Anti-pædobaptists (to the amount of 100 congregations), in England and Wales, in 1689; and ratified and adopted by a Baptist Association met at Philadelphia, in 1742; chapter 27. Also a "Short Treatise on Church Discipline," appended to it by the latter. Chapters 3 and 4.

But although, as has been already said, no reason is formally assigned, or even hinted, in the writings of the Reformers, for laying aside the imposition of hands in the ordination of Ruling Elders; it is not, perhaps, difficult to conjecture how it happened. One mistake, I suspect, naturally led to another. They began by considering the office as a temporary one; or, rather allowing those who bore it, if they saw fit, to decline sustaining it for more than a single year. There was a new election of these Elders annually. The same individuals, indeed, if they were acceptable to the people, and were willing to continue to serve the Church, might be re-elected for a series of years, or, if they consented, even for life. But this seldom occurred. There was, for the most part, annually, a considerable change in the individuals, and, annually, a new ordination. The tenure of the office being thus temporary, and, in many cases, but for a single year; no wonder that there should seem to the discerning and pious men who took the lead in organizing the Reformed Churches, some incongruity between this annual renewal of the official investiture and obligation, and setting apart men to the office in question, each time, with the very same formalities which attended the ordination of ministers of the Gospel, whose tenure of office was for life. This incongruity, it is probable, struck them with so much force, that they could not reconcile it with their feelings to set apart to their office, these temporary incumbents, with the same rites and solemnity which they employed in ordaining ministers of the Word and Sacraments.[5] Nor is it matter of wonder that such feelings should have had an influence on their minds. Those who take such a view or the tenure of the office in question as they did, will never be very cordial or decisive either in addressing those who bear it, or in setting them apart, as men consecrated for life to the service of the Church. But that in the

---

5. This representation is not wholly gratuitous. It appears from the *Compendium Theologim Christianae* of Marek, and from the opinion of Frederick Spanheim, quoted with approbation by De Moor, the Commentator on Marck, that all three of these divines of the Reformed Church had no other objection to the laying on of hands in the ordination of Ruling Elders, than that which I have suggested. – De Moori, *Com. Perpet.* Vol. vi. p. 330.

Church of Scotland,[6] and in the Presbyterian Church in this country; where, it is believed, correct views of the office of Ruling Elder, as perpetual, are universally received, the scriptural mode of setting apart to this office should have been so long and so generally disused, is a fact for which it is not easy to assign a satisfactory reason.

We are now prepared to take a brief survey of the arguments by which the propriety of ordaining Elders by the imposition of hands may be maintained. They are such as the following:

1. We find, throughout the whole Jewish history, that solemnly laying the hands on the head of a person who was intended to be particularly honoured, blessed, or devoted to sacred functions, was a rite of frequent, not to say constant, use; and even in cases in which the conveyance of the miraculous gifts of the Holy Spirit could not possibly have been designed.

2. The inspired Apostles, in organizing the New Testament Church, took as their model the Synagogue system of government, to which the first Christians had been all their lives accustomed.

3. It is certain that in every Jewish Synagogue there was a bench of Ruling Elders; and it is just as certain that these Elders were always ordained by the imposition of hands.

4. There is not a single instance of an ordination, to any ecclesiastical office whatever, of which we have any account in the New Testament, in which the ceremony of the laying on of hands does not appear to have been used.

5. The first Deacons, though not intrusted with an office so purely spiritual, or so arduous, as that of Ruling Elder, were yet, as all acknowledge, set apart to the Diaconate by the imposition of hands. Of course, those who bear a superior office ought not to be introduced to it with less solemnity.

6. To imagine that there is any peculiar meaning or mysti-

---

6. At what period in the history of the Church of Scotland it was that the annual election of Elders was laid aside, and the office made permanent, it has not fallen in the author's way to obtain information. He is disposed to believe, however, that the change took place either late in the sixteenth, or early in the seventeenth century.

cal influence in the laying on of hands, which is above the dignity of the Ruling Elder's office, involves, at once, a superstitious estimate of a simple, emblematical act, and an unworthy degradation of an important order in the Christian family.

Accordingly, it is observable, that almost all classes of writers whose judgment in reference to this matter is worthy of particular notice, freely concede the propriety of setting apart both Ruling Elders and Deacons in the manner for which I contend; and scarcely offer any other reason for omitting it, than that such has been "long the custom" of the Reformed Churches, and that the ceremony is not "essential" to a valid ordination. The following specimen of the manner in which the subject is treated by such writers, will be quite sufficient to establish my position.

The very learned authors of the *Theses Leydenses,* who were zealous Presbyterians, in speaking of the biennial election of Ruling Elders and Deacons, in the Church of Holland, acknowledge that, in the Apostolic Church, those offices were both perpetual, and concede that the different plan adopted among themselves was an imperfection;[7] plainly intimating, that their mode of ordaining these officers had grown out of this imperfection.

The foreign Protestants, who established themselves in London, during the reign of Edward the sixth, not only had Ruling Elders and Deacons in all their Churches; but also uniformly ordained them by the imposition of hands, as we have seen in the preceding chapter.

The Rev. John Anderson, of Scotland, the able and zealous defender of Presbyterianism against Rhind, who lived a little more than a century ago, speaking of the ordination of Ruling Elders by the imposition of hands, has the following passage: "Nobody doubts it is very lawful; and, for my own part, I heartily wish it were practised; but I deny that it is absolutely necessary, there being no precept enjoining it."[8]

The Rev. Archibald Hall, also of Great Britain, and a

---

7. *Synopsis Purioris Theologia*. Disput. 42. p. 621.
8. *Defence*, &c. Chap. ii. Sect. vi. p. 179.

thorough-going advocate for Presbyterian order, speaks on the same subject in the following terms: "The call of Ruling Elders, like the call of the Elders who 'labour in the word and doctrine,' consists in two things, viz., election and ordination. Their election should be popular, and their ordination judicial, and performed with laying on of hands." And, in a subsequent page, he expresses an opinion that Deacons ought to be ordained in the same manner.[9]

The venerable John Brown, of Haddington, one of the most decisive, consistent and devoted Presbyterians that ever lived; – after giving an account of the nature and warrant of the office of Ruling Elders, observes: "Their ordination ought to be transacted in much the same manner, as that of teaching Elders, or Pastors."[10]

The learned and pious Dr. Cotton Mather, delivers the following opinion on the subject before us: "The imposition of hands in the ordination of a Church officer, is a rite not only lawful to be retained; but it seems by a divine institution directed and required; so that although the call of a person to Church office may not become null and void, where that rite may have been omitted, as it is in the Seniors and Deacons in most of the Reformed Churches; yet we cannot approve the omission of it. A ceremonial defect may be blameworthy."[11]

The Rev. President Dwight, gives an opinion concerning the ordination of Deacons, which is decisive of his opinion concerning that of Ruling Elders, in favour of which latter class of officers, he very explicitly, as we have before seen, declares his judgment. He speaks thus:

"Deacons are to be ordained by the imposition of hands, and by prayer.

"'When the brethren had set these men before the Apostles,' Luke informs us, 'they prayed and laid their hands upon them.'

---

9. *Scriptural View of the Gospel Church*, Chapters 12 and 15, pp. 67, 102.
10. *Compendious View*, Book vii. Chapter ii, p. 640.
11. *Magnalia*, Vol. ii. p. 218.

"This also is an authoritative example of the manner in which Deacons are to be introduced into every Church. It is the example of inspired men; and was, therefore, the pleasure or the Spirit of God. There is no hint in the New Testament, nor even in ecclesiastical history, that they were ever introduced in any other manner. At the same time, there is no precept, revoking, or altering the authority, or influence of this example. It stands, therefore, in full force; and requires that all persons chosen by the Church to this office, should be consecrated to the duties of it in the same manner.

"It is to be observed, further, that if any such alteration had existed in periods subsequent to the apostolic age, it would have been totally destitute of any authority to us. This mode of consecration has, in fact, been disused in New England, to a considerable extent. For this, however, there seems to have been no reason of any value. So far as I have been able to gain information on the subject, the disuse was originated at first, and has been gradually extended by mere inattention; nor is it capable, so far as I know, of any defence."[12]

These are a few of the authorities which might be quoted in favour of the same general position. In fact, I have met with no Presbyterian or Independent writer, who believed in the propriety of the imposition of hands in any case of ordination, who did not either explicitly, or virtually grant, that there was no reason for withholding this ceremony in the case of Ruling Elders, but the custom of the Church, or some similar consideration.

On the supposition, then, that the imposition of hands ought always to be employed in the ordination of Ruling Elders, the question naturally arises: Whose hands ought to be laid on in such ordinations? And here, if we attend to the simplest principles of all government, it would seem that we could scarcely be at a loss for a satisfactory answer.

It seems to be a fundamental principle in every department, both of the natural and moral world, that every thing must be considered as capable of begetting its like. If this be so, does

---

12. *Theology Explained and Defended*, Vol. iv. p. 291.

it not follow as a plain dictate of common sense, that, in ordaining Ruling Elders, the members of the Session already in office should lay on hands, with the Pastor, in setting apart an additional number to the same office? In other words, if there be such a body already in existence in the Church, the hands of the parochial Presbytery ought to be laid on, in adding to its own number; – and the "right hand of fellowship" given, at the close of the service, by each member of the Session, to each of his newly ordained brethren. This appears to me equally agreeable to reason and Scripture, and highly adapted to edification. And if there be no Eldership already in the Church in which the ordination takes place, then the Presbytery, upon proper application being made to them, ought to appoint at least one minister, and two or more Ruling Elders, to attend, at the time and place most convenient, to perform the ordination. How much more impressive and acceptable would be such a scene, than the cold and naked manner in which this service is too often performed!

A question may here arise in the minds of some whether those Elders who, when ordained, had no hands laid on them, may, without impropriety, join in the imposition of hands on the heads of their younger brethren, who may be ordained in this manner. To this question, beyond all doubt, we may confidently return an affirmative answer. They may unite in the imposition of hands, without the least scruple, and with the utmost propriety. All reasonable men grant, that the rite in question though rational and scriptural, is not essential to a valid ordination. Our venerable Fathers of the Scotch Reformation did not deem the imposition of hands necessary, even in the ordination of Ministers of the Gospel; and, therefore, in their First Book of Discipline did not prescribe it. Elders, therefore, who have been regularly set apart to their office, agreeably to the Formula prescribed in the Presbyterian Church, have received an ordination completely valid. They are fully invested with the office, and with all the powers and privileges which it includes. It is contrary to the whole genius of the Gospel to make a mere ceremonial defect fatal to the substance of an otherwise regular investiture. If Elders who have been thus ordained, be deemed competent to any part of their official work, they are competent to every part; and, of course, to partake in the solemnity which I am here endeavouring to recommend.

If the foregoing principles be correct, then Ruling Elders ought also to lay on hands, with the Pastor, in the ordination of Deacons; their office as Rulers vesting them with full power for this act, and rendering it strictly proper. But inasmuch as Deacons make no part of the parochial Presbytery, and are not vested with any portion of the function of spiritual government; it does not seem proper that they should lay on hands in any case of ordination. In that of Ruling Elders, it would be manifestly incongruous; since their office is altogether unlike. But even in the ordination of Deacons, it would be inconsistent with regular order. Ordination is an act not only official, but also authoritative. It is an act of government: but to no participation in this are Deacons appointed. This office, as we have seen, is highly important, and requires much wisdom, piety, prudence, and diligence; but their sphere of duty is entirely different from that of those who are "set over the flock in the Lord," and who are appointed to "watch for souls as they that must give account."

If, after this whole discussion, any should be disposed to ask, what additional advantage may be expected to flow from ordaining our Elders by the imposition of hands, and with similar external solemnities to those which are employed in setting apart ministers of the Gospel – I answer: It will be a return to scriptural example, and primitive usage – which is always right, and will, we have reason to hope, by the grace of God, be connected with a blessing. It will be doing warranted and appropriate honour to a class of officers too long deprived of their due estimation and authority when the people see those whom they have elected to this office, devoutly kneeling before the Lord, and the hands of the parochial Presbytery laid on their heads, with fervent prayer, and with a solemn charge and benediction, they will naturally attach to the office itself more importance, and to those who bear it, more reverence. Nay, perhaps it is not unreasonable to believe, that such solemnities may be made the means of salutary impressions on the minds even of their immediate subjects. If the writer of these lines does not greatly mistake, he has known the solemnities attending the ordination of Pastors, productive of deep and lasting impressions, both on the ordained and the spectators. But he has no recollection of ever witnessing any such result from our comparatively cold and lifeless mode of setting apart the official Rulers in Christ's house. "This is a lamentation, and shall be for a lamentation."

A claim has been recently made with regard to the Ruling Elder, in respect to the point of Ordination, which, perhaps, ought to be cursorily noticed in this connection. The claim is, that Ruling Elders, when present, as members of Presbytery, ought always to unite with Teaching Elders, or Pastors, in the imposition of hands, in the ordination of Pastors. After the most careful and impartial examination that I am able to give this subject, I feel warranted in affirming, that such a claim or practice was never known or heard of in any Presbyterian Church on earth until within a very few years, and in a remote part of our own country. I say such a practice was never known or heard of in any *Presbyterian* Church. Among Independents, indeed, it has been both contended for and practised; as it naturally resulted from their erroneous views of the nature and functions of the office. But among Presbyterians it was never thought of until recently. And as the practice is wholly without precedent, so I believe it to be contrary to essential Presbyterian principle. I arrive at this conclusion, with unwavering confidence, from the following considerations.

I. It is evident from the word of God, and is expressly recognized in our Formularies, that the Pastoral office is the highest in the Christian Church; and, of course, it ought to be so exhibited in all our ecclesiastical proceedings. Every thing, therefore, which tends to destroy all distinction between Pastors and Ruling Elders; to hold them up to view as one in order and in power, tends, in fact, to supersede the Eider's office in its primitive design and function. It was this mistake which had nearly banished that office from the Church fourteen hundred years ago; and the recurrence of the same mistake, if adopted, will result in the same calamity again. It is manifest that this office can never occupy its appropriate place, nor render to the Church its appropriate services, when its real nature is misapprehended, and when it is confounded with another and a very different office. Ruling Elders have no authority to preach the Gospel, or to administer sacraments. How, then, can they with propriety unite in those symbolical acts which imply the imparting of this authority to others? And how can they take the ordained minister by the hand, on rising from his knees, and say, "We give you the right hand of fellowship, to take part of this ministry with us?" Is the Ruling Elder ever called a *minister* in the language of our public formularies? Is his office ever styled a *ministry?* With what propriety, then, can he take part in such a significant and authoritative act?

II. If the office of the Teaching and Ruling Elder are the same: if they are officers of the same order, and possess the same rights and authority, then it is plain, every Church Session may, without scruple, ordain Pastors, as well as Ruling Elders; and, if this be admitted, we may bid farewell to the Ruling Elder's office in any thing like its present peculiar form. It is true, some advocates of the new claim, perceiving that the adoption of the new principle would be so serious an invasion of the present constitution of the Church, have forborne to carry it to this length. But if the first step in this innovation, embracing the radical principle, be admitted, it is not difficult to foretell that every other will speedily follow.

III. For the last three hundred years, since the Ruling Elder's office has been revived and established in the Reformed Churches, this class of officers has scarcely ever been themselves ordained with the imposition of hands, and, of course, have not been called upon, in their turn, to impose hands on others. That which made no part of the ceremonial of their own induction into office, it was evident they could not regularly be allowed to partake in, in investing others with a different and higher office. It is true, this omission in the ordination of Ruling Elders is not to be commended, as I have stated in a former part of this chapter; but still this admitted fact must be considered as conclusive against the new claim, so far as the usage of the Church furnishes any index of duty

IV. The testimony of the whole Presbyterian Church, in all periods and countries, is conclusive against the whole claim in question. It is not only certain that Ruling Elders themselves have not been, for the last three centuries, usually ordained with the imposition of hands; but it is equally manifest that, during the whole of that period, no regular Presbyterian Church has ever set the example of allowing Ruling Elders to lay on hands in the ordination of Pastors.

(1.) In the Church of *Scotland,* under the First Book of Discipline, which occupied an authoritative place between the years 1560 and 1578, no one pretends that Ruling Elders laid on hands in the ordination of Teaching Elders or Pastors. The fact is know to be, that in the First Book of Discipline, and during its reign, there was no laying on of hands at all, either prescribed or in use in the ordination even of Pastors. During that time this rite was repudiated as unnecessary, if not improper. It was supposed to be connected, in the apostolic age, with the miraculous gifts of the Holy Spirit, and to be no longer either appropriate or suitable when those gifts were considered as having ceased. Concerning this period, then, there is no need of adding another word. No one has ever ventured to assert, that, during that period, Ruling Elders either claimed or exercised the right in question.

(2.) It is equally certain that the same thing may be made out as to the period under the Second Book of Discipline; that is, that from the formation of that book in 1578, until the meeting of the Westminster Assembly in 1643, both the claim and the exercise of this right were unknown in the Church of Scotland. On this subject no witness can be accounted either more competent or more credible than the celebrated *David Calderwood,* the venerable historian of the Church of Scotland, whose piety, talents, learning and indefatigable labours and sufferings in that Church are universally known. The *Altare Damascenum* of that great man was published in 1623, of course just twenty years before the Westminster Assembly met, and while the writer was under a sentence of banishment in Holland, for his fidelity to the Presbyterian cause.

The *Altare Damascenum* is a controversial work, directed to the refutation of many adversaries. Among these, *Tilenus,* once a Presbyterian and Calvinistic Profssor in the Seminary at *Sedan,* but then an apostate from the truth, and bitterly and blindly bigoted against all that he had formerly espoused, was one of the most forward and conspicuous. *Tilenus* objected to the Presbyterian system, because Ruling Elders were not considered as having a right to lay on hands in the ordination of Pastors: – that they were members of the Presbytery, and yet, in an ordination performed by the Presbytery, were not allowed to take part in this significant and solemn act. Calderwood explicitly admits the fact, that they *did not,* in any case, partake in this act; but denies the consequence which Tilenus draws from it. He contends that Elders might, if there were any *necessity for it,* lay on hands, without infringing any essential principle, as, in his opinion, that act was not an essential part of ordination, and did not really convey, in itself, either authority or grace. But he adds, "I concede that that imposition of hands which is joined with prayer and benediction, is *confined* to Pastors or Teaching Elders *only*. Nevertheless, as a sign of consent and assistance, the Ruling Elders *might* lay on hands. They *do not* lay them on because it is not necessary: nor, indeed, do *all* the co-Presbyters of any one Classis (or Presbytery) lay on hands, but only a part in the name of the rest. Even one might act in the name of all." "Finally," says Calderwood, "though we should grant this act (the laying on of hands) to be a sacrament, and that the administrators of this sacrament are Pastor-Presbyters *only* – still the others (the Ruling Elders) will not thereby be excluded from the Presbytery, (1 Tim. iv. 14) because the laying on of hands *does not belong to them,* for the imposition of hands may be called the imposition of the hands of the Presbytery, although each and every one of the Presbytery have not the power of imposing hands. It is enough that the leading part of the Presbytery have that power; just as the tribe of *Levi* is said to offer incense, when it was the prerogative of the Priests only."

(3.) The celebrated *Alexander Henderson,* one of the most conspicuous and influential leaders of the Church of Scotland, in his work entitled, *The Government and Order of the Church of Scotland*, published in 1641, in speaking of the minute details observed in the ordination of Pastors, says, Section II.: "The minister cometh from the pulpit, and, with as many of the *ministers* present as may conveniently come near, lay their hands upon his head, and, in the name of Jesus, do appoint him to be the Pastor of that Church."

(4.) In another treatise, by the well known *Samuel Rutherford,* entitled, *A Peaceable Plea For Paul's Presbytery in Scotland*, published in 1642, the same fact is repeatedly brought out, and the practice defended on scriptural grounds, as well as the nature of the ministerial office. He says, "Every where, in the word, where Pastors and Elders are created, there they are ordained by *Pastors,"* p. 37. "Ordination of Pastors is *never* given to people, or believers, or to *Ruling Elders,* as is clear from 1 Tim. v. 22; Titus i. v; Acts vi. 6; xiii. 3; 2 Tim. i. 6; 1 Tim. iv. 14," p. 190. In this Treatise, Rutherford argues on the principle that if believers who are not Pastors, may ordain Pastors, they may again depose and excommunicate, "which, says he, are the highest acts of jurisdiction; and then may they preach and baptize, not being called as *Ministers,* then may the Sacraments be administrate where there are no Pastors, which is absurd even to the separatists themselves," p. 57.

(5.) The excellent *James Guthrie,* of Sterling, in his *Treatise of Elders and Deacons*, observes: "Howbeit the execution of some decrees of the Church assemblies, – such as *the imposition of hands,* – the pronouncing the sentence of excommunication – the receiving penitents – the intimation of the deposition of ministers, and such like, *do belong to ministers alone."*

(6.) In the Westminster Assembly of Divines, the testimony borne on this subject is perfectly clear and explicit. Their language is: "Every minister of the word is to be ordained by imposition of hands and prayer, and fasting, by those *preaching Presbyters* to whom it doth belong. 1 Tim. v. 22; Acts xiv. 23, and xiii. 3."

(7.) With the uniform language of the Church of Scotland, and the decisive judgment of the Westminster Assembly, the recorded opinion of the venerable *Calvin* perfectly harmonized. Calvin's language on this subject is too explicit and pointed to admit of doubt or controversy: "The imposition of hands in the ordination of ministers is *confined to Pastors alone."* Instit. bib. iv. Cap. iii. sect. 16. And this, by the way, may be considered as a sufficient index of the practice of the Church of *Geneva,* in which Calvin had a patriarchal authority.

In accordance with all these, it is notorious that our venerated Fathers, who framed the present Formularies of the Presbyterian Church in the United States, and who might be supposed best to know the import of their own work, never claimed or allowed for Ruling Elders the right in question. In no branch of European or American Presbyterianism was such a claim ever heard of, until very lately, in a small portion of our Body.

In vain is it alleged, then, that the language of our prescribed form of ordination seems to imply that *all the members of the Presbytery* shall lay hands on the head of the candidate, and take him by the hand, with an official salutation on rising from his knees. That none but the stated, permanent *ministerial* members of the Presbytery are intended by these terms, is perfectly manifest, from the common laws of language; from all the sources whence these formularies were derived; and, above all, from the uniform acknowledged practice of their framers themselves for more than fifty years: for it was more than half a century from the time of the adoption of our present constitution, before the new claim in question was proposed or thought of.

CHAPTER FOURTEEN

Of the Resignation of Ruling Elders, Their Removal From One Church to Another, and the Method of Conducting Discipline Against Them

As it is a fundamental principle of the Presbyterian Church that the office of Ruling Elder is permanent; that when a man is once set apart to it, he is always an Elder, while he lives, unless deposed by regular constitutional process; a variety of questions, naturally resulting from this principle, claims our notice. Among these, some of the more obvious and important will be briefly considered in the present chapter.

A Ruling Elder, after being regularly and solemnly set apart to his office, with, perhaps, as full an intention of faithfully performing its duties to his life's end, as ever man had, may lose his health, and thus become physically and permanently unable to perform those duties. Or he may become, unavoidably, so situated, with regard to his temporal business as to render the regular fulfilment of his duties altogether impracticable. In this case, the individual supposed may resign his place in the Session; in other words, he may cease to be an acting Overseer, or Inspector and Ruler of that Church. He will, of course, still retain his place and privileges as a regular member of the Church; but he will no longer take any part in its spiritual government. This is so reasonable a provision, that it can scarcely be thought to require either illustration or defence. We all know that a Teaching Elder, or Minister of the Word and Sacraments, after being for a time a Pastor, may, if the state of his health, or any other circumstance should imperiously demand it, resign his pastoral charge, and retire, as long as the cause of his resignation continues to operate, to private life. He who does this, it is well known, though he ceases to be a Pastor, still continues to be a minister, fully invested with the powers of an "Ambassador of Christ." He may still, if he think proper, reside within the bounds of the congregation which he formerly served; and he may, occasionally, if mutually convenient and agreeable, minister to them in sacred things. But he is no longer their minister; and he may never think proper again to take a pastoral charge.

All these principles apply to the Ruling Elder. If he verily think that he cannot any longer perform the duties of his office in a manner acceptable either to the Head of the Church, or to his people; he may withdraw from active service. When he does this, however, he does not lay down his office. He does not cease to be an Elder. He only ceases to be an acting Elder. If his health should ever be restored, or his temporal circumstances undergo a favourable alteration, he may resume the duties of his office, and again take his place in the Session from which he withdrew, or some other, without a new ordination. When an Elder thus wishes to resign his station, he is to give official notice of his desire to the Session; they are to declare, if they think proper, their acceptance of his resignation; the whole transaction is to be distinctly recorded in the Sessional Book; and report made to the Presbytery that the individual in question has ceased to be an acting member of that Session.

Again; an Elder may become wholly incapable of serving the Church with which he is connected, by the entire loss of his popularity. He may not have become either heterodox in his theological opinions, or so irregular in any part of his practice, as to render himself liable to process or deposition from office; and yet he may, by indiscretions, or by undignified conduct, so lose the respect and confidence of the people, or, in a moment of prejudice or passion, the popular feeling, without any just ground of bitune on his part, may be so strong against him, that he may be no longer able to serve the Church either acceptably, or to edification, as a spiritual Ruler. In either of these cases, he ought voluntarily to resign his place in the Session, as stated in the preceding paragraph; and the Session, after taking a vote of acceptance on the resignation, ought distinctly to record the same in the minutes of their proceedings, and make regular report of it, for the information of the Presbytery. In all this there will be recognized an almost exact similarity to the usual course of proceeding, when a Pastor is sensible that he has become unpopular, and wishes to resign his charge.

It may be, however, that the Elder, whose popularity is thus prostrated, may not be sensible of his real situation; may be unwilling to believe that he is not popular, and may, therefore, refuse, even when requested, to resign his station. In this case, the course prescribed in our Form of Government, is, that the Session make due report of the whole matter to the Presbytery, giving due notice to the Elder in question of the time and place at which it is intended to make the report; and that the Presbytery decide, after due inquiry and deliberation, whether he ought to resign, or continue his connexion with the Session. On the one hand, no Church ought to be burdened by the incumbency of an unpopular and obstinate Elder, who, instead of edifying, is injuring it. And, on the other hand, no innocent and really exemplary Elder ought to be abandoned to the fury of popular prejudice, and permitted to be trampled under feet, when, perhaps, he ought to be sustained and honoured for his fidelity.

Further; Ruling Elders, like other Church members, may find it their duty to remove their residence from the bounds of the Church which called them to office, to another. Such cases not unfrequently arise. The question is, when they do occur, how is the official standing of such a removing Elder to be disposed of? He, of course, when he goes, ought to take with him a regular certificate of good standing, as a private Christian, and a dismission and recommendation to the Church to which he removes. The certificate ought also to bear an attestation of his regular standing as an Elder, and of his official as well as personal dismission from his former Church. With this certificate he will repair to the Church to which he is recommended, and will, of course, be received as a private member in good standing. If the existing Eldership and members of the Church to which he removes, think it for their edification that he be introduced into their Session, he may be elected in the manner "most approved and in use in that congregation;" that is, either by a nomination by the Session, or by a popular vote of the Church members; and if thus elected, introduced to an official relation to that people, not by a new ordination, which ought never to be repeated; but by being regularly installed as their Elder. This is effected by the candidate appearing in the face of the congregation, as one about to be ordained; answering in the affirmative the fourth question directed to be put to candidates for the Eldership at their ordination; the members of the congregation publicly professing to receive him as their spiritual Ruler, agreeably to the last question, in the same formula; declaring him one of the Ruling Elders of that Church; and closing with prayer for the Divine blessing on the transaction.

It may be, however, that when an individual, who has served one congregation as an Elder, removes into the bounds of another, that other may not, on the whole, think best to elect him as one of their Elders. They may already have as many as they think there ought to be in one Church. Or his character, though unexceptionably good, may not be such as to promise great benefit by taking him into their parochial Presbytery. In this case, they are under no obligation to elect him one of their Elders. And if they do not think best to employ him in this character, he may live among them as a private member of the Church. At this he ought to take no offence. It would be a hard case, indeed, if Churches were not left at liberty to act agreeably to their own views of propriety and duty in such cases. If a preaching Elder, or Pastor, be liberated from his pastoral charge, and remove his residence within the bounds of another Church, however excellent his character, that Church is not bound to employ him. To suppose it bound, would indeed be ecclesiastical slavery. A preacher inferior to him, in every respect, might be preferred. Every Church must be left to its own unbiased choice. Still the Elder, as well as the minister, in the case supposed, though in retirement, and without official employment, retains his office, and is capable of being employed in that office, whenever the judicatories of the Church think proper to avail themselves of his services.

When Ruling Elders become chargeable with heresy or immorality, and, of course, liable to the discipline of the Church, they are amenable to the bar of the Church Session. By that body they are to be arraigned and tried. Process against them is to be conducted according to the same general rules which regulate the trial of private members of the Church, excepting that, as their character is, in some respects, more important, and their example more influential, than the character and example of those who bear no office in the Church; so there ought to be peculiar caution, tenderness, and care in receiving accusations, and in commencing process against them. "Against an Elder," says the inspired Paul, "receive not an accusation, but before two or three witnesses." If, therefore, any person observe or hear of any thing in a Ruling Elder which he considers as rendering him justly liable to censure, he ought by no means immediately to spread it abroad but to communicate what he has observed or heard to the Pastor of the Church, and take his advice as to the proper course to be pursued; and if the Pastor cannot be seen and consulted, then similar consultation and advice should be had with one, at least, of the brother Elders of the supposed delinquent: and all this, before any hint respecting the alleged delinquency is lisped to any other human being.

As the Church Session is the tribunal to which the Ruling Elder is, at least in the first instance, always amenable; so it is generally proper that he should be tried by that judicatory. Yet where there is any thing peculiar or delicate in the case of process against an Elder, a Presbytery should be consulted.

There are cases, however, so very peculiar as to preclude the possibility of an impartial trial, and sometimes, indeed, of any trial at all, before the Session. A few such cases may be specified.

An instance occurred, a few years since, in which there were only two Elders in a certain Church Session, and the moral conduct of both these Elders became impeached. It was, of course, impossible to try them in the usual manner.

In another case, the Session was composed of two Elders beside the Pastor. These Elders were their own brothers. One of them was charged with immoral conduct; and it was judged altogether improper that any attempt should be made to try the delinquent in that Session.

In a third class of cases, when process against members of Church Sessions had been commenced, it was found that so many of the brother Elders of the delinquents were cited as witnesses, that there was no prospect of a dispassionate and impartial trial by the remainder.

In all these cases, it was wisely judged proper to apply immediately to the Presbytery, to take the several causes in hand, and to commence and issue process.

It has been sometimes proposed, in exigencies similar to those which have been stated, without applying to the Presbytery, to call in the aid of the Eldership of a neighbouring Church, and to submit the case to their decision. To this course there are two objections. First, the constitution of the Presbyterian Church knows of no such body. It has no where provided for the formation of a parochial tribunal in such a manner. And, secondly, the adoption of this plan would be to set one Church as a judge over a neighbouring sister Church.

To avoid this incongruity, it has been sometimes proposed to form a tribunal for the trial of delinquent Elders, by selecting one or two of the same class of officers, from each of several neighbouring Sessions. This was intended as an expedient to avoid the impropriety of setting one Church in judgment over another. But this expedient, besides that it is unauthorized by any constitutional provision, is liable to the charge of a selection of judges which may not always be fair and impartial. It is far better on every account, and especially more in harmony with the nature of the case, and with the spirit of our general principles to go immediately to the Presbytery. That body is the natural resort in all cases in which the Church Session is unable, in its ordinary structure and situation, to perform the contemplated work.

CHAPTER FIFTEEN

Advantages of Conducting Discipline on the Presbyterian Plan

It is not forgotten, in entering on this chapter, that most denominations of Christians are so far prejudiced, and sometimes so blindly prejudiced, in favour of their own particular government and formularies, that their judgment in reference to this matter can seldom be regarded as impartial. The writer of this Essay, though he does not allow himself to indulge in such prejudices, yet does not claim to be wholly free from them. Instead, therefore, of troubling the reader with his bare impressions and preferences in regard to the Presbyterian mode of conducting discipline – which would, of course, go for nothing – it is proposed to present such a series of principles and reasonings as will enable the intelligent inquirer to judge for himself how far the conclusions of the writer are sustained by solid argument.

I. And, in the first place, the plan of discipline for which we plead, is founded, essentially, on the principle of representation, which, in a greater or less degree, pervades all human society. When a community of any extent wishes to frame laws for its own government, by whom is this service usually performed? By the whole body of citizens, wise and unwise, orderly and disorderly, coming together, and debating on the propriety and the form of every proposed enactment? No, never. An attempt of this kind would soon show the plan to be equally foolish and impracticable. Again; when a Court is to be formed, for applying the laws already in force, to human actions, of what materials is this tribunal commonly composed? Does any one ever think of summoning the whole mass of the male population, excepting the culprit, or the complainant, whose cause is to be tried, to come together, and decide on the case? Who would ever expect either a tranquil or a wise decision from such a judicial assembly? In both these cases, the good sense of men, in all civilized society, dictates the choice of a select number of individuals, representatives of the whole body, and supposed to possess a competent share of knowledge, wisdom, and integrity, to form the laws of the community; and another body, smaller, indeed, but constituted upon similar principles, judicially to apply them when enacted. And so in every department of society. The representative system was one of the earliest that appeared in the progress of mankind. It is recommended by its reasonableness, its convenience, its wisdom, and its efficiency. In fact, the more deeply we look into the history and state of the world, the more clearly we shall see that large bodies of men cannot take a step without it.

And, as this system pervades all civil society; so we may say, without fear of contradiction, that it equally pervades the whole economy of redemption and grace. Is it not reasonable, then, that we should find it in the visible Church? If we did not, it would, indeed, be a strange departure from a general principle of Jehovah's kingdom.

The Presbyterian plan, then, of conducting the government of each congregation, is recommended by its conformity with this, almost universal, principle. It deposits the power of applying the laws which Christ has enacted, and given to His people, not with the whole professing population of the Church; but with a select body of the communicants, most distinguished for their piety, knowledge, judgment, and experience. It does not make judges indiscriminately of the young and old, the enlightened and the ignorant, the wise and the unwise. It selects the exemplary, the pious, the prudent, the grave, and the experienced, for this important work. "It sets those to judge who are most esteemed in the house of God." This is the theory; and, in most cases, we suppose, the actual practice. And where it is really so, who does not see that there is every security which the nature of the case admits, that the judgment will be the most calm, judicious, and edifying, that the amount of wisdom and of piety in that Church could pronounce?

The inconvenience, nay, the positive mischiefs, of committing the judgment, in the most delicate and difficult cases of implicated Christian character, to the whole mass of Christian professors, have been alluded to in a preceding chapter. And the more closely they are examined, the more serious will they appear. No confidential precaution; no calm, retired inquiry; no deliberate consultation of sensitive feelings, with fidelity, and yet with fraternal delicacy, can possibly take place, in ordinary cases, but by the adoption of an expedient, which amounts to the temporary appointment of Elders. On the contrary, upon any other plan, the door is wide open for tale-bearing; for party heat; for the violation of all those nicer sensibilities which in Christian society, are of so much value; and after all, for a decision with which, perhaps, no one is satisfied. It would, truly, be passing strange, if a sober, wise, and consistent decision should be pronounced by such a tribunal. We are surely, then, warranted in setting it down as one of the manifest advantages of conducting discipline on the Presbyterian plan, that, by the adoption of the representative system, it provides, in all ordinary cases, for the purest, the wisest, and the most edifying decisions of which the nature of the case admits.

II. Further; as was hinted, in a preceding chapter, this method of conducting discipline presents one of the firmest conceivable barriers against the ambition and encroachments of the clergy. It is not intended again to enlarge on the liableness of ministers of the Gospel to feel that love of power which is natural to man. Very few of them, it is believed, in this land of religious liberty, have ever really aimed at ecclesiastical encroachment. But as laws are made for the disobedient; and as ministers are but men; so that system of ecclesiastical polity may be considered as the best, which, while it is attended with the greatest amount of positive advantage, is adapted most effectually to obviate those evils to which human nature is exposed.

Now, it is evident, that the method of conducting discipline at present under consideration, assigns to every Pastor a Council, or Senate of pious, wise, prudent men, chosen from among the body of the communicants; and though not strictly laymen, yet commonly so viewed, and, at any rate, carrying with them the feelings of the mass of their brethren. The Pastor is simply the chairman of this body of six, eight, or ten men, who are charged with the whole spiritual rule, and "without whose counsel nothing is done in the Church." He can carry no measure but with their consent. He can neither admit nor exclude a single member, without their concurrence. If he engage in any sinister or foul plan, as many are fond of supposing the clergy inclined to attempt, he certainly cannot accomplish it, either in his own Church, or in neighbouring Churches, unless he can prevail on these men to join with him in conspiring to elevate himself, at their own expense. Will he be likely to work such a wonder as this? At any rate, there seems to be the best barrier against it, that the nature of human society admits.

The same general safeguard pervades all the Judicatories of the Presbyterian Church. In all of them Ruling Elders have a place, and in all of them, excepting the General Assembly, the Elders, if the theory of our system were carried into perfect execution, would be a majority. In the General Assembly alone, if completely full, they would stand on an equality in votes with the Pastors. And these Ruling Elders are not merely present in all these bodies. They mingle in all the business; are appointed on all committees and have every possible opportunity of becoming acquainted, in the most intimate manner, with all that is proposed or done. There can be no concealment. The proceedings of all our Judicatories, excepting the Church Session, where the Elders form an overwhelming majority, are open and public as the light of day. And every Ruling Elder has at his disposal a vote as potent as that of his most eloquent and learned neighbouring Pastor.

It may be asked, then, whether there is not here a barrier against clerical ambition and encroachment as fixed and firm as can well be conceived or desired? It is, undoubtedly, a far more firm barrier than is presented by the popular plan in use among our Independent brethren. For as, in every Church, a majority of the members have but little discernment, and are, of course, easily influenced and led; so an artful, designing Pastor, if such an one should appear in a Church thus constituted, might generally succeed in conciliating to his own person and schemes a majority of the votes, to the utter discomfiture of the more wise, pious, and prudent portion of the members. But, upon the Presbyterian plan, it is precisely this best class of his Church members who are associated with him in authority and counsel who are with him, ecclesiastically speaking, abroad and at home, in the house and by the way, in going out and in coming in; from whose notice he cannot escape, and without whose cooperation he can do nothing. Truly, this is the very last method that designing, ambitious ministers would adopt to forward their projects! Nothing could be conceived more unfriendly to corrupt schemes, than such a band of official colleagues. And accordingly, as we have more than once seen, in the foregoing chapters, the honest and pious old Ambrose, of the fourth century, expressly tells us, that it was a wish to get rid of such colleagues, on the part of the Teaching Elders, that first led to the gradual disuse of Ruling Elders in the Church, after the first three centuries.

III. Again; as the Presbyterian plan of administering discipline is adapted to present one of the strongest conceivable barriers against clerical ambition, so it also furnishes one of the best securities for preserving the rights of the people. And here nothing will be said on the supposed congeniality between the Presbyterian form of Church Government, and the republican, representative systems under which we live; and the alleged tendency of the former to prepare men for understanding, prizing, and maintaining the latter. I say, on these allegations I shall not dwell; not because I do not consider both as perfectly well founded; but because the discussion might be deemed, by some readers invidious; and because it forms no necessary part of my argument. Independently of these considerations, it may be confidently maintained, that the Presbyterian plan of administering discipline, furnishes far better security for preserving unimpaired the rights of private Christians, than any plan with which we are acquainted. It is not forgotten that this assertion will appear a paradox to many; but it rests, nevertheless, on the most solid grounds.

There is no oppression more heavy, no tyranny more unrelenting, than that of an excited, infuriated popular assembly; no body with which the rights and privileges of an inculpated individual are less safe; especially when headed and controlled by an eloquent, artful, and highly popular Pastor, who has taken part against that individual. Suppose, then, as the annals of Independency have too often exemplified, that a member is on trial for some alleged delinquency, before a Church of that denomination. Suppose the alleged offence to be one which has deeply alienated from him his Pastor, and all the particular friends of the Pastor. Suppose these, as one man, rise up against him, and resolve to crush him. And suppose this Pastor to be so generally admired and beloved by his people, that he is able to command an overwhelming majority of their votes, in support of all his favourite measures. What chance would such an accused person stand of an impartial trial before such a tribunal? Not the smallest. He might be guilty, indeed, and deserve the heaviest sentence; but even if innocent, his acquittal, in such circumstances, could be anticipated by none. He must become the victim of popular resentment; and if he thus fall, he has no remedy. There is no tribunal to which he can appeal. He must lie down under the oppressive sentence. And there he must lie as long as he lives. He cannot regularly (that is, according to that ecclesiastical rule which pervades all religious denominations), go to another Church; for the supposition is that he is excommunicated, and cannot be recommended as in "good standing" to any other ecclesiastical body. He must submit to the operation of the sentence, however unjust, until the excited and impassioned body which laid it upon him, shall be disposed to relent, and consent to remove the deadly weight.

It is not denied that there may be moments of prejudice and passion in the Presbyterian Church, in which even the grave and experienced Elders may be so wrought upon by different sorts of influence, as to dispense justice very imperfectly, or, even, in a particular case, to refuse it entirely. But then, in every such case, upon the Presbyterian plan, there is an immediate and perfect remedy. An individual who supposes himself wronged, may appeal to a higher tribunal, where his cause will be heard by judicious, enlightened, impartial men, who had no concern in its origin, and who, if wrong have been done, may be expected to afford prompt and complete redress. The oppressive sentence may be reversed. He may be reinstated, in spite of popular excitement, in all his Christian privileges; and even, where his own reluctance, or that of his former connexions, may forbid his return to the bosom of the same congregation in which he recently received such treatment; yet he may easily and regularly be attached to a neighbouring one of the same denomination, and thus find the whole difficulty satisfactorily removed.

It is not asserted then, that other Churches, in the exercise of discipline, do, in fact, more frequently injure and oppress the subjects of their discipline than the Presbyterian Church. Such an assertion, indeed, might, perhaps, be made without invidiousness; inasmuch as decisions formed and pronounced by the popular voice may be deemed, without disparagement to the individuals who form them, less likely to be wise, and impartial, than when formed by a select body of enlightened and pious judges. But on this point no comparative estimate will be attempted. It is, however, confidently asserted, that when such wrong, as that of which we speak unhappily occurs, the Presbyterian system affords more complete relief from oppression, and, therefore, furnishes more fixed security for the rights of the people, than is found in any other denomination. No single man, in our Church, whatever title he may bear, can, by his single, perhaps capricious, *veto*, deprive a professing Christian of his privileges as a Church member; nor can it be done by a feverish, popular assembly, impelled by its own prejudice or passion, or held under the sovereign control of one man. The best array of piety, wisdom, and knowledge which the society affords, must sit in judgment in the case, and even if this judicatory should give an unjust sentence, the religious rights of the individual are not prostrated or foreclosed; but may be reviewed by an impartial tribunal, and every privilege which he ought to enjoy, be secured.

IV. Further; the plan of conducting Church government with the aid of Ruling Elders, secures to Ministers of the Word and Sacraments, counsel and support in all their official proceedings, of the best possible kind. Supposing ministers of the Gospel to be honest, pious, disinterested, and zealous in their appropriate work; to have no disposition, at any time, to encroach on the rights of others; and to be above the reach of that passion and prejudice, which are so apt to assail even the honest, and which need a check in all; even suppose ministers of the Gospel to be above the reach of these evils; still they need counsel, information, and support in a multitude of cases, and cannot, with either safety or advantage, proceed without them. In all the affairs of the Church, it is of the utmost importance that the interests of the whole body be constantly consulted, and that the whole body act an appropriate part in conducting its affairs. As there are no privileged orders to be aggrandized and elevated; so there are no ecclesiastical secrets to be kept; no private or selfish schemes to be tolerated. The more completely every plan is laid open to public view, understood, and appreciated by every member, sustained by unanimous and willing effort, and made to promote the knowledge, purity, and order of the whole, the better.

Of course, that plan of ecclesiastical regimen which is best adapted to attain these ends, and to attain them in the most certain, direct, quiet, and comfortable manner, is most worthy of our choice.

Such a plan it is firmly believed, is the Presbyterian. In every department of official duty, the Pastor of this denomination has associated with him, a body of pious, wise, and disinterested counsellors, taken from among the people; acquainted with their views; participating in their feelings; able to give sound advice as to the wisdom and practicability of plans which require general co-operation for carrying them into effect; and able also, after having aided in the formation of such plans, to return to their constituents, and so to advocate and recommend them, as to secure general concurrence in their favour.

This is an advantage, strictly speaking, peculiar to Presbyterianism. For although other forms of Church government provide for associating laymen with the clergy in ecclesiastical business; yet, according to them, there is no divine warrant for it. It is a mere human expedient, to meet an acknowledged exigency, for which those who make this acknowledgment suppose that the law of Christ makes no provision. And the human provision which they thus make is, manifestly, liable to many objections. It consists either in constituting the whole body of the communicants the Pastor's counsellors – which is liable to all the objections stated at Large in a former chapter – or, in providing for him a committee, or small delegation of laymen, who may be changed every year, or oftener, and, of course, may have very little experience; and in some Churches these lay delegates are not required to be communicants, or even baptized persons; and, consequently, may have no real ecclesiastical responsibility for their conduct.

V. The method of conducting discipline under consideration, has also the advantage on the score of *despatch and energy,* as well as of wisdom and the security of equal rights.

Where all the discipline that is exercised is in the hands of a single individual, without appeal, it must be confessed that, in this case, provision for despatch and energy cannot be, at least in theory, more perfect. But where it is in the hands of the whole body of the Church members, there is no saying how long litigation may be protracted, or in what perplexities and delays the plainest case may be involved. There are so many minds to be consulted, and every case, upon this plan, is so open to capricious or malignant interposition, that it is impossible, in ordinary circumstances, to calculate results, or to foresee an end.

Even on the Presbyterian plan, there is no doubt that delay and perplexities may, in some cases, arise. But where the whole management of discipline, from its inceptive steps to the consummation of each case, is entirely committed to a select body of pious, intelligent, prudent, and experienced men, accustomed to the work, and aware of the dangers to which their course is exposed, we may reasonably calculate on their decisions being as speedy, as unembarrassed, and as much lifted above the temporizing feebleness, or the tempestuous irregularity and confusion, incident to popular management, as human infirmity will allow.

VI. The plan of conducting discipline by means of a succession of judicatories, admitting of appeal, provides for redressing many grievances which do not appear, otherwise, to admit of a remedy. According to the Independent, or strictly Congregational system, as suggested in a preceding page, when a member of a Church has been unjustly censured or cast out, he has no appeal. There is no tribunal to which he can apply for relief. Yet his case may be an exceedingly hard one, loudly calling for redress. The cause of religion in his neighbourhood may be suffering severely by the situation in which he is placed. Ought there not to be some regular and adequate method of meeting and removing such a difficulty? In such of the Churches of Connecticut as have entered into the plan of Consociational union, such a method has been, to a certain extent, provided. But it has been by adopting, to precisely the same extent, a leading principle of Presbyterianism. When difficulties arise in a particular Church, a tribunal is formed, by a number of neighbouring ministers, together with one or more lay-delegates, from each of the Churches represented, who may review, and, if need be, redress the alleged grievance. This is a Presbyterian feature in their system, and, so far as it goes, excellent and effectual. In the judgment, however, of the venerable President Dwight, this plan is still defective, and defective precisely in the point at which it stops short of Presbyterianism. The opinion which this distinguished Congregational Minister has expressed, in reference to the subject before us, will best appear by presenting it in its connexion. It is as follows:

"There are many cases in which individuals are dissatisfied, on reasonable grounds, with the judgment of a Church. It is perfectly obvious, that, in a debate between two members of the same Church, the parties may, in many respects, stand on unequal ground. One of them may be ignorant; without family connexions; in humble circumstances; and possessed of little or no personal influence. The other may be a person of distinction;

Advantages of Discipline on the Presbyterian Plan 261

opulent; powerfully connected; of superior understanding; and of great personal influence, not only in the Church, but also in the country at large. As things are in this world, it is impossible that these persons should possess, in any controversy between them, equal advantages. Beyond all this, the Church itself may be one party, and a poor and powerless member the other. In this case, also, it is unnecessary to observe, the individual must labour under every supposable disadvantage, to which a righteous cause can be subjected. To bring the parties in these, or any similar circumstances, as near to a state of equality as human affairs will permit, it seems absolutely necessary that every ecclesiastical body should have its tribunal of appeals; a superior Judicature, established by common consent, and vested with authority to issue finally all those causes, which, before a single Church, are obviously liable to a partial decision.

"Such a tribunal, in all the New-England States, except this (Connecticut), is formed by what is called a Select Council; that is a council mutually chosen by the contending parties. This has long appeared to me a Judicatory most unhappily constituted. The parties choose, of course, such persons, as they suppose most likely to favour themselves. If, therefore, they commit no mistake in the choice, the Council may be considered as divided in opinion, before it assembles; and as furnishing every reason to believe, that it will not be less divided afterwards. Its proceedings will frequently be marked with strong partialities; and its decisions, if made at all, will, not unfrequently, be those of a bare majority. Coming from different parts of the country, it will have no common rules of proceeding. After its decisions, its existence ceases. Its responsibility vanishes with its existence; as does also the sense of its authority. As the members frequently come from a distance, it can have no knowledge concerning those numerous particulars, which respect the transactions to be judged of, and the characters, interests, views, and contrivances of those who are immediately concerned. As individuals, these members may, in some instances, have much weight; and in certain circumstances, may, by their wisdom and piety, do much good. But all this must arise solely from their personal character. As a Council, as a judicatory, they can scarcely have any weight at all for as they disappear when the trial is ended, they are forgotten in their united character; and having no permanent existence, are regarded with no habitual respect, and even with no prejudice in their favour. Very often, also, as they are chosen on partial principles, they are led, of course, to partial decisions; and leave behind them very unhappy opinions concerning ecclesiastical government at large.

"In this State (Connecticut), a much happier mode has been resorted to, for the accomplishment of this object. The tribunal of appeal is here a Consociation; a standing body; composed of the settled Ministers within an associational district, and Delegates from the Churches in the same district; a body always existing; of acknowledged authority; of great weight; possessed of all the impartiality incident to human affairs; feeling its responsibility as a thing of course; a Court of Record, having a regular system of precedents; and, from being frequently called to business of this nature, skilled, to a good degree, in the proper modes of proceeding.

"The greatest defect in this system, as it seems to me, is the want of a still superior tribunal, to receive appeals, in cases where they are obviously necessary. These, it is unnecessary for me to particularize. Every person extensively acquainted with ecclesiastical affairs, knows that such cases exist. The only remedy provided by the system of discipline established in this State, for those who feel aggrieved by a Consociational judgment, is to introduce a neighbouring Consociation, as assessors with that which has given the judgment, at a new hearing of the cause. The provision of this partial, imperfect tribunal of appeals, is clear proof that those who formed the system perceived the absolute necessity of some appellate jurisdiction. The judicatory which they have furnished of this nature is perhaps the best which the Churches of the State, would at that, or any succeeding period, have consented to establish. Yet it is easy to see that, were they disposed, they might easily institute one which would be incomparably better.

"The only instance found in the Scriptures of an appeal,

actually made for the decision of an ecclesiastical debate, is that recorded in the fifteenth chapter of the Acts, and mentioned for another purpose in a former discourse. A number of the Jews in the Church at Antioch, insisted that the Gentile converts should be circumcised and be obliged to keep the law of Moses. Paul and Barnabas strenuously controverted this point with them. As no harmonious termination of the debate could be had at Antioch, an appeal was made "to the Apostles and Elders at Jerusalem." But, as I observed, in the discourse mentioned, it was heard and determined by the Apostles, Elders, and Brethren. As this judicatory was formed under the direction of the Apostles themselves, it must be admitted as a precedent for succeeding Churches; and teaches us, on the one hand, that an appellate jurisdiction is both lawful and necessary in the Church; and, on the other, that it is to be composed of both Ministers and Brethren, necessarily acting, at the present time, by delegation."[1]

In this quotation, and in the remarks which preceded it, a reference, it will be perceived, is principally had to cases in which individual private members have considered themselves as aggrieved by the decisions of particular Churches. But the same remarks, in substance, are applicable to those cases in which difficulties arise between Ministers and their Congregations, or between two neighbouring Congregations of the same name. No form of Church government provides for the settlement of such difficulties so promptly or so well as the Presbyterian. Independency, strictly so called – that is Independency, in strict adherence to its essential principles – furnishes, for such evils, no remedy whatever. Other sects furnish a nominal or partial remedy, by investing some official individual with power to constitute a tribunal for settling such controversies. But the choice of the members of this tribunal is usually committed entirely to that individual, and it is, of course, in his power to make it, like a "packed jury," in the hands of a corrupt returning officer, a mere instrument of oppression. But, in the Presbyterian Church, every difficulty of this kind is committed, for adjustment,

---

1. *Theology Explained and Defended*, Vol. iv, pp. 399-401.

to a permanent, responsible body – a body whose proceedings may be reviewed and examined; whose organization or members cannot be changed at the will of a corrupt individual who may choose to tamper with them; and whose decisions are not merely advisory, but authoritative.

VII. Finally; the Presbyterian method of conducting the government of the Church, is most friendly to the spread of the Gospel, and furnishes peculiar facilities for union and efficiency of action, in promoting the great objects of Christian benevolence.

It has been sometimes, indeed, alleged in opposition to this, that Presbyterianism is naturally, and almost necessarily, cold and formal; and that Congregationalism has been found, in fact, more favourable to zeal and activity in spreading the Gospel. It is by no means intended to depreciate either the zeal or the activity of our Congregational Brethren. Justice demands that much be said in commendation of both. And it will be no small praise to any other denomination to be found successfully emulating the intelligence, enterprise and perseverance which they have often manifested in pursuing the best interests of the Redeemer's kingdom. But when the organization of the Presbyterian Church is examined, one would think that prejudice itself could scarcely deny its peculiar adaptedness for united, harmonious, and efficient action, in every thing which it might become convinced was worthy of pursuit.

In order to enable this Church to act with the utmost energy and uniformity, throughout its entire extent, there is no need of any new organization. It is organized already, and in a manner, as would seem, as perfect as possible for united and harmonious action. A delegation from every Church meet and confer, several times in each year, as a matter of course, in Presbytery. What opportunity could be imagined more favourable for forming and executing plans of co-operation, among all the Churches thus united, and statedly convening? They have the same opportunity, and every advantage, of meeting at pleasure, that can be enjoyed by a voluntary association; with the additional advantage, that they act under a system of ecclesiastical rules and authority, which enable them to go forward with more energy and uniformity in their adopted course. If a more extended union of Presbyterian Churches than of those which belong to a single Presbytery be desired, for any particular purpose, the regular meetings of the Synods, each comprising a number of Presbyteries, afford the happiest opportunity, without any new or extra combination, of effecting the object. The representatives of, perhaps, one hundred and fifty Churches, assembled in their ecclesiastical capacity, and in the name of Christ, could hardly be conceived to convene in circumstances more perfectly favourable to their co-operating, in any worthy and hallowed cause, with one heart, and with the most perfect concentration of effort. And when we extend our thoughts to the General Assembly, the bond of union, counsel and co-operation for more than two thousand Churches, all represented, and combined in the same cause, we see a plan which, in theory at least, it would seem difficult to adapt more completely to union of heart and hand in any good work. The most admirable combination, with every possible advantage, exists beforehand. Nothing is in any case wanting, but the animating Spirit necessary for applying it to the proper objects. The machinery, in all its perfection, is already constructed, and ready to be set in motion. Only let the impelling principle, which is necessary to set all moral combinations into vigorous movement, be present, and operate with due power, and it may be asserted, that a more advantageous system for ecclesiastical enterprise was never devised.

It is not a sufficient reply to this statement to say, that the Congregational Churches of New England, have, in fact, done more within the last thirty years, in the way of contribution and effort, for extending the Redeemer's kingdom, than any equal number of Churches of the Presbyterian denomination in the United States. It is impossible to contemplate the intelligence, harmony of feeling, and pious enterprise of the mass of our Congregational Brethren, without sentiments, at once, of respect and gratitude. But is not the general fact alluded to, chiefly referable to other causes than the form of their Church government? No one, it is believed, can doubt, for a moment, that this is the case. Their Church government is, manifestly, less adapted to promote union and effective co-operation than most others. But their intelligence, their piety, their common origin, their homogeneous character, their compact situation, and the sameness of the instruction, the excitements, and the agencies which they enjoy, have all tended to prepare them for united and harmonious co-operation. Only give to the members of Churches organized on the Presbyterian plan the same advantages, the same natural principles of cohesion, the same intellectual and moral stimulants, and the same pervading spirit, and can any one believe that there would be found less union, and less energy in pursuing the best interests of man? We must deny the connexion between cause and effect, before we can doubt that there would be more of both. It has been sometimes, indeed, said, as a supposed exemplification of the unfavourable influence of Presbyterianism, that the Churches called Presbyterian in South Britain have generally declined, both in orthodoxy and piety, within the last hundred years; while the Independents have generally and happily maintained their character for both. But the fact is, that when the English Presbyterians gradually fell into those errors, for which the greater part of them are now distinguished, they, at the same time, gradually renounced the Presbyterian form of government, although they retained the name. There are not now, and have not been, for many years, any real Presbyterians in England, excepting those who are, directly or indirectly, connected with Churches in Scotland. After all, it is not pretended that the Presbyterian form of Church government can, of itself, infuse spiritual life and activity into an ecclesiastical body; but that where vitality, and zeal, and resources exist, there is no form of ecclesiastical organization in the world so well adapted to unite counsels, and invigorate efforts, as that under which we are so happy as to live.

It makes no part however, of the design of the author of this volume to assail or to depreciate the ecclesiastical order of other denominations. On the contrary, wherever he finds those who evidently bear the image of Christ, and who appear to be engaged in advancing His kingdom, whatever form of Church order they may prefer, he can hail them with unqualified affection as Christian Brethren. The truth is, he would not have alluded to any other portion of the Christian Church than that with which he is more immediately connected, had it appeared possible, without doing so, fully to illustrate the character and advantages of our own form of government. His ardent wish is, not to alienate, by high claims, or unkind language; but rather to conciliate and bind together by everything that can minister to brotherly love. And his daily prayer is, that all the Evangelical Churches in our land may be more and more united in principle and effort, for extending that "kingdom which is not meat and drink, but righteousness and peace and joy in the Holy Ghost."

THE END.

www.ingramcontent.com/pod-product-compliance
Lightning Source LLC
Chambersburg PA
CBHW060501090426
42735CB00011B/2064